THINKING WITH
ST. JOHN PAUL II

JP2 LECTURES 2020/2021

JP2 LECTURES 2020/2021

Edited by Dariusz Karłowicz

THINKING WITH
ST. JOHN PAUL II

GIANFRANCO RAVASI,
JOHN FINNIS,
ROWAN WILLIAMS,
MAREK A. CICHOCKI,
JOHN CAVADINI,
FRANÇOIS DAGUET,
CHANTAL DELSOL,
RÉMI BRAGUE,
RENATO CRISTIN,
DARIUSZ GAWIN

ANGELICUM UNIVERSITY PRESS
FUNDACJA ŚWIĘTEGO MIKOŁAJA
Rome—Warsaw 2021

Angelicum University Press
Fundacja Świętego Mikołaja
Rome—Warsaw 2021
Published by the St. John Paul II Institute of Culture at the Pontifical
University of St. Thomas Aquinas in Rome—Angelicum.
Founded at the Angelicum, the St. John Paul II Institute of Culture is run
in cooperation with the Saint Nicholas Foundation.
www.angelicum.it/institutes/st-john-paul-ii-institute-of-culture

Angelicum University Press
Largo Angelicum, 1—00184 Rome, Italy
editoria@pust.it—www.angelicumpress.com

Fundacja Świętego Mikołaja
Koszykowa 24/7—00553 Warsaw, Poland
redakcja@teologiapolityczna.pl—www.teologiapolityczna.pl
www.mikolaj.org.pl

ISBN: 978-83-62884-79-7 (print)
ISBN: 978-83-62884-83-4 (ebook)

Managing editors: Marta Broniewska, Mikołaj Marczak
Copy edited by Linklab, Trieste, Italy; T Studio Oxford, Oxford,
United Kingdom
Designed and typeset by Kachergis Book Design
Cover design by Michał Strachowski, Dariusz Karłowicz

On the centenary of Pope St. John Paul II's birth, 18 May 2020, the St. John Paul II Institute of Culture was established at the Faculty of Philosophy of the Pontifical University of Saint Thomas Aquinas in Rome (Angelicum). The Institute is a joint initiative of the Saint Nicholas Foundation, the Futura-Iuventa Foundation (both based in Poland) and the Angelicum, and is financed entirely by private donations.

Our special thanks go to: Danuta and Krzysztof Domarecki, Jolanta and Mirosław Gruszka, Adam Krauze, Wojciech Piasecki, Dorota and Tomasz Zdziebkowski, without whose support the activities of the Institute would not be possible.

The Honorary Donors of the volume "Thinking with St. John Paul II" are: Łukasz Cybula, Rafał Kania, Wojciech Piasecki, Paweł Turno, Dorota and Tomasz Zdziebkowski.

The development of the St. John Paul II Institute of Culture in Rome and the publication of this book have been supported by: Mirosława Adamczak, Rev. Jan Andrzejczak, Rev. Przemysław Artemiuk, Maria Augustyniak, Michał Balcerzak, Maria Klonowska-Baranowska and Andrzej Baranowski, Bartłomiej Bargiel, Anna Baterowicz, Maria and Artur Bazak, Nikodem Bernaciak, Maciej and Agnieszka Bernacik, Wojciech Bogusławski, Paweł Bochnia, Krzysztof Bożym, Fr. Radosław Broniek O.P., Ewa Bugaj, Michał Buraczewski, Krzysztof Bystram, Paulina and Piotr Chołd, Bogumiła Cichońska, Agata and Michał Cierkoński, Łukasz Cybula, Robert Czernisz, Ewa Czumakow, Dorota and Piotr Dardziński, Urszula and Dariusz

Dąbrowski, Paweł K. Długosz, Rev. Witold Dorsz, Paweł Drobny, Róża and Marcin Dziekiewicz, Agnieszka and Marcin Dziurda, Jacek Ebertowski, Maria Fijałkowska, Dominik Filipek, Katarzyna and Bartosz Fingas, Anna and Andrzej Fister-Stoga, Małgorzata Flis, Fr. Norbert Frejek SJ, Agnieszka and Piotr Gajda, Krzysztof Galeja, Paweł Gałuszka, Maria Gintowt-Jankowicz, Joanna, Paweł and Michał Gładysz, Dariusz Góra, Paweł Górnikowski, Mariusz Grunt, Jolanta and Mirosław Gruszka, Antonina and Filip Grządkowski, Rev. Bp. Jacek Grzybowski, Marta Gugała, Michał Haake, Magdalena and Maciej Hajdul, Andrzej Iwaniuk, Tomasz Iwasiów, Jadwiga Jakubas-Przewłocka, Rev. Wiesław Jankowski, Krzysztof Jański, Maciej Jesionkiewicz, Teresa Juszczyk, Rev. Przemysław Kaczkowski, Karol Kalinowski, Jan Kałuża, Łukasz Kamiński, Ewa and Dariusz Karłowicz, Zofia and Janusz Karłowicz, Adrian Kędzierski, Maria Klamut† and Andrzej Klamut, Grzegorz Klimczak, Sandra and Krzysztof Knigawka, Dominik Kolbusz, Piotr Kołodziej, Maria Kołosowska, Maria and John Kontak, Marek Korczyński, Jacek Koronacki, Wojciech Kowalczyk, Grzegorz Kowalski, Stanisław Kowolik, Maciej Kozakiewicz, Adam Krauze, Robert Krawczyk, Rev. Janusz Królikowski, Radosław Krupka, Rafał Kuks, Róża and Bernard Kulisz, Małgorzata and Damian Kulisz, Michał Kulisz, Dorota Kuncewicz, Marek Kuzaka, Monica Georgii-Lassak and Franz Lassak, Adam Lausch-Hołubowicz, Tomasz Lechowski, Rev. Piotr Lidwin, Krzysztof Lipiec, Małgorzata Lipska-Schydlo, Witold J. Lukaszewski, Anna Łabno, Małgorzata Łukasiewicz-Traczyńska, Anna Madej, Katarzyna Majcherek, Dariusz Makać, Joanna Żak-Markiewicz and Zbigniew Markiewicz, Rev. Waldemar Matusiak S. Chr., Przemysław Matusik, Jan Melon, Rev. Edward Jan Michowski SVD, Ryszard Mikietyński, Mikołaj Mikołajczyk, Anna and Paweł Mościcki, Grażyna Mozol, Mateusz Nagórski, Anna Nawrot, Krzysztof Nowak, Maria and Grzegorz

Nowak, Marek Nowakowski, Sławomir Nowotny, Bartłomiej Orzeł, Wojciech Orzewski, Przemysław Osiak, Ryszard Paciorek, Joanna and Jakub Paciorek, Ewa and Jarosław Paradowski, Jan Pawelec, Adam Pawłowicz, Grzegorz Pacek, Agata Petrovschi, Elżbieta Pękala, Jan Pięta, Olga Płaszczewska, Marek Podgórny, Patryk Pogoda, Jan Polkowski, Paweł Porucznik, Andrzej Pruś, Adam Raszewski, Grzegorz Ratajczak, Wiesław Ratajczak, Paulina and Adrian Rec, Izabela Augustyn-Reza and Mariusz Reza, Marek Ringwelski, Anna Romanowska, Agnieszka and Marek Rosicki, Sabina and Damian Rowiński, Izabela and Piotr Rudnicki, Izabela Rutkowska, Aleksy Rybiński, Monika and Jerzy Sagan, Magdalena and Jacek Sało, Fr. Tomasz Samulnik O.P., Rev. Marcin Schmidt, Jakub Sendor, Anna and Michał Siciarek, Tomasz Sienicki, Danuta and Jacek Silski, Adam Skutnik, Paweł Słup, Joanna and Paweł Sobolewski, Małgorzata Sochańska, Maciej Sokołowski, Piotr Stawiński, Zbigniew Stawrowski, Tomasz Stefanek, Anna and Marek Sterniczuk, Andrzej Stępień, Mariusz Sulkowski, Piotr Szawlis, Anna Szeliga, Tomasz Szocik, Bogumiła Szponar, Adam Szymanowski, Piotr Szymanowski, Rafał Szymański, Dariusz Szymczak, Anna Tancinco, Agnieszka Tarnowska, Kamilla Thiel-Ornass, Roman Tomanek, Wojciech Tomczyk, Małgorzata Łukasiewicz-Traczyńska and Krzysztof Traczyński, Agata and Wojciech Trebnio, Tamara Trojanowska, Daniel Trojnar, Paweł Turno, Katarzyna and Zbigniew Tyszkiewicz, Magdalena and Paweł Ukielski, Urszula and Andrzej Wacławczyk, Wojciech Walczyk, Elżbieta and Jan Walewski, Bartosz Wesołowski, Katarzyna Węgrzyn, Weronika Wieczorek, Anna Wilińska, Alina and Piotr Winiarski, Remigiusz Witkowski, Elżbieta Włostowska, Krzysztof Wojciechowski, Teresa Woźniak, Jan Wółkowski, Wiesław Zaczkowski, Dariusz Zgutka, Wiesława Żyszkowska, and many more Donors who wish to remain anonymous. Your support is of greatest importance to us. Thank you most warmly!

TABLE OF CONTENTS

Foreword. Thinking with St. John Paul II   xi
DARIUSZ KARŁOWICZ

Why Christianity Needs Culture   1
CARDINAL GIANFRANCO RAVASI

John Paul II and the Foundations of Ethics   20
JOHN FINNIS

Faith in the Modern Areopagus   51
BISHOP ROWAN WILLIAMS

European Identity: North and South, East and West—
the Main Dividing Lines   74
MAREK A. CICHOCKI

Pope St. John Paul II, the Second Vatican Council,
and the Crisis of Modernity   95
JOHN CAVADINI

Political Theology from St. Thomas Aquinas to
John Paul II and Benedict XVI   115
FRANÇOIS DAGUET, O.P.

The End of Christendom   138
CHANTAL DELSOL

The Place and Relevance of Art in the Modern World   155
RÉMI BRAGUE

Formal Europe and Vital Europe. Tradition as
Ground of Identity   176
RENATO CRISTIN

The Phenomenon of "Solidarity"   200
DARIUSZ GAWIN

Index   223

DARIUSZ KARŁOWICZ

FOREWORD

Thinking with St. John Paul II

The dispute over whether St. John Paul II deserves the label "the Great" does not seem difficult to resolve. The sanctity of his life, the depth and range of his teaching, the scale of his pastoral mission, and, finally, the impact he had on the world, leave no doubts that we are dealing here with an extraordinary pontificate.

However, doing justice to the unique meaning of St. John Paul II's life and thought is only the beginning of the road. After all, we are talking about a work that is not, and should not become, closed—but one which is instead a calling. The question of what happens with his heritage is in an obvious way directed at us, at the generations formed by St. John Paul II, at the people upon whom, to a great degree, the continuation of his work depends. What should we do to make sure we do not waste this heritage?

More research is definitely needed to better understand what St. John Paul II wrote and what he did. Taking into account the immensity of his achievements we can confidently assume that research about this pontificate has only started. But the life and thought of Karol Wojtyła are much too serious a matter to leave only to historians. We need St. John Paul II not only as an object of research but also as a witness to Christ, as a thinker, artist, spiritual guide, an expert on (and critic of) modernity, an adviser, and, finally, a still-living source of ever-relevant inspiration.

This is why when, on 18 May 2020, we founded the St. John Paul II Institute of Culture within the Faculty of Philosophy at the Pontifical University of St. Thomas Aquinas (Angelicum) on the 100th anniversary of John Paul II's birth, it was our goal to create a living center of reflection upon the most important problems of the contemporary Church and the world—a place where we will not only think about St. John Paul II but also *with* him.

The Angelicum—a world-renowned university whose roots reach all the way back to the *studium conventuale* led by Thomas Aquinas, where the young Karol Wojtyła wrote his doctorate, today a place where young people from nearly 100 countries study— seemed like the natural place for taking up deep and serious reflection inspired by the teaching of John Paul II. A year after opening the St. John Paul II Institute of Culture we were able to announce a one-year, interdisciplinary program—the JP2 Studies, within which we invite students to the Angelicum to join seminars and lectures in the academic year 2021–2022.

I am honored to present you with a collection of ten lectures from the JP2 Lectures series that were delivered in the first year of the Roman St. John Paul II Institute of Culture. We invite the most outstanding thinkers in our time who are in dialogue with the thought of St. John Paul II to take part in this cycle of lectures. They reflect upon both what is intriguing and living in his thought, as well as what is particularly important, beautiful, and difficult today in the contemporary Church and the world.

I would like to express my gratitude to the outstanding thinkers who made their contributions to this volume. I hope that the wonderful texts collected here illustrate the idea of our plan for this lecture series in the future. The JP2 Lectures were inaugurated by the President of the Pontifical Council for Culture, Cardinal Gianfranco Ravasi, who lectured on Christian reflection upon contemporary culture; there is also the penetrating study of John Paul II's ethics by Professor John Finnis (University of Oxford/ University of Notre Dame); followed by Bishop Rowan Williams's (University of Cambridge/University of South Wales) essay about faith in the modern Areopagus, taking its inspiration from St. Paul's visit to Athens; Professor Marek Cichocki's (Collegium Civitas in Warsaw) lecture is on the spiritual geography of Europe; Professor John Cavadini's (University of Notre Dame) lecture is on St. John Paul II, the Second Vatican Council, and the crisis of modernity; the chapter by Professor François Daguet, O.P. (Institut Catholique de Toulouse) covers the history of Christian theology from St. Thomas Aquinas to Benedict XVI; Professor Chantal Delsol's (Université Paris-Est Marne-la-Vallée) reflection deals with the end of the Christian world; Professor Rémi Brague's (Sorbonne/Ludwig-Maximilians-Universität München) lecture is on the meaning of art in Christianity and beyond; Professor Renato Cristin's (Università di Trieste) lecture is on the competing conceptions of European identity; and finally, last but not least, Professor Dariusz Gawin's (Institute of Philosophy and Sociology of the Polish Academy of Sciences) lecture is on the meaning of the Polish "Solidarity" movement (1980–1981). These are not only outstanding texts but they also present extremely important aspects of an entire spectrum of topics that we would like to tackle in the future JP2 Lectures cycles.

In closing, I would like to sincerely thank the authorities of the Angelicum for their great kindness with which the initiative of establishing the St. John Paul II Institute of Culture was met and the support they provide in its daily operation. I especially direct my gratitude to the Rector of the Angelicum in the years

2017–2021, Professor Michał Paluch, O.P., to the current Rector Professor Thomas Joseph White, O.P., to the Dean of the Faculty of Philosophy Professor Serge-Thomas Bonino, O.P., and the first Director of the Institute, Professor Ryszard Rybka, O.P., as well as to the many other professors and employees of the Angelicum who helped the Institute get off the ground. From among the latter I should mention the Dean of the Faculty of Theology, Professor Catherine Joseph Droste, O.P., the Dean of the Faculty of Social Sciences, Professor Alejandro Crosthwaite, O.P., as well as Benedict Croell, O.P., who deserves special thanks for his unflagging and indispensable support.

I also extend my deep thanks to the priests who agreed to join me in hosting the consecutive, monthly JP2 Lectures during the academic year 2020–2021 and in conducting the discussions that accompanied them. I thank the Professors: Hyacinthe Destivelle, O.P., Dominic Holtz, O.P., Piotr Janas, O.P., Justin Schembri, O.P., Ezra Sullivan, O.P., and Mariusz Tabaczek, O.P.

I would like to express my gratitude to the anonymous sponsors from Poland whose generosity made the St. John Paul II Institute of Culture possible. I would also like to thank all our friends and donors by singling out the main patrons of the St. John Paul II Institute of Culture, the members of the Founders' Council: Danuta and Krzysztof Domarecki, Jolanta and Mirosław Gruszka, Wojciech Piasecki, Dorota and Tomasz Zdziebkowski.

Last but not least I would like to gratefully mention the team of organizers from the Saint Nicholas Foundation in Warsaw, who worked with the St. John Paul II Institute of Culture to bring these JP2 Lectures to viewers and readers around the world. The people I have in mind were in charge of organizing the lectures, arranging translations and making them available online, and the work connected with the preparation of this publication. I thank with all my heart the Director of the Foundation, Joanna Paciorek, along with Aleksandra Bogucka, Marta Broniewska, Natalia Chruścicka, Małgorzata Czajkowska, Monika Dąbrowska, Karol Grabias, Tomasz Herbich, Monika Madej-Wójcik, Mikołaj Marczak, Hanna Nowak, Mikołaj Rajkowski, Izabela Stawicka, Michał Strachowski, Adam Talarowski, and Krzysztof Wojciechowski.

THINKING WITH
ST. JOHN PAUL II

JP2 LECTURES 2020/2021

CARDINAL GIANFRANCO RAVASI

WHY CHRISTIANITY NEEDS CULTURE

The thematic horizon proposed by the title is too vast and complex to allow an exhaustive treatment or a complete descriptive map, as is clear from the immense bibliography. The socio-cultural landscape, unlike that of past eras, is indeed mobile and marked by accelerating developments, new phenomena, and a frenetic evolution of the fundamental structures themselves. Such an evolution begins, first and foremost, with a necessary premise, however obvious, concerning the very notion of "culture."

1. "Culture": An Anthropological Concept

When the term was coined in eighteenth-century Germany (*Cultur*, which later became *Kultur*), the underlying concept was clear and defined: it embraced the high intellectual horizon, the aristocracy of thought, art, science, and humanism. For decades, however, this category has been "democratized;" it has expanded its boundaries and taken on more anthropological characteristics in general, so much so that the adjective "transverse" has now been adopted to indicate the multiplicity of areas and human experiences that it "crosses through."

Indeed, classifications can embrace entire systems. Let us think of subjective-personal patrimony as well as cognitive-intellectual and practical (philosophical, scientific, literary, artistic, technical, all the way down to bodybuilding, etc.). But let us also think of the immense objective-historical sphere (prehistoric, classical, medieval, renaissance, modern culture, and so forth), as well as social (farming, industrial, mass, etc.), national (Italian, French, Russian, English, etc.), and continental (African, Asian, Latin American, and so on). And yet, this fluidity and generality or, if you will, "generalism" brings us back to the classical conception when other very significant synonymous terms were in force: think of the Greek *paideia*, the Latin *humanitas*, or our "civilization" (preferred, for example, by Pius XII). Indeed, despite being of Latin origin, the Latin term *cultura* is attested to only by Cicero in *Tusculanae disputationes* (I, 3) as *agri cultura*, that is to say, cultivation of the fields, and metaphorically applied to philosophy, *cultura animi*.

It is in this broader and more anthropological perspective that the word "culture" had already been accepted with conviction by the Second Vatican Council which, just as in the magisterium of Paul VI, is repeated ninety-one times in its documents. Starting from the Council itself with *Gaudium et Spes*, the theme was subsequently developed in various documents of the Magisterium, including encyclicals and apostolic exhortations, to arrive at further authoritative ecclesial texts, up to *Evangelii Gaudium* of Pope Francis. In this way, a real thematic rainbow has been made that can also acquire a theological and pastoral value. As St. John Paul II expressed in his address to the General Assembly of the United Nations (1995), "any culture is an effort of reflection on the mystery of the world and in particular of man: it is a way of giving expression to the transcendent dimension of human life. The heart of every culture is constituted by its approach to the greatest of mysteries, the mystery of God."[1]

---

1. John Paul II, *Address to the 50th United Nations General Assembly* (United Nations Headquarters New York), para. 9 (5 October 1995). English version available at: https://www.vatican.va/

Along these lines—starting in the 1950s—the theological-pastoral theme of inculturation developed, which the same pontiff defined in *Slavorum Apostoli* (1985) as the "incarnation of the Gospel in native cultures as well as their introduction into the life of the Church,"[2] a dialogical movement of exchange, therefore, whereby—as the pope himself had declared to the bishops of Kenya in 1980—"a culture, transformed and regenerated by the Gospel, produces from its own tradition original expressions of life, celebration, and Christian thought." The term "inculturation" has thus taken on a connotation above all on the theological level as a sign of interpenetration between Christianity and cultures in a fruitful encounter, gloriously attested to by the meeting of the Christian theology of the first centuries and the classical Greco-Roman heritage, and forcefully reaffirmed by the aforementioned *Evangelii Gaudium*.[3]

A significant corollary is that of interculturality, a dynamic category that presupposes a different approach than just "multiculturality." The latter is a static reality of mere juxtaposition or coexistence, as happens in the various ethnic neighborhoods of many metropolises. Interculturality, on the other hand, is based on the recognition of diversity as a necessary and precious flowering of the common "Adamic" root, without, however, losing one's own specificity. What is proposed, then, is attention, study, and dialogue with civilizations that were previously ignored or remote, but that are now prominently appearing in a cultural limelight that has been hitherto occupied by the West (consider Islam, but also India and China), an appearance that is facilitated not only by the current

---

content/john-paul-ii/en/speeches/1995/october/documents/hf_jp-ii_spe_05101995_address-to-uno .html.

    2. John Paul II, *Slavorum Apostoli* (Vatican City, 2 June 1985), para. 21. Available at: https:// www.vatican.va/content/john-paul-ii/en/encyclicals/documents/hf_jp-ii_enc_19850602_slavorum-apostoli.html.

    3. Francis, *Evangelii Gaudium* (Vatican City, 24 November 2013), para. 68-70. Available online at: https://www.vatican.va/content/francesco/en/apost_exhortations/documents/papa-francesco_esortazione-ap_20131124_evangelii-gaudium.html.

globalization, but also by means of communication capable of crossing every frontier (of which the computer network is the paramount symbol).

These cultures, which are "new" for the West, demand an interlocution, often imposed by their dominating presence, so much so that now there is a tendency to speak of "glocalization" as a new phenomenon of planetary interaction. We must, therefore, propose a complex commitment to encounter and dialogue, to cultural and spiritual exchange, which we could represent—in Christian theology—precisely through the same fundamental characteristic of Sacred Scripture and in particular of the Gospel.

2. Gospel and Culture

In order to develop our theme on a general theological level, it is necessary to refer to a central and structural thesis of biblical and, in particular, evangelical Revelation. The Word of God is not a sacred aerolite that swoops down from heaven, but rather the interweaving of divine *Logos* and historical *sarx*: "the Word became flesh" (*John* 1:14).[4] This is a radical contrast with the Greek conception, which did not allow the eternal and transcendent *Logos* to be confounded by immersing itself in the temporality and materiality of history. In the Bible, on the other hand, we are in the presence of a dynamic exchange between Revelation and various civilizations, from nomadic to Phoenician-Canaanite, from Mesopotamian to Egyptian, from Hittite to Persian and Greco-Hellenistic, at least as far as the Old Testament is concerned; New Testament Revelation intersects with Palestinian and Diaspora Judaism, with Greco-Roman culture, and even with the pagan cults.

St. John Paul II, in 1979, affirmed before the Pontifical Biblical Commission that, even before becoming flesh in Jesus Christ, "the

---

4. All Biblical quotations in this text are taken from the New American Bible Revised Edition (NABRE).

divine Word Itself had become human language, assuming the modes of expression of the various cultures which, from Abraham to the Seer of the Apocalypse, offered the adorable mystery of God's saving love the possibility of becoming accessible and comprehensible to the various generations, despite the manifold diversity of their historical situations."[5] The same experience of fruitful exchange between Christianity and cultures—which gave rise to the inculturation of the Christian message in distant civilizations (one need only think of the work of Matteo Ricci in the Chinese world)—has also been constant throughout the Tradition beginning with the Fathers of the Church, both in their dialogue with classical culture and with the theme of *synkatabasis/condescensio* used to describe Revelation and the Incarnation.

In testimony to this cultural and spiritual encounter, it suffices to quote a passage from the First Apology of St. Justin (2nd century): "The entire human race were partakers of the divine *Logos*; and those who lived according to the *Logos* are Christians, even though they were thought atheists; as, among the Greeks, Socrates and Heraclitus, and others like them".[6] As evocatively stated by the English Catholic writer Gilbert K. Chesterton: "All Christian iconography represents the saints with their eyes open to the world, while Buddhist iconography represents every being with its eyes closed."[7] There are, therefore, two different typologies regarding our theme. On the one hand, there is a more exquisitely transcendental, absolute conception, which, by closing its eyes, seeks to go beyond the world, history, time, and space, with its fragility, its finitude, its limits, its weightiness. On the other hand, there is the Christian

---

5. John Paul II, *Address to the Members of the Pontifical Biblical Commission* (26 April 1979). Available online at: https://www.vatican.va/content/john-paul-ii/en/speeches/1979/april/documents/hf_jp-ii_spe_19790426_pont-com-biblica.html.

6. Justin Martyr, *First Apology*, XLVI, 2-3.

7. G.K. Chesterton, *Orthodoxy* (London: John Lane Company, 1908), 74. The actual quote is: "The opposition exists at every point; but perhaps the shortest statement of it is that the Buddhist saint always has his eyes shut, while the Christian saint always has them very wide open."

vision which is deeply innervated within various societies and in the multiplicity of cultures, so much so as to constitute an often unavoidable dialoguing presence.

With a little freedom, we could therefore reformulate the Johannine assertion as follows: "the Word became culture," in the general anthropological sense indicated above. Indeed, Jesus Himself, precisely because He is true man as well as true God, is the *Logos* who became a Jew (*John* 4:22; 19:21), set within precise historical and geographical coordinates (a Galilean in the first thirty years of the first century under a regime of Roman imperial occupation), bound to the social status of "layman" (of the tribe of Judah and not of Levi: *Hebrews* 7:14; 8:4), professionally a carpenter (*Mark* 6:3) at first, and later an itinerant preacher. He is mentally structured according to Semitic cultural characteristics, as attested to by His language that privileges paratactic and parallelistic *logia*, parabolic symbols, and corporeality, unlike the Greek world that relied on syllogistic subordination, speculative abstraction, and interiority.

The very heart of His message, the "Kingdom of God" (*Mark* 1:15), is based on a theme typical of the Old Testament that drew on the socio-political components of the Near East and was configured as God's dynamic plan of salvation within time (history) and space (creation). The same historical existence of Jesus intersected with the events of a society in whose fabric He was placed both in harmony (as attested to by the so-called "Third Quest" and the historiographic criterion of "continuity") and as an explosive catalyst, with His not only theological but also cultural originality (as confirmed by the historiographic criterion of "dissimilarity" and "embarrassment"). A "marginal Jew," yes, to use the well-known expression of John P. Meier,[8] but also an unprecedented and explosive presence, as the final double sentence of His trial bears witness.

---

8. J. P. Meier, *A Marginal Jew. Rethinking the Historical Jesus* (vols. 1–3, New York: Doubleday-Random House, 1991-2001); (vols. 4–5, New Haven and London: Yale University Press, 2009-2016).

On the other hand, He had indeed wanted His message to be "inculturated," starting precisely from His primary destination to Israel: "I was sent only to the lost sheep of the house of Israel" (*Matthew* 15:24); "Go rather to the lost sheep of the house of Israel" (*Matthew* 10:6). But He will then reach, with His Church, the entire *ecumene* in the Easter commissioning: "Go, therefore, and make disciples of all nations" (*Matthew* 28:19). And this is what St. Paul will do in an exemplary way, incarnating the Christian message in the Greco-Roman civilization with a complex and sophisticated operation of inculturation, even with all the reactive difficulties that this work entailed (*Acts of the Apostles* 17:16–34). In this way, three striking metaphors used by Jesus, real coded compendia of inculturation, were actualized in history and culture: the salt in the food (*Matthew* 5:13), the yeast in the dough (*Matthew* 13:33), and the seed in the earth (*John* 12:24).

3. General Changes of the Cultural Paradigm

From the foundation we now move on to contemporary ramifications by casting a glance at some cultural paradigm shifts which are characteristic of our postmodern era. We shall do this through two movements, the first of which comprises a path of a general illustrative nature, while the second will be decidedly more circumscribed and entrusted to some particularly significant symbols. An initial survey concerns the erosion of cultural, moral, and spiritual identities, as well as the fragility of new ethical-social and political models, the changeability and acceleration of phenomena, and their almost gaseous fluidity (now codified in the well-known symbolism of "liquidity" proposed by the sociologist Zygmunt Baumann). These phenomena evidently also affect anthropology, particularly that of the youth. The theme is obviously complex and admits multiple analyses and results. We shall only indicate the phenomenon of the fragmented "ego," linked to the primacy of emotions, to what is more immediate and gratifying, and to the linear accumulation of things rather than to a deepening of meanings. Indeed, society tries to satisfy all needs but extinguishes great desires and eludes projects with a broader scope, thus creating a state of frustration, and above all, distrust in the future. Personal life is full of consumption and yet remains empty, faded, and sometimes even spiritually extinct. Thus, narcissism flourishes, that is to say, self-referentiality that has various symbolic emblems such as the "selfie," the headset, or even the standardized "pack," the nightclub, or bodily exteriority. But there is also the antithetical drift of radical rejection expressed through protest as an end in itself or in generalized indifference, but also with the fall into drug addiction or suicide at a young age.

A new phenotype of society thus takes shape. In order to attempt a meaningful exemplification—referring for the rest to the endless sociological documentation elaborated in a continuous way—we propose a synthesis through a line from the philosopher Paul Ricoeur: "We live in an age when the bulimia of means corresponds to the atrophy of the ends." Indeed, the primacy of the instrument over the meaning dominates, especially if it is ultimate and global. Let us think of the prevalence of technology (so-called "technocracy") over science; or of the dominance of finance over the economy; of the increase in capital rather than productive and working investment; of the excess of specialization and the absence of synthesis in all fields of knowledge, including theology; of mere management of the State with respect to true political planning; of the virtual instrumentation of communication that replaces personal encounters; of the reduction of relationships to mere sexuality that marginalizes and ultimately removes *eros* and love; of religious devotional excess that numbs rather than nourishes authentic faith; and so on.

Finally, let us just address the religious question with an evocation. "Secularity" is a typical value of Christianity on the basis of the evangelical axiom, "Render unto Caesar what is Caesar's and unto God what is God's," but also of the Incarnation itself, which does not erase the *sarx* for a spiritualistic *gnosis*. Precisely for this reason, any theocracy or hierocracy is not Christian, just as sacral fundamentalism is not, despite the recurring temptations to that effect. There is, however, also a "secularism" or "secularization," a widely studied phenomenon[9] that is clearly opposed to a coexistence with religion. And this happens through various paths: we shall highlight two of the more subtle ones (explicit persecution is, of course, more evident, but it is present in circumscribed areas). The first is the so-called "apatheism," that is to say, religious apathy and moral indifference for which the fact that God exists or does not exist is altogether irrelevant, just as ethical categories are hazy, interchangeable, and subjective. This is what is well-described by Pope Francis in *Evangelii Gaudium*: "Priority is given to the outward, the immediate, the visible, the quick, the superficial and the provisional. What is real gives way to appearances. [...] [This has meant] the invasion of ways of thinking and acting proper to other cultures which are economically advanced but ethically debilitated".[10] The pontiff also introduces the second path, connecting it to the first one: "[It] tends to reduce the faith and the Church to the sphere of the private and personal. Furthermore, by completely rejecting the transcendent, it has produced a growing deterioration of ethics, a weakening of the sense of personal and collective sin, and a steady increase in relativism. These have led to a general sense of disorientation".[11]

In practice, there is an endorsement of the idea that religiosity is only an interior and personal spirituality, an experience to be relegated among the volutes of incense and the shining of candles in the

9. See, for example, the imposing and famous study by C. Taylor, *A Secular Age* (Cambridge, MA: Harvard University Press, 2007).

10. Francis, *Evangelii Gaudium*, para. 62.

11. Ibid., para. 64.

sacred space of temples, separated from the pulsating square. These two aspects of the "new atheism" do not exclude, of course, the presence of a more conservative atheism still bound to critical and even sarcastic attack (à la Hitchens, Dawkins, Onfray, Odifreddi, and so on), or the figure of the so-called "nones," who erase all religiosity, paradoxically relying, however, on pagan rituals...

These are just a few points of analysis regarding phenomena that become as many pastoral challenges and that expand to further important issues such as the concepts of "human nature" and "truth," with the related issue of gender, or such problems as those raised by ecology and sustainability (see *Laudato Si'*),[12] to which young people are particularly sensitive, or the effect of a flattened economy on a finance that creates an enormous accumulation of capital, but also its "virtual" fragility, generating serious social crises and, in connection, the scourge of unemployment or poorly paid underemployment. In this regard, the message of the encyclical *Fratelli Tutti* is explicit.[13] We also think of more specific themes such as the link between aesthetics and culture, particularly the importance of new musical languages for young people and, more extensive in scope, the link between art and faith and so on.

It is important, however, to reiterate that attention to sociocultural paradigm shifts must never be an act of mere denunciation, nor the temptation to retreat into sacred oases, nostalgically going back to an idealized past. The world in which we now live is full of turmoil and challenges to the faith, but it is also endowed with great human and spiritual resources of which young people are often the bearers: it is enough to mention lived solidarity, volunteerism, universalism, a yearning for freedom, victory over many diseases,

12. Francis, *Laudato Si'* (24 May 2015). Available online at: https://www.vatican.va/content/fran cesco/en/encyclicals/documents/papa-francesco_20150524_enciclica-laudato-si.html.

13. Francis, *Fratelli Tutti* (Vatican City, 3 October 2020). Available online at: https://www .vatican.va/content/francesco/en/encyclicals/documents/papa-francesco_20201003_enciclica-fratelli-tutti.html.

the extraordinary progress of science, and testimonial authenticity required by many, even non-believers, from religions or politics, and so on. But this is another very important chapter to be written in parallel to the one drafted thus far and which lies outside the limited approach we have chosen.

4. Two Specific Itineraries: Science and Computer Communication

As we have announced, we shall now try to narrow down the vast and varied horizon evoked thus far, introducing two itineraries that we can consider fundamental in contemporary life, those of science and communication. These are the paths that the younger generations, in particular, are enthusiastically following, convinced that herein lie the most well-founded answers to so many of their expectations. Indeed, these are fascinating paths, even if still in their infancy, which are capable of creating real revolutions. Let us start with an incursion, however simplified, into the field of science with three examples. First of all, genetics, with the discovery of DNA and its flexibility and even its changeability, which has recorded different results: on the one hand, research has been developed with the aim of eliminating diseases; on the other hand, however, the use of genetic engineering has been hypothesized to improve and change the anthropological phenotype, envisaging a future with a radically modified human genome. It is in this further perspective that the still confusing landscape of trans- and post-humanism is opened.

This manipulation of DNA generates a delta of questions of various kinds, for now only futurological, starting from the basic question about the human species itself: will these new anthropological phenotypes still be classifiable in the genus *homo sapiens sapiens*? The questions become burning at the theological and ethical level: are these interventions in the heart of human life compatible, and therefore justifiable, with the biblical vision of man as deputy or viceroy or "image" of the Creator, or are they to be classified under the capital-original sin of wanting to be "like God," in the act of Adamic hubris judged in chapter 3 of Genesis?

A second area where research is moving forward in a decisive way is that of neuroscience. For the Platonic-Christian tradition, mind/soul and brain belong to different planes, one metaphysical, the other biochemical. The Aristotelian-Christian conception, while recognizing the substantial autonomy of mind from brain matter, admits that the latter is an instrumental condition for the exercise of mental and spiritual activities. A more "physicalistic" model, widespread in the contemporary horizon, does not hesitate instead, also on the basis of evolutionary theory, to radically reduce mind and soul to a neuronal datum, which is, however, already impressive in itself: our brain, which weighs only 120–180 grams, contains a galaxy of a hundred billion neurons, as many as the stars of the Milky Way.

Faced with this complexity, we are content to underline that human identity also takes the stage here. This identity certainly has in the brain-mind (however the connection is understood) a fundamental meeting point whereby, if this reality is structurally influenced, one will go in the direction of redefining the human being. The sequence of philosophical, theological, and ethical problems stretches out then excessively: where to situate in such an approach the will, consciousness, freedom, responsibility, decision, calibration between external and intrinsic impulses, interpretation of acquired information and, above all, the origin of thought, of symbolism, of religion, of art, and, in the final analysis, the "ego"?

This perspective leads us, seamlessly, to a third equally impressive and delicate example, that of "thinking machines," i.e. artificial intelligence. At present, so-called robotics is generating increasingly autonomous machines. There is no doubt that this has positive repercussions in the fields of medicine, production, management, and administration. But, precisely in this last sector, questions arise about the future of work, which is conceived in the classical and biblical vision as a component of hominization itself (the "cultivating and caring" and the "naming" of living and non-living beings), the lack of which therefore generates a social and personal imbalance. This imbalance is then intensified if a privileged class of inventors, programmers, and owners of similar machines appears.

The questions are perhaps more urgent on the anthropological side, since already today some machines have a remarkable ability to "appropriate" language, thus creating information autonomously. There is, then, an even more significant ethical side of things. What moral values can be programmed into the algorithms that lead the thinking machine to decision-making processes in the face of scenarios that are presented to it and in respect of which it must make a decision capable of affecting the lives of human creatures? The concerns regard in particular so-called "strong artificial intelligence" (artificial general intelligence or Strong AI) whose systems are programmed for an autonomy of the machine up to the point of improving and recreating on its own the range of its services, so as to achieve a certain "self-awareness."

Until now, the clear distinction between a machine with artificial intelligence and a human person has seemed stable, according to the assertion of the American philosopher of language John Searle (b. 1932) for whom computers possess syntax but not semantics; in practice they do not know what they are doing.[14] But the prospects of the aforementioned "strong artificial intelligence," which is convinced that it can cross this line of demarcation with the advent of machines that are not only thinking but also self-aware, shuffles the

---

14. Searle presented this point in the famous 1980 thought-experiment known as the "Chinese room argument" first discussed in "Minds, Brains and Programs," *Behavioral and Brain Sciences* 3 (1980): 417-57, and then in "Is the Brain's Mind a Computer Program?", *Scientific American* 262, no. 1 (1990).

cards and requires new attention and examination, but also some demythologizing.

5. The Infosphere

The second itinerary that contemporary culture and society have embarked upon is so significant in its results that some believe it has already created a new anthropological phenotype. We refer to the question of mass communication. One of the best contemporary "digital" philosophers, Luciano Floridi of the University of Oxford, has acutely grasped this phenomenon in his book *The Fourth Revolution: How the Infosphere is Reshaping Human Reality*.[15] After the previous major turning points in history and modern science, namely, the three anthropological revolutions (the Copernican, Darwinian, and psychoanalytic), a computer revolution enters the scene, which manages to change the global coordinates of democracy itself, as well as of culture.

By now presupposed is the reference to the first steps taken by the Canadian scholar Marshall McLuhan (1911–1980) with his primordial considerations on the counterpoint between content and communication, with the axiom, which is now abused to the point of stereotype, according to which even "the medium is the message," for which, as the Canadian scholar joked in one of the essays from *The Mechanical Bride*, "Today it is not the classroom nor the classics which are the repositories of models of eloquence, but the ad agencies."[16] But we have gone far beyond that. Indeed, the most significant sign of the change underway regarding the balance between content and communication is that now communication is no longer a medium similar to a prosthesis that increases the functionality of our senses, allowing us to see or hear farther away

15. L. Floridi, *The Fourth Revolution: How the Infosphere is Reshaping Human Reality* (Oxford: Oxford University Press, 2014).
16. M. McLuhan, *The Mechanical Bride: Folklore of Industrial Man* (New York: Vanguard Press, 1951).

(tele-phone, tele-scope, tele-vision), but it has become a total, global, collective environment, an atmosphere that we cannot but breathe, not even those who delude themselves into thinking they can escape it, precisely, an "infosphere."

Thus, today's communication is no longer an "extension of ourselves," as McLuhan intended, but the passing to a new "human condition," to an unprecedented anthropological model whose traits are controlled by this all-encompassing reality of which the Internet is the ruling banner.[17] Even Galileo with the telescope only believed to "extend" visual capabilities, but in the end created a revolution not only cosmological but also epistemological and anthropological for which man was no longer the center of the universe (the "Copernican Revolution"). We are, therefore, immersed in a "creation" that is different from the primordial "creation."

In it there are already many new full-fledged citizens, those who, since 2001, with Mark Prensky, have been called digital natives,[18] compared to those of previous generations who at most can aspire to be "digital migrants," unable—as happens precisely to immigrants—to lose the old accent. Immersed in this new general and global "environment," it remains increasingly difficult and senseless to adopt apocalyptic rejection. However, it is necessary to be sensitive and critically surveilled so as not to become "info-obese," i.e. totally integrated.

One should not, therefore, plunge into an impossible isolationism or into radical criticism. However, it is necessary to advance some reservations. At the purely linguistic level, a basic problematic phenomenon immediately emerges: similar to the citizens of the biblical Babel, we risk not understanding each other and becoming unable to dialogue, having become victims of a sick communication, excessive in quantity and quality, often wounded by violence,

17. "The Extension of Man" was the subtitle of McLuhan's 1964 essay, "Understanding Media".
18. M. Prensky, "Digital Natives, Digital Immigrants," *On the Horizon* 9, no. 5 (October 2001).

approximation and clinging to stereotypes, to excess and vulgarity, and even to falsification. We need, therefore, a campaign of linguistic ecology: authentic "communication," as indicated by the Latin root, is a making available to the other (*cum*) a *munus*, that is to say, a "gift," a "mission." It is, therefore, a sharing of values, of confidences, of contents, of emotions.

A further reservation to be pointed out concerns another computer phenomenon, which is at first sight positive, namely the exponential multiplication of data offered. Indeed, this can lead to an agnostic relativism, to an intellectual and moral anarchy, to a decrease in the capacity for critical selective examination. The hierarchies of values are upset, the constellations of truths are dispersed, reduced to a game of variable opinions in an immense basket of information. The principle that the philosopher Thomas Hobbes had formulated in his famous *Leviathan* (1651) is actualized in an unexpected way: "*Auctoritas non veritas facit legem.*" It is the powerful and dominant authority that determines ideas, thought, choices, behavior, and not the objective truth itself. The new authority is precisely the prevailing public opinion, which obtains more space and is more effective within the enormous mass of data offered by computer communication and which, in this way, creates "truths." Emblematic of the drift to which one can be led is the triumph of fake news, the lie that having taken root, being insisted on, and proliferated on the Internet, regenerates as pseudo-objective truth.

Another critical note points to the degeneration underlying a component that is in itself positive. Under the apparent "democratization" of communication, under the deregulation imposed by the globalization of information technology, which would seem to be a principle of pluralism, under the same multiplicity of content previously mentioned, a subtle operation of standardization and control is actually hidden. It is not for nothing that the management of networks is increasingly entrusted to the hands of tycoons or "mega-corporations" or centers of power that can skillfully and knowingly orient, shape, and mold for their own use (and for the use of their market and interests) content and data, thus creating new models of behavior and thought. Examples are the recent cases related to the instrumental socio-political use of Facebook data or to the external data breach in the electoral events of one nation.

A final critical observation concerns the acceleration and multiplication of contacts, but also their reduction to virtuality. As mentioned earlier, we are plunged into a "cold" and solitary communication that explodes into forms of exasperation and perversion. On the one hand, we have the sellout intimacy of the "chat line," or Facebook, or to stay in the television sphere, that of so-called reality programs; we have the violation of subjective conscience, of interiority, of the personal sphere. On the other hand, the result is a more pronounced loneliness, a basic incomprehension, a series of misunderstandings, a fragility in one's own identity, a loss of dignity. It has been observed that as soon as computers multiplied and satellite dishes flourished on the roofs of houses, people shut themselves in their homes and lowered their shutters. Paradoxically, the effect of moving towards virtual reality and media worlds has been one of separation from one another and the death of living, direct dialogue in the "village."

Faced with such a problematic horizon, there can be a strong temptation to discouragement and an attitude of resignation, convinced of the unstoppability of a similar process destined to create a new human standard. The disembodied attitude of those who shut themselves up in their own little old world, content to follow the rules of the past, deploring the degeneration of the present age, is certainly not Christian. For young people, then, this is *par excellence* their world in which they were born and are at ease.

The French philosopher and sociologist Edgar Morin—while observing that the new means that have arisen to distinguish reality from manipulation and truth from lies, such as photography, cinema, and television, have been used in many cases precisely to foster illusion, manipulation, and lies—has demonstrated, along with many other scholars of these phenomena, how the new communication can ultimately generate a richer and more complex reality that is even more fruitful in human terms.[19] This is what we often experience on the ecclesial level as well, in proclamation and pastoral engagement through the new "media."

It is, therefore, essential to continue to develop a theological and pastoral reflection on communication itself in the age of the Internet and on the ways in which the proclamation of the Gospel can be grafted onto it. At its basis, then, is the conviction that the Net is a "domain" endowed with great spiritual potential. It is necessary to continue research for the construction of a grammar of pastoral communications. This solicitation must involve not only the "technicians" of the digital civilization but also ecclesial workers in their continuous and constant encounter with the contemporary anthropological profile of the digital native and the new social society, and therefore, in a privileged way, with the world of young people.

We conclude our look at the need for the Church to pay attention to culture with a statement made by an exemplary witness who reminds us of the need to combine humanism and technology and, therefore, faith and contemporary culture, namely—Steve Jobs, the founder of Apple who, not long before his death in 2011, said: "Technology alone is not enough. It's technology married with the liberal arts, married with the humanities, that yields the results that make our hearts sing."[20]

translated from Italian by Peter M. Falco

---

19. E. Morin, *L'esprit du temps* (Paris: Armand Colin, 2008).

20. At the iPad 2 unveiling, S. Jobs said: "It is an Apple's DNA that technology alone is not enough—it's technology married with the liberal arts, married with the humanities, that yields us the results that make our heart sing."

CARDINAL GIANFRANCO RAVASI—born in Merate, Italy, in 1942. Appointed as cardinal at the consistory in 2010. Currently he is one of the most eminent officials of the Roman Curia presiding over: the Pontifical Council for Culture, the Pontifical Commission for Sacred Archeology, and the Pontifical Commission for the Cultural Heritage of the Church. Close collaborator of Pope Benedict XVI and Pope Francis.

JOHN FINNIS

JOHN PAUL II AND THE FOUNDATIONS OF ETHICS

Although this lecture will recall some leading elements of the book *The Acting Person* where they illuminate a papal document, the lecture, with that exception, will scarcely touch upon the pre-papal writings of John Paul II. Instead it will focus on his first encyclical, *Redemptor Hominis*, his encyclical *Laborem Exercens*, and his encyclical *Veritatis Splendor*, with occasional mention of other statements he made as Pope. Those three encyclicals set forth a conception of the foundations of ethics that deserves and repays study.

They also illustrate one of the most important propositions of Christian teaching: the proposition, repeatedly affirmed by St. Thomas, that some important elements of Christian teaching restate and make more widely available the equivalent teachings of sound philosophy. One example is the truth that the universe is created *ex nihilo* by a transcendent act of reason, will and executive power effecting the transcendent choice to create and, specifically, to create *this* universe rather than any of the countless possible alternatives.

Another example is what sound philosophy affirms as the foundational moral principles and precepts, those that St. Paul had in mind in *Romans* 2:14 when he taught that all those peoples to whom the Law revealed to Moses and Israel was not revealed are nevertheless able, by nature—by natural reason in the form of conscience—to make moral judgments which correspond to the revealed Law. Many passages in *Romans* and other epistles indicate that Paul is speaking about the Law set forth in the Decalogue, not the many other parts of the Mosaic Law, which in the tradition carried forward by St. Thomas have been called its "ceremonial and judicial precepts," as opposed to its "moral" part. Considered philosophically, the precepts of the Decalogue—with the exception of the *determinatio* of the period of rest as one day in seven—are precepts of natural law. That is, they are standards which (as Paul is saying to the Roman Christians) are accessible to human reason unaided by revelation—accessible either in the form of conscience (see *Romans* 2:15) or of philosophy. Paul emphasizes this accessibility by saying that "Gentiles who do not have the Law do *by nature* (*physei*) what the Law requires, and so are a law unto themselves" because "the content [*ergon*] of the Law is written on their hearts (*kardías*; *cordibus*), while their conscience (*syneideseôs*; *conscientia*) also testifies [...]." (I will come back later to the words "heart" and "conscience.")

Fundamental to ethics (or, to say the same thing: at the foundations of ethics) is the constitution, the make-up, the nature and essence of the human person who can be morally good or morally bad. Ethics is founded on realities affirmed by metaphysics, ontology, and anthropology—on the given realities of human nature. But in the order of discovery, as St. Thomas says more than once, metaphysics comes last and, as he emphasizes countless times from his earliest to his latest works, the *nature* of a dynamic reality/being is *known* (discovered) by knowing the being's *capacities*, and these are known only by knowing its *activities*, its acts, its actuations of those capacities, and acts are known and understood only by knowing *their objects*. And as Aquinas makes clear in his formal discussion of the first principles of ethics in the *Prima Secundae*, the objects of human acts are intelligible goods, the goods that the first principle of practical reason directs us to and practical reason's other first principles identify.[1] But what is good or defective in the pursuit of goods is *the* subject-matter of ethics. Therefore: we know human nature adequately, philosophically, metaphysically, by first understanding it ethically.

This conclusion, if not—or not explicitly—all the reasoning towards it, inspires (I believe) all John Paul II's pre-papal philosophical work on the nature of the human person and of human acts.

So I will consider first some main elements and conclusions of his analysis of the acts of human persons. Then I will consider the implicit or perhaps explicit methodology deployed in that analysis: the adoption of the internal point of view, the self-understanding of the deliberating, intending and choosing person. After which, I will consider what was left under-developed in Karol Wojtyła's philosophical work on human nature, the study of intelligible human goods and of the good way of pursuing and actualizing them: the study that is properly called ethics.

Most of the following lecture will be philosophical, but I will not rigorously exclude the doctrinal and the theological—that is, propositions and reflections based on revelation.

---

1. See St. Thomas Aquinas, *Summa Theologiae, Prima Secundae*, q. 94, a. 2. Although *obiectum* does not appear in q. 94, this article, in speaking of *inclinationes ad bona*, is speaking of their *obiecta* according to the axiom stated in *ST*, I, q. 105, a. 4c: "*Velle enim nihil aliud est quam inclinatio quaedam in obiectum voluntatis, quod est bonum universale*" (where "*universal*" does not mean "in general or in the abstract" but "not a particular as such"; human life, for example, is a universal, but so is ice-cream or trumpet-playing). See also the discussion in *ST*, I-II, q. 51, a. 1c of the *obiecta* of *inclinationes* and *potentiae*, with mention of *principia iuris communis* which are *seminalia virtutum*. See my *Aquinas: Moral, Political and Legal Theory* (Oxford: Oxford University Press, 1998), 86–94.

1. *Laborem Exercens* (1981)

The original Polish edition of Karol Wojtyła's *The Acting Person* has, I gather, the subtitle: "An Attempt at Constructing Catholic Ethics on the Basis of Max Scheler's Philosophy"—a subtitle neither used nor mentioned in the English edition published ten years later, in 1979. Leaving aside all questions about the relationship between Scheler's philosophy and John Paul II's, on which much has been written, none of which am I concerned to assess, the point I wish to make is that the book was conceived not simply as a phenomenology or study of the personal experience of acting, of being an acting subject, but as at least a foundation for ethics—a study of one of the fundamentals of ethics. Here and throughout my lecture I take "ethics" to be a critical reflective understanding of the morality of choices, dispositions and actions, and thus of what it is for a person to be *morally* good or *morally* bad. There is only a nuance of difference between "ethics" and "morality," and I tend to use the terms "ethical" and "moral" interchangeably. That interchangeability is found also in, for example, *Laborem Exercens*.[2] A foundation of ethics is a foundation of morality because ethics is fundamentally a theoretical (though also practical, and so: *practical*-theoretical) study of morality, a study in which the decisive question is: what are the true standards by which I can assess my own actual or prospective choices as morally sound or unsound (immoral), and thus too assess, in like terms, my way of life, and indeed *myself*.

Leaving aside for a moment the question of the true standards, to which I will return, I focus in this first section on the relationship between choices, acts, ways of life, and "selves," that is, persons—in the first instance myself—as self-determining and self-shaping

2. See John Paul II, *Laborem Exercens* (Vatican City, 14 September 1981), para. 6: "human work has an ethical value of its own"; para. 9: "the dignity of human work […] its specific *moral* value" (cf. Italian *morale* and Latin *ethica* [!]). Available online at: http://www.vatican.va/content/john-paul-ii/en/encyclicals/documents/hf_jp-ii_enc_14091981_laborem-exercens.html.

by choice. This is the matter or topic which the book *The Acting Person* takes as its main concern, and which is fundamental to the encyclical *Laborem Exercens*. That was John Paul II's third encyclical, explicitly linked to his first, *Redemptor Hominis* (which we will consider in the next section) and is implicitly in close relation to the book. *Laborem Exercens*, published in September 1981 with the subtitle "on Human Work, on the nineteenth anniversary of *Rerum Novarum*," has as one of its primary themes the Catholic social teaching on property and thus on socialism and communism and exaggerated or normless capitalism and economism. Here I shall ignore all that, despite its value, in order to focus on the other primary theme: "human work."

The encyclical identifies with precision its own "guiding thread": "the mystery of creation."[3] For by work, human persons fulfil, develop or realize themselves, that is, we each share in God's creation of us, even when the work—what we are working on, or working at—is humble in its "objective character" as work.[4] (One should recall here that in speaking of divine, transcendent creation we need not depart from the strictly philosophical. For strictly philosophical arguments show that the universe must have its explanation in such a transcendent act.)

The encyclical deploys, throughout, a distinction between "work in the subjective sense" and "work in the objective sense." It has nothing to do with the distinction between "objective" truth and mere "subjective" opinion, opinion strongly held and affirmed but

---

3. Ibid., para. 12; see also para. 4.

4. Note the cautionary words at the end of *Laborem Exercens,* para. 4: "As man, through his work, becomes more and more the master [*dominus*] of the earth, he nevertheless, in every case and at every phase of this process [*progressionis*], remains within the Creator's original ordering [*in via illius primigeniae ordinationis, a Creatore datae, manet constitutus*]. And this *ordinatio* remains necessarily and indissolubly linked with the fact that man was created, as male and female, 'in the image of God'. This *ordo rerum* [the Italian, English, etc., here have, questionably, 'process'] is at the same time universal [...] it embraces all human beings, every generation, every phase of economic and cultural development [*progressus*], and, at the same time, it is an *ordo efficitur* [again, questionably, 'process takes place'] within each human being, in each conscious human subject [...]."

lacking in objectivity, that is, lacking in truth. The encyclical's distinction reflects the fact that work has two aspects, two dimensions, two *rationes*. In the "objective sense," work is directed towards an external object, for example, some part of the world's resources; and it transforms that external object with another external object— for example, with some machine created by someone's (perhaps by someone *else's*, another person's) work—and results in another external object, the finished product. Even when work is taken, as the encyclical intends, in a more generic sense, as including all forms of chosen activity in this world of time—including even (I believe) the activity and work of contemplation—there is an "objective" aspect: the chosen activity as an observable phenomenon in time and space.

Thus, I think, the idea of "external" objects is to be understood as including anything external to the will, to the act of deliberating and choosing: prayer and contemplation, as outcomes of an act of choice, are external to one's will, even though they are observable only to the person who is praying or contemplating. I believe that this is the case (the fact of the matter) even though the observing is in a sense internal, and even though—as Elizabeth Anscombe brilliantly emphasized—*we know what we are doing* without having to "observe" what we are doing.[5] One *can* observe what one is doing, but one does not *need* to, for one already (before observing) knows what one is doing, because in doing it one is carrying out the plan (the proposal, the set of envisaged ends and means) that one shaped up in deliberating and adopted by choosing. In saying this, I have gone beyond what the encyclical says and *perhaps* even beyond what John Paul II thought, or thought out. Yet what I am saying is entirely in line with his thought, his "phenomenological" interest and "personalist" intent. Section 4 of *Laborem Exercens* introduces the "objective aspect" of work in these words:

5. See my essay "On Hart's Ways: Law as Reason and as Fact," in J. Finnis, *Philosophy of Law: Collected Essays Volume IV* (Oxford: Oxford University Press, 2011), 230–56, see particularly 235–9.

Work understood as a "transitive" activity, that is to say, an activity beginning in a human subject and directed towards an external object, presupposes a specific dominion by man over "the earth" and, in its turn, it confirms and develops that dominion.[6]

The word "transitive" suggests, of course, its opposite, "intransitive."
Not wishing, however, to impose his own philosophical vocabulary
on the Church, John Paul II abstains in the encyclical from using
the term "intransitive," even though it is a or even *the* key term in
his own philosophical explanation of what the encyclical calls the
"subjective" aspect of work. The subjective aspect or *ratio* of work is
explained in section 6 of *Laborem Exercens*:

> Man has to subdue the earth and dominate [i.e., have dominion over] it, be-
> cause as the "image of God" he is a person, that is to say, a subjective being
> capable of acting in a planned and rational way, capable of deciding about
> himself [*deliberandum de se*], and with a tendency to self-realization [*eoque
> contendem ut de se ipsum perficiat*]. *As a person, man is therefore the subject
> of work.* As a person he works, he performs various actions belonging to the
> work process; independently of their objective content, these actions must
> all serve to realize his humanity, to fulfil the calling to be a person that is his
> by reason of his very humanity. [...] And so this "dominion" spoken of in
> the biblical text being meditated upon here refers not only to the objective
> dimension of work but at the same time introduces us to an understand-
> ing of its subjective dimension. Understood as a process whereby man and
> the human race subdue the earth, work corresponds to this basic biblical
> concept only when throughout the process man manifests himself and
> confirms himself as the one who "dominates." This dominion, in a certain
> sense, refers to the subjective dimension even more than to the objective
> one: this dimension conditions the *ethical* nature of work. In fact there is no
> doubt that human work has an *ethical value* of its own [*in labore humano vis
> ethica insit*], which clearly and directly remains linked to the fact that the
> one who carries it out is a person, a conscious and free subject, that is to say
> a subject that decides about himself [*de se ipso deliberans*].[7]

---

6. John Paul II, *Laborem Exercens*, para. 4.
7. Ibid., para. 6 (emphasis in original).

"This truth, which in a sense constitutes the fundamental and perennial heart of Christian teaching on human work"[8] is made clear in the explanation of the good of work in section 9:

[...] as such, [work] is a good thing for man. It is not only good in the sense that it is useful or something to enjoy; it is also good as being something worthy, that is to say, something that corresponds to man's dignity, that expresses this dignity and increases it. If one wishes to define more clearly the ethical meaning of work, it is this truth that one must particularly keep in mind. Work is a good thing for man-a good thing for his humanity—because through work man *not only transforms nature,* adapting it to his own needs, but also *achieves fulfilment* as a human being and indeed, in a sense, becomes "more a human being."[9]

This "perfecting, realizing, developing of oneself" (*se ipsum perficiens*) is a theme of the treatment of work in Vatican II's *Gaudium et Spes*:

Just as [human activity] proceeds from man, so it is ordered towards man. For when a man works he not only alters things and society, he develops himself as well. He learns much, he cultivates his resources, he *goes outside of himself and beyond himself.* Rightly understood, this kind of growth is of greater value than any external riches which can be garnered [...] Hence, the norm of human activity is this: that in accord with the divine plan [*consilium*] and will, it should harmonize with the genuine good of the human race [*genuino humani generis bono*], and that it allow men as individuals and as members of society to pursue their total vocation [*integrae suae vocationis*] and fulfil it.[10]

It would be no surprise to learn that in 1964–65 Archbishop Wojtyła had an input into that part of *Gaudium et Spes*, and certainly it is a part that is reflected in the central chapter of his book

8. Ibid.

9. Ibid, para. 9.

10. Second Vatican Ecumenical Council, Pastoral Constitution on the Church in the Modern World *Gaudium et Spes* (Vatican City, 7 December 1965), para. 35 (emphasis added). Available online at: https://www.vatican.va/archive/hist_councils/ii_vatican_council/documents/vat-ii_const_19651207_gaudium-et-spes_en.html. Note that this section of *Gaudium et Spes* is quoted in section 26 of *Laborem Exercens*.

The Acting Person, originally published in 1969. For that chapter begins with the proposition that "the performance of an action brings fulfillment," and with the comment: "All the essential problems considered in this study seem to be focused and condensed in the simple assertion of fulfillment in an action."[11] And at the same time the author invites us to notice that the idea of "fulfillment in an action" bears upon "our previous discussion of the person's transcendence in the doing of an action."

What is this transcendence of the person by the person? It seems reminiscent of the statement in section 35 of *Gaudium et Spes* that in activity man goes outside of himself and beyond himself (*extra se* and *supra se*). Neither the statement nor the idea is mere poetry or metaphor. The transcendence that Wojtyła often has in view he regularly calls "vertical transcendence," and his distinction between "horizontal" and "vertical" transcendence corresponds (is equivalent) to his distinction between "objective" and "subjective" *rationes* of work, and to his distinction between the "transitive" and "intransitive" aspects of action. To repeat: *horizontal transcendence is what the objective ratio of work seeks and the transitive aspect of action is intended to achieve.* Just as by perceiving and knowing objects we in a sense get outside ourselves, so too we get outside ourselves by intending and willing (choosing) objects (including events and states of affairs) beyond ourselves or, more strictly, beyond our willing.

Vertical transcendence, on the other hand, is the fact of self-determination. As a person, one transcends one's structural boundaries by one's capacity to exercise freedom.[12] This transcendence is "associated with self-government and self-possession."[13] It is a matter of one's "ascendancy over [one's] own dynamisms,"[14] over all the

---

11. K. Wojtyła, *The Acting Person,* trans. Andrzej Potocki (Dordrecht, Boston & London: D. Reidel Publishing Company, 1979), 149.

12. Ibid., 119.

13. Ibid., 131.

14. Ibid., 138.

natural dynamisms of body and mind (*soma* and *psyche*),[15] over all the natural dynamisms of emotion and desire and aversion that are in themselves merely things that happen in or happen to oneself (i.e., that *take place* in me) and are not *me acting* although they belong to me just as much as the dynamism of action itself belongs to me.[16] When I act, they are integrated into that superior type of dynamism and receive from it a new meaning and a new quality that is properly personal.[17]

Let me explain in my own words what I understand by "vertical transcendence" in *The Acting Person* (and therefore also by "subjective *ratio* of work" in *Laborem Exercens*). Free choice (what *The Acting Person* calls "free will") is more, much more, than what the ancients and the post-Christian moderns understand by freedom of choice: freedom from compulsion and freedom to do as one pleases. What, instead, is presupposed in *Deuteronomy* 30:18 ("I set before you life or death, blessing or curse: *choose* life") or in *Ecclesiasticus* (*Sirach*) 15:14 ("When God in the beginning created man he made him subject to his own free choice: if you wish you can keep the commandments"), and in the whole of the Gospel, as well as in John Paul II's references to freedom, is the following: I can choose between alternative options/proposals that I have shaped up in deliberation, *open* alternatives in that there is *no factor save my choosing* that settles which alternative I choose—no factor, whether it is a system of desires or preferences (as the typical Anglo-American philosopher would have it), or "selfish genes," or the superior reasonableness or moral rightness of one alternative and the wrongness of the other(s), or any other "sufficient reason." So my free choices—precisely because they are not the product of what was there in my wants, preferences, habits, or other such dynamisms—*create*. This

15. Ibid., 197.
16. Ibid., 80.
17. Ibid., 197.

creativity of choice is the essence of what *Laborem Exercens* calls "transcendence," a term we already find in the title of section 3 of Chapter Three of *The Acting Person*: "Free will as the basis of the transcendence of the acting person."

In understanding this creativity, we also understand what *The Acting Person* calls the "intransitivity" of action. In my own words: one's free choices establish, create one's own identity or character—not, of course, one's identity as male or female, or (somewhat differently) as slave or free, identities that are not within one's power to choose for oneself. Thus one's choices are not only transitive, i.e., transiting out from one's will into one's behavior and one's efficacy in shaping things and events in the world. They are also intransitive: each free choice is an act by which I who am choosing constitute myself the person I will henceforth be, as the person I will remain unless and until (if ever) I repent of that choice, either formally by contrition and resolve to amend my ways, or informally by making a new choice incompatible with the former one.

Thus we have reached another distinctive theme of the analysis of action in *The Acting Person*, that is, what that book calls the *persistence* of actions:

In the inner dimension of the person, human action is at once both transitory and relatively lasting, inasmuch as its effects, which are to be viewed in relation to efficacy and self-determination, that is to say, to the person's engagement in freedom, last longer than the action itself. The engagement in freedom is objectified [...] in the person and not only in the action, which is the transitive effect. [...] Human actions once performed do not vanish without trace: *they leave their moral value*, which constitutes an objective reality intrinsically cohesive with the person, and thus a reality also profoundly subjective.[18]

---

18. Ibid., 151 (emphasis added).

I interject to make two interpretative observations. First, I think "moral value" here is equivalent to "ethical value" in *Laborem Exercens* 6, quoted above. Second, I think the term "objective" in the just-quoted sentence of *The Acting Person* does not correspond to "objective" as we saw it in *Laborem Exercens* 4, but rather to the meaning of "objective" that simply intensifies the predicate "true," "real," "really," etc., not merely imaginary. When, however, John Paul II goes on "also profoundly subjective" he *is* anticipating the language of *Laborem Exercens* 4. (So there was here, it seems, a sort of punning on "objective.") In the same exposition in *The Acting Person* we read:

> It is in the modality of morality that this objectification becomes clearly apparent, when through an action that is either morally good or morally bad, man, as the person, himself becomes either morally good or morally bad. In this way we begin to glimpse the meaning of the assertion that "to perform the action brings fulfillment." [...] Implied in the intentionality of willing and acting, in man's reaching outside of himself towards objects that he is presented with as various goods—and thus values—here is his simultaneous moving back into *his ego, the closest and most essential object of self-determination.* [...] because of self-determination, an action reaches and penetrates into the subject, into the ego, which is its primary and principal *object.*[19]

This explanation of what *Laborem Exercens* will call the subjective *ratio* of work and action (and the philosophical writings call the intransitive aspect of action) explains the subject (the chooser and doer) as the object, the intransitive object, of the choosing and doing (the choice and action). This corresponds to the sense in which, as *Laborem Exercens* repeatedly says, one deliberates about oneself, *deliberat de se ipso.* It is elaborated in Chapter Three of *The Acting Person*:

> [...] the person is, owing to self-determination, an object for himself, in a peculiar way being the immanent target upon which man's exercise of all

19. Ibid. 150–1 (emphasis added).

his powers concentrates, insofar as it is he whose determination is at stake. He is in this sense, the primary object or the nearest object of his action. Every actual act of self-determination makes real the subjectiveness of self-governance and self-possession; in each of these interpersonal structural relations there is given to the person as the subject—as he who governs and possesses—the person as the object—as he who is governed and possessed. This objectiveness is, as may be seen, the correlate of the person's subjectiveness and, moreover, seems to bring out in a specific manner subjectiveness itself.[20]

And later he says that the subject is not only the primary and nearest object of his or her action but is also the basic, most direct and innermost object.

But these statements, like the talk of deliberating *de se ipso* (about oneself) are not to be taken as subscribing to any theory— call it a theory of fundamental option—which holds that one disposes of oneself only by a fundamental option which is not a choice to do this or do that particular act, but somehow a radical choice for self or for God, a "total disposal" of the self "in the depths of the self" where (these theorists say) the self is "totally present to itself," so that no particular choice or act can be said to be of itself a mortal sin. John Paul II's theory of the intransitive object of action is in fact radically opposed to that theory of fundamental option. For, in the very midst of his insistence on the directness and immediacy of that intransitive object, and on the ego as that intransitive object, he makes the essential *caveat* (proviso):

Nevertheless, the objectification of the subject does not have an intentional character in the sense in which intentionality is to be found in every human willing. When I will, I always desire *something*. Willing indicates a turn toward an object, and this turn determines its intentional nature. In order to turn intentionally to an object we put the object, as it were, in front of us (or we accept its presence).[21] […] in self-determination we do not turn to the

---

20. Ibid., 108.

21. Here there occurs the sentence: "Obviously it is possible to put in this position our own ego as the object and then to turn to it by a similar volitional act, the act of willing. But this kind of

ego as the object, we only impart actuality to the, so to speak, ready-made objectiveness of the ego which is contained in the intrapersonal relation of self-governance and self-possession. This imparting of actuality is of fundamental significance in morality, that specific dimension of the human, personal existence which is simultaneously both subjective and objective. It is there that the whole reality of morals, of moral values, has its roots. [...] The objectification that is essential for self-determination takes place *together with* the intentionality of the particular acts of the will. When I will *anything*, then I am also determined by myself. Though the ego is *not* an intentional object of willing its objective being is contained in the nature of acts of willing. It is only thus that willing becomes self-determination.[22]

The references in *Laborem Exercens* to deliberating and deciding *de se ipso* have a similar implication: this deliberating is not some mysterious act of self-disposal in which the very objective intended is total self-disposal before God.[23] Rather, the deliberating *de se ipso* is the very same deliberating that precedes any free choice, for example, the choice to engage in this specific work or project—say, of my writing or your reading this text—and to do it well, for this

---

intentionality does not properly appertain to self-determination. For in self-determination ..." In a discussion of John Paul II and fundamental option theories, one would wish to provide an exegesis of this. But for present purposes it is enough that the context excludes every theory in which choices of particular actions are treated as not disposing of the self.

22. K. Wojtyła, *The Acting Person*, 109 (emphases added); see also 309, last sentence of n. 40.

23. The phrase "*deliberans de se ipso*" occurs in St. Thomas just once, in *ST*, I-II, q. 89, a. 6c, in the famous passage about the seven-year-old pagan whose first act of free will/choice is either a mortal sin or an act of conversion *ad debitum finem* and *ad Deum*. This is the passage to which supporters of fundamental option theory have appealed—mistakenly, however; for when Aquinas comes to describe that act of conversion, in q. 113, a. 7 ad 1 and aa. 4 and 6, he makes clear that this is not a matter of the total self-disposal imagined by fundamental-option theorists, but instead the down-to-earth reality of a free choice to "consent" to two particulars: faith in God and detestation of sin. As I say elsewhere (see my *Aquinas*, 41n): "Even though a single choice (Aquinas thinks) cannot form a habitual disposition in the strict sense (which is formed by reiteration of acts: I-II q. 51 a. 3), still a choice lasts in, and shapes, one's will(ingness) until one repudiates or repents of it (see e.g. *De Veritate* q. 24 a. 12c). Although their emotional character and culture can be profoundly shaped before they reach the age of reason [...], children cannot make free choices until they reach that age; and when one does reach it, one is immediately {*statim*} confronted with the rational necessity of deliberating, so far as one can, about oneself {*de seipso*} and about the direction, the integrating point, of one's whole life {*salus sua*}, so that one treats oneself as an end in oneself to which other things are related as quasi-means {*de seipso cogitet, ad quem alia ordinet sicut ad finem*}, and either do or fail to do 'what is in oneself {*quod in se est*}': I-II q. 89 a. 6c & ad 3; II Sent. d. 42 q. 1 a. 5 ad 7; *De Malo* q. 7 a. 10 and 8."

or that purpose. The deliberating *de se ipso* is an implication of any serious choice; for any serious choice, however specific its topic, is a self-disposal, a formation of character, a (partial) creation (or reinforcement, or destruction) of character—and lasts beyond the time of the action and, being a spiritual reality, can last into eternity. Thus the whole section on the subjective *ratio* of work[24] ends like this:

In the final analysis it is always man who is the purpose of the work, whatever work it is that is done by man—even if the common scale of values rates it as the merest "service," as the most monotonous, even the most [marginalizing][25] work.

In "Human Acts," a paper I gave in Rome, at a Congress on Moral Theology in 1986,[26] I devoted some pages to theologians (I mentioned Timothy O'Connell and Josef Fuchs) who:

[...] deny that one can know oneself in, and by reflection upon, one's choices and actions. They propose an account of the person, and of knowledge, according to which the self is a reality radically unaffected by many fully free choices and actions, a reality which, unlike choice and action, remains inaccessible both to consciousness and even to reflective knowledge.

At the end of my exposition and critique I sum up by saying:

By thus rejecting an epistemology dominated by the image of taking a look, or gazing, or confronting, we rejoin the perennial methodology: whatever is known is known insofar as it is in act; the character of soul is known by the soul's capacities, but those capacities are known by and in their actuations. And, more specifically, [in the words of Wojtyła's *The Acting Person*,

---

24. John Paul II, *Laborem Exercens*, para. 6.

25. The Vatican's English translation here has "alienating," but the versions of this text in other languages more accurately say "marginalizing" (Italian *emarginante* or similar; Latin *opere* [...] *in societatis partes secundarias potissimum detrudente*). The whole burden of the analysis is that work in which man expresses his self-determination, self-governance and self-possession is not alienating, however menial. Work can only be degrading or alienating when all incentive to creativity and responsibility, and thus all personal satisfaction, is removed because one is in no way working "for oneself" (*in re propria*): see *Laborem Exercens*, para. 5.

26. See my "Human Acts," republished in J. Finnis, *Intention and Identity: Collected Essays Volume II*, (Oxford: Oxford University Press, 2011).

p. 11] action constitutes the specific moment whereby the person is revealed. Action gives us the best insight into the inherent essence of the person and allows us to understand the person most fully.[27]

2. *Redemptor Hominis* (1979)

The first paragraph of this first encyclical of John Paul II, which opens with the words: "The Redeemer of man, Jesus Christ, is the centre of the universe and of history," closes by quoting that Redeemer: "God so loved the world that he gave his only Son, that whoever believes in him should not perish but have eternal life."[28] Here I shall focus only on the encyclical's anthropology of action, as it appears from the document's repeated phrase "intellect, will, conscience and freedom," as in: "[…] freedom's root [is] in man's soul, his heart, and his conscience;"[29] "we are speaking of each man […] in all the unrepeatable reality of what he is and what he does, of his intellect and will, of his conscience and heart;"[30] and "man's deepest sphere […] the sphere of human hearts, consciences and events."[31]

What are *intellect, will, conscience* and *heart*?

In the New Testament, in line with the Old, the term *kardía* (Latin *cor*) signifies the seat, center or source of physical, spiritual and mental life, of the whole "inner life" of thinking, feeling and volition, often taken inclusively, but in specific contexts indicating either (a) thought, understanding, doubting, and so forth, or (b) willing and deciding, being tempted, and so forth, especially morally significant decisions or choices and their aftermath, purity of heart or guilty hearts, or (c) desires, emotions, loves, resentments, and so forth.[32] St. Thomas surveys some strategic texts such

27. Ibid., 134–6.
28. John Paul II, *Redemptor Hominis* (Vatican City, 4 March 1979), para. 12. Available online at: http://www.vatican.va/content/john-paul-ii/en/encyclicals/documents/hf_jp-ii_enc_04031979_redemptor-hominis.html.
29. Ibid.
30. Ibid., para. 24.
31. Ibid., para. 10.
32. See W. F. Arndt, F. W. Gingrich, and F. W. Danker (ed.), *A Greek-English Lexicon of the*

as Psalm 84:2(3): *cor meum et caro mea exultaverunt*, and assigns *cor* to the intellectual appetite, *caro* ("flesh") to the sensitive appetite.[33] However, when considering the variant lists in *Deuteronomy 6*, *Matthew* 22, *Mark* 12 and *Luke* 10 on the call to *love* with "heart, soul, mind, strength/powers," he unhesitatingly says that, since love (*dilectio*) is an act of will, *cor* corresponds to will, especially the intending of ends, above all the ultimate end; and that "mind" is a matter of intellect, moved by will, and "soul" is the lower appetite(s), while "strength" signifies the executive powers external to one's inner willing, desiring, understanding and so forth.[34] He might have given more prominence to those fundamental sayings of the Lord, recounted in *Matthew* 15 and *Mark* 7—with interesting variations which illustrate the reliance of each on memory and apostolic [eye-witness] oral preaching, not on either of them redacting the other's text—when he explains to his close disciples his controversy with Pharisees who were denouncing failure to wash before eating: it is from inside, from the heart, that immoral actions come, deeds shaped up in and by the heart.[35]

So I think we should understand *Redemptor Hominis* like this. Intellect and will are the essential elements in self-determining choices and actions, choosings and actings. "Heart" includes those but is not redundant, for it includes also the life of emotion and feeling which accompanies all human understanding and willing, somewhat as images accompany all human mathematical thinking even though the mathematician knows that they are not what is being considered and indeed partly misrepresent what is being considered—a line that can be seen or imagined cannot be what a line is defined to be: length without breadth. Although section 54

New Testament and other Early Christian Literature (Chicago & Cambridge: University of Chicago Press, 1979), s.v. *kardia*.

33. St. Thomas Aquinas, *Summa Theologiae, Prima Secundae*, q. 24, a. 3c.

34. Ibid., q. 44, a. 5c.

35. *Matthew* 15:1-20, especially 18-19; *Mark* 7:1-23, especially 21.

of *Veritatis Splendor* will treat the term "heart" as a name for conscience, in *Redemptor Hominis* "conscience," that important New Testament word put into circulation by Peter[36] and Paul,[37] is essentially, and more specifically, one's *understanding* of the *proposals for action* that deliberative understanding shapes up as options, for choosing between. But conscience is a *specialized* understanding: an understanding that *measures* those proposals against the *standards* of honesty, justice and other elements of integral reasonableness (*prudentia*), and ultimately by reference to what orientations of one's will are or are not open to integral human fulfillment.

For we cannot understand ethics, or a project like *The Acting Person*, or a more complete project like *Veritatis Splendor*, unless we enter into the viewpoint not of observers but of the deliberating and choosing person himself or herself—of oneself, one's own thinking about what to do, and deciding/choosing what to do (whether one has judged it morally good or judged it morally bad, "in conscience"). This viewpoint has the academic name "the internal point of view." It is what is referred to at a key point in *Veritatis Splendor*:

> *The morality of the human act depends primarily and fundamentally on the "object" rationally chosen by the deliberate will*, as is borne out by the insightful analysis, still valid today, made by Saint Thomas. In order to be able to grasp [understand] the object of an act which specifies that act morally, it is therefore necessary to place oneself *in the perspective of the acting person*. [...] that object is the proximate end of a deliberate decision [*delectionis*; *un choix*] which determines [i.e., settles] the act of willing on the part of the acting person.[38]

---

36. *1 Peter* 3:16, 21; cf. 2:19.

37. *1 Corinthians* 8:7, 19; 10:29; *2 Corinthians* 1:12; 4:2; 5:11; *Romans* 2:15; 9:1; 13:5; *1 Timothy* 1:5, 19; 3:9; 4:2; *Titus* 1:15; *2 Timothy* 1:3; *Acts of the Apostles* 23:1. Perhaps earliest, in (as it seems) Apollos's sermon, *Hebrews* 9:9, 14; 10:22; approved by Paul: 13:19(!), 22–24 (very probably: despatching the annotated sermon from Ephesus to Corinth); cf. *Acts of the Apostles* 18:24—19:1; *1 Corinthians* 16:12.

38. John Paul II, *Veritatis Splendor* (Vatican City, 6 August 1993), para. 78 (italics in original). Available online at: http://www.vatican.va/content/john-paul-ii/en/encyclicals/documents/hf_jp-ii_enc_06081993_veritatis-splendor.html.

We can and should go so far as to say that as an acting person one has, in the act of choosing, infallible knowledge of the object, that is, of what one is choosing, though even a moment later one may have partly forgotten or begun misrepresenting to oneself what one chose.[39]

3. *Veritatis Splendor* (1993)

This encyclical is significant above all as doctrinal, magisterial and apostolic. But it is also theological. And like all sound theology (as the encyclical *Fides et Ratio* will say five years later),[40] it consciously seeks to be also sound philosophy. It seems to me—but this is certainly open to discussion—that the original conceiving of *The Acting Person* as "an attempt at constructing Catholic ethics on the basis of Scheler's philosophy" is evidence of two things. First, that Karol Wojtyła considered that the Neo-Scholastic Thomistic presentations of ethics with which he was familiar were *deficient* in not, or not sufficiently, adopting the *internal point of view*—the viewpoint of the acting person—in expounding the structure of the human person and human freely chosen action. So he turned elsewhere, to Scheler, in hope of finding more inwardness, thus at least implicitly conforming to the actual method of St. Thomas by acknowledging that adequate critical knowledge of actions precedes, in the epistemological order, an adequate critical knowledge of nature, in this case human nature and structure. Second, resort to Scheler's philosophy was of little or no help—indeed, I venture to think, it was a distraction—in recovering what the Neo-Scholastics

---

39. You will have noticed that I always use the pronoun "one" in the English, not the American way: it is in the first-person, equivalent in meaning to "I". This first-person usage is the best way— indeed the only safe way—to present, to understand and to analyze the acts of an acting person or generically of the acting person: as they are understood and created by that person (for good or ill)—"in the perspective of the acting person," as *Veritatis Splendor* says.

40. Cf. John Paul II, *Fides et Ratio* (Vatican City, 14 September 1998), para. 68: "moral theology requires a sound philosophical vision of human nature and society, as well as of the general principles of ethical decision-making." Available online at: https://www.vatican.va/content/john-paul-ii/en/encyclicals/documents/hf_jp-ii_enc_14091998_fides-et-ratio.html.

had lost: an accurate understanding of the truly intelligent and intelligible *human goods* that are what first principles of practical understanding and reason direct us to, as St. Thomas expounded, though not with unblemished clarity of exposition, in question 94 articles 2 and 3 of the *Prima Secundae*.[41] To speak of "fulfillment in our actions," as *The Acting Person* does right from the outset, is implicitly to speak of human goods (as we saw in the passage quoted above[42]). But much remained to be made explicit and critically defended. The project of *Veritatis Splendor*, announced in 1987 and completed six years and six days later, but certainly meditated earlier and longer, summoned John Paul II to an articulated, albeit incompletely articulated, exposition of *those* fundamentals of ethics.

The second of the three chapters of *Veritatis Splendor*—the longest, running from section 28 through section 83—deals in sequence with four main currents of thought converging on dissent from the Church's constant moral teaching.

The first of the four currents broadly concerns notions of autonomy or liberty, in relation to Christian ideas of human freedom, divine and natural law, and human nature. One element in this current concerns:

> [the] denial that there exists, in Divine Revelation, a specific and determined moral content, universally valid and permanent. The word of God would be limited to proposing an exhortation, a generic *paraenesis* [exhortatory preaching] which the autonomous reason alone would then have the task of completing with normative directives which are truly "objective," that is, adapted to the concrete historical situation [...] [but which are not] part of the proper content of Revelation, and would not in themselves be relevant for salvation.[43]

Related to this is the notion that there is no divine and natural law, properly speaking, other than the law of love (of God and

---

41. St. Thomas Aquinas, *Summa Theologiae, Prima Secundae*, q. 94, a. 2, 3.
42. See above note no. 18 to the passage from Wojtyła, *The Acting Person*, 151.
43. John Paul II, *Veritatis Splendor*, para. 37.

neighbor), beyond which the Church has nothing definite to teach about human conduct, and gives us just exhortations and orientations or ideals. Related sub-currents of dissent maintain that the Church's moral teaching uses an outdated and false concept of nature, and is physicalist or biologistic rather than truly human and reasonable. Against all these, the encyclical defends the humanity and reasonableness, as well as the divinely revealed character, ratified by Christ, of the *natural moral law demanding respect in every choice and act for the fundamental* goods of human nature.

These fundamental human goods were already referred to in the encyclical's first chapter, in section 13's meditation on Christ's response to the man who asked what he must do to inherit eternal life, a response recalling the man to the Commandments:

> The different commandments of the Decalogue are really only so many reflections of the one commandment about the good of the person, at the level of the many different goods which characterize his identity as a spiritual and bodily being in relationship with God, with his neighbour and with the material world. [...] The commandments of which Jesus reminds the young man are meant to safeguard the good of the person, the image of God, by protecting his goods. "You shall not murder; You shall not commit adultery; You shall not steal; You shall not bear false witness" are moral rules formulated in terms of prohibitions. These negative precepts express with particular force the ever urgent need to protect human life, the communion of persons in marriage, private property, truthfulness and people's good name. The commandments thus represent the basic condition for love of neighbour [...].[44]

"Human life, the communion of persons in marriage, private property, truthfulness and people's good name": this is a list of fundamental human goods that is clearly neither fully clarified and stabilized philosophically, nor exhaustive. Yet it is a valuable pointer to the need for, and I would add the availability of, such a clarified and adequate list.

---

44. Ibid., para. 13.

After alluding in section 44 to "the Thomistic doctrine of natural law" as something long "included in" the Church teaching on morality, in section 48 *Veritatis Splendor* returns to the fundamental goods that (although the encyclical does not say so) are the subject of Thomas' teaching on the first principles of the natural law.[45] Here John Paul II is directly confronting that current of theological opinion which accuses the Christian doctrine on sex and marriage and human life of confusing biological laws with moral laws—physicalism, biologism, and so forth.[46] Part of a complex response says:

> It is in the light of the dignity of the human person—a dignity which must be affirmed for its own sake—that reason grasps the specific moral value of certain goods towards which the person is naturally inclined. And since the human person cannot be reduced to a freedom which is self-designing, but entails a particular spiritual and bodily structure, the primordial moral requirement of loving and respecting the person as an end and never as a mere means also implies, by its very nature, respect for certain fundamental goods [...].[47]

It is not the fact that we are naturally inclined to these goods that makes them morally normative, but rather the truth that the *objects* of such inclinations, objects such as life and marital communion (marriage), are intrinsic elements of one's human dignity as a being—a person—inseparably both bodily and spiritual (*corpore et anima unus*):

> [...]natural inclinations take on moral relevance only insofar as they refer to the human person and his authentic fulfilment, a fulfilment which for that matter can take place always and only in human nature.[48]

When question 94, article 2 of the *Prima Secundae* is text-critically transcribed and translated, we find that St. Thomas already identified marriage—not sexual intercourse or procreation—as the basic human good that should be listed after life and health.[49]

45. See once again St. Thomas Aquinas, *Summa Theologiae, Prima Secundae*, q. 94, a. 2.
46. John Paul II, *Veritatis Splendor*, para. 47 and 48.2.
47. Ibid., para. 48.3.
48. Ibid., para. 50.
49. J. Finnis, *Aquinas*, 82, 97–8.

I shall say here very little about the second and third of the four currents of erroneous theological opinion. The second concerns conscience, taken up in sections 54–64. No teacher who has identified a course of conduct or kind of action as truly wrong can then rationally add: "But if you judge it in your conscience not to be wrong for you, it is not wrong for you." Such a bishop or other teacher merely contradicts himself, and in all probability is merely in bad faith, trying in vain to conceal the fact that he does not believe what he professes to teach. In view, however, of what is said about conscience in and in relation to section 303 of *Amoris Laetitia*,[50]—that an individual's conscience confronting the divine and Gospel commandment against adultery can "recognize with sincerity and honesty what for now is the most generous response which can be given to God, and come to see with a certain moral security that it [understood: carrying on with the adultery in a civil purported second marriage] is what God himself is asking amid the concrete complexity of one's limits, while not yet fully the objective ideal"[51]—it is right to notice Saint John Paul II's description of false teaching in *Veritatis Splendor*:

[…] some authors have proposed a kind of double status of moral truth. Beyond the doctrinal and abstract level, one would have to acknowledge the priority of a certain more concrete existential consideration [which], by taking account of circumstances and the situation, could legitimately be the basis of certain exceptions to the general rule and thus permit one to do in practice and in good conscience what is qualified as intrinsically evil by the moral law. A separation, or even an opposition, is thus established in some cases between the teaching of the precept, which is valid in general, and the norm of the individual conscience, which would in fact make the final decision about what is good and what is evil. On this basis, an attempt is made to legitimize so called "pastoral" solutions contrary to the teaching of the

50. See Francis, *Amoris Laetitia* (Vatican City, 19 March 2016), para. 303, as well as para. 37, 298, and 304. Available online at: https://www.vatican.va/content/dam/francesco/pdf/apost_exhortations/documents/papa-francesco_esortazione-ap_20160319_amoris-laetitia_en.pdf.

51. Francis, *Amoris Laetitia*, para. 303.

Magisterium, and to justify a "creative" hermeneutic according to which the moral conscience is in no way obliged, in every case, by a particular negative precept. No one can fail to realize that these approaches pose a challenge to the very identity of the moral conscience in relation to human freedom and God's law.[52]

Sections 57–64 (and section 117) offer a long and careful refutation of this corrosive error.

The third current is the claim that nothing morally matters, or matters for salvation, other than a person's "fundamental option" for Good, or goodness in general, an option which is only imperfectly reflected, and never definitively, in one's specific or particular choices and acts. To this John Paul II replies (I paraphrase) that the real fundamental option is *faith*, a fundamental choice by which man is indeed:

> capable of giving his life direction and of progressing, with the help of grace, towards his end, following God's call. But this capability is actually exercised in the particular choices of specific actions, through which man deliberately conforms himself to God's will, wisdom and law.[53]

So the fundamental option is "revoked when man engages his freedom in conscious decisions to the contrary, with regard to morally grave matter."[54]

The fourth current is the current most carefully identified and discussed, and specifically condemned formally and twice over, in *Veritatis Splendor*, where it is named "proportionalism" or "teleologism"; one might also call it consequentialism (to use the term successfully and helpfully minted by Elizabeth Anscombe). It was only in and after late 1968 that Catholic theologians began denying, publicly and with more or less philosophical arguments, that there is any moral precept (natural or revealed) that absolutely excludes a kind of action specifiable (identifiable) by reference only to its

52. John Paul II, *Veritatis Splendor*, para. 56.
53. Ibid., para. 67.
54. Ibid.

intentional-behavioral elements—a kind of action such as killing an innocent person, apostasy, sex acts with a person to whom one is not married, etc.—where the identification or specification does not depend upon a prior *moral* assessment of such actions as unjust, unchaste, immoderate or the like.[55] The dissenting but numerous theologians and pastors confronted in *Veritatis Splendor* asserted that true and Christian morality's precepts do not prohibit such an action except when it is, in the circumstances (situation), *disproportionate*, that is, seems in those circumstances likely to cause, overall and in the medium or long term, *more* human (pre-moral) bad than human (pre-moral) good—and therefore is in the relevant particular circumstances unjust, unchaste, immoderate or the like. According to that line of thought, a particular action cannot be judged (or assessed in conscience) to be, in the circumstances, wrong until one has *weighed* all the particular acting person's motivations and circumstances (including the likely overall, long-term consequences)—and then its wrongness is simply its *disproportionate* harmfulness or likely harmfulness relative to the morally relevant "values" or human goods. Without such an individualized assessment of proportionality, no general precept or "commandment"

55. In dating the momentous change of mind by a majority of priest-scholar moral theologians, a key date is April 1966, when the theologians of Pope Paul VI's Commission on Population, Family and Birth-rate found that a majority of them thought that the Church's teaching that contraception is intrinsically immoral was reformable and mistaken, and went on to explain that opinion by a theory that particular acts of contracepted marital intercourse could be morally assessed only when considered in relation to a whole lifetime of marital relations between these spouses in question. As I say in Finnis, *Moral Absolutes: Tradition, Revision and Truth* (Washington, DC: Catholic University of America Press, 1991), 89: in these 1966 documents "the contraceptive act and the contracepted sexual act constitute only one act, whose moral character is derived entirely from the moral character of the sexual act. This in turn attains its essential moral character from the 'totality' constituted of itself, the series of contracepted acts of which it forms a part, and the non-contracepted acts which there have been or may be in the course of a married lifetime. This theory, [...]—on which the church was meant to have reversed its teaching on contraception and promulgated a new teaching that contraception is often morally obligatory—could not withstand a touch of rational reflection and has rightly disappeared without trace. Or rather, it collapsed into the general proportionalist theory that the morality of a choice can be assessed only by taking into account *all* the circumstances, a totality far wider, of course, than the supposed 'totality' constituted by the couple's imagined series of marital acts past, present, and future."

can truly be more than a *reminder* of important values and *ideals* or orientations for considering what love of God and neighbor calls for *in the situation* in which the choice whether or not to engage in a particular act (of non-marital sex, abortion, euthanasia and so forth) is to be assessed. That assessment, to repeat, is to be made, said these theologians, *in the light of the proportions of good and bad, value and disvalue, foreseeable in the likely overall, long-term outcomes of the alternatives*—of engaging or alternatively not engaging in that act in that (kind of) situation.

So these theorists accepted the labels "proportionalist" or "teleological" because the "proportionate reason" for choosing an act—even an act of a kind hitherto judged intrinsically immoral—is that choosing and doing so has, and seems likely (in the circumstances) to attain, the *telos*, the purpose or goal, of doing greater good or at least lesser evil overall, net and in the long term.

Already in its response to the first current back in section 52, *Veritatis Splendor* had distinguished between negative and positive precepts, and reaffirmed St. Thomas' teaching that only *negative* moral precepts decisively or exceptionlessly direct us *semper et pro semper,* always and on every occasion, without exception. Affirmative precepts if true are always in play, but their application is always relative to circumstances—they direct us *semper sed non pro semper*, always but not on every occasion. The *negative* precepts identifying and prohibiting intrinsically evil acts do not say merely that it is wrong to act contrary to a virtue—for example, to kill *unjustly*, or to engage in an *unchaste or impure* sex act. Rather, these precepts exclude, without exception,[56] "specific," "concrete," and "particular" *kinds of behavior*.[57] These kinds of behavior are excluded by the relevant negative moral precepts (and are contrary to virtue) without first being identified by their opposition to virtues,

56. John Paul II, *Veritatis Splendor*, para. 52, 67, 76, and 82.
57. Ibid., para. 49, 52, 70, 77, and 79-82.

and without consideration of particular circumstances, and without regard to the good intentions someone may have for choosing to engage in behavior of this kind.

In line with his philosophy of action, which in its essentials is also St. Thomas' philosophy of action, John Paul II here makes clear that in speaking of *behavior* he does not mean behavior that might be engaged in even by someone incapable of making a free choice—performances that might be recorded on a video-camera. Rather, in explaining what is meant by "the object of a given moral act," he makes it clear that here, when we speak of *behavior* we mean precisely the possible object of deliberate or free choices, the behavior as envisaged by the choosing subject. I have already partly quoted the passage, and repeat it now:

> In order to be able to grasp the object of an act which specifies that act morally, it is therefore necessary to place oneself *in the perspective of the acting person.* The object of the act of willing is in fact a freely chosen kind of behaviour. [...] By the object of a given moral act, then, one cannot mean a process or an event of the merely physical order, to be assessed on the basis of its ability to bring about a given state of affairs in the outside world. Rather, that object is the proximate end of a deliberate decision which determines the act of willing on the part of the acting person.[58]

In short: behavior is of a morally relevant kind in virtue of *the description it has in the deliberation of a person who could choose to do it.*[59]

These paragraphs of *Veritatis Splendor* deploy the classic terminology used, but also freely departed from, by St. Thomas: intention, object, and circumstances. The key to understanding this is that the terms "intention" and "object" correlate with the terms "end" and "means": one intends to accomplish some deed or outcome X *by* doing Y, that is, by means of Y. Here "means" refers not

---

58. Ibid., para. 78.

59. Of course, this description will be affected by what the acting person assesses as needed to bring about a desired/intended state of affairs in the world. Deliberation attends to (supposed/envisaged) causal efficacy.

to some instrument but to some action (perhaps using an instrument). And so we have the set of relationships already expounded by Aristotle in his *Metaphysics* and by Aquinas in his *Commentary on the Sentences*: in short, all ends (except the most ultimate) are also means, and all means (except the most initial: beginning to flex one's muscles) are also ends.[60] So there is only a relative distinction between *intention* (which is, by definition, "of ends") and *object* (which in this context is, by definition, the "chosen means"). Sometimes "intention" is used broadly to include "objects," as in St. Thomas' famous discussion of self-defense, in which he launches the notion of the *duplex effectus*—results that are *intended* either as end *or as means*, and results that, in the acting person's plan and proposal are *neither* ends nor means but are foreseen and accepted as *side-effects*. In this broad sense of "intention," the objects of a chosen act are the *close-in* intentions of the person who chose it. And sometimes, as in *Veritatis Splendor* beginning with the third sentence of section 74, "intention" is used more narrowly and distinguished from "object," just as "ends" are distinguished from "means" even though for almost all practical purposes ends are means and means are ends.[61] Intentions when thus distinguished from objects are of further-out, more ultimate aims, ends, motives.

The requirement of reason is that *all* one's broad-sense intentions—including those that in the narrow sense are object(s) rather than intention(s)—must be in line with reason, and none of them a willing (intending or choosing) of the destruction or damaging of a fundamental human good. In that sense, there are means that no

---

60. See my *Aquinas*, 31–2, 35, 142 n. 43, 165–6, etc.

61. The terminology of sections 74–82 is established in section 74: "But on what does the moral assessment of man's free acts depend? What is it that ensures this ordering of human acts to God? Is it the *intention* of the acting subject, the *circumstances*—and in particular the consequences—of his action, or the *object* itself of his act? This is what is traditionally called the problem of the 'sources of morality.' Precisely with regard to this problem there have emerged in the last few decades new or newly revived theological and cultural trends which call for careful discernment on the part of the Church's Magisterium." See John Paul II, *Veritatis Splendor*, para. 74.

end can justify, and evils one may not choose even for the sake of good, and it is not enough to have good intentions and a just concern for long-term consequences including side-effects. *Bonum* only *ex integra causa, malum ex quocumque defectu*—from wrongness of end *or* wrongness of means *or* injustice of side-effects.

The rightness or wrongness of the nuclear bombing of Nagasaki is settled not *merely* by establishing whether the intentions were free from hatred and were concerned only with long-term human wellbeing (including Japanese wellbeing) *and* whether the medium-term consequences were in many respects fairly likely to be good. One must ask not only about intentions and circumstances but also about object: did the planners of the operation need for its success the destruction of (lots of) non-combatants and therefore choose their destruction as a means, that is, have that killing as their object (that is, in the broad sense of intention, as one of their intentions)?

I have been summarizing in the language of the tradition—fully understood from a rigorously internal, moral, never *merely* physical or behavioral point of view—what John Paul II means by *kind of behavior*, by *human act*, and by *object of the human act* when the recalls in *Veritatis Splendor* that there are:

acts which in the Church's moral tradition have been termed "intrinsically evil" (*intrinsece malum*): they are such *always and per se*, in other words, on account of their very object, and quite apart from the ulterior intentions of the one acting and the circumstances.[62]

The main conclusion and central teaching of *Veritatis Splendor* is set out in section 79 and repeated almost verbatim in section 82:

One must therefore reject the thesis, characteristic of teleological and proportionalist theories, *which holds that it is impossible to qualify as morally evil according to its species—its "object"—the deliberate choice of certain kinds of behaviour or specific acts, apart from a consideration of the intention for which*

---

62. John Paul II, *Veritatis Splendor*, para. 80 (emphases in original); see also para. 81.

the choice is made or the totality of the foreseeable consequences of that act for all persons concerned.[63]

As a Magisterial act, this condemnation is rested *primarily* on the revealed scripture and tradition of Christian faith.[64] But the Encyclical also outlines (without expounding) a philosophical critique of the relevant proportionalist or teleologist theories. Such theories propose to determine "proportions" among the "pre-moral" goods and evils expected to result from a choice, but *Veritatis Splendor* points out "the impossibility of evaluating all the good and evil consequences and effects" by any *rational* "weighing" or "measuring".[65]

We might put it like this: the goods and harms which are intrinsic to persons and their associations only begin in this life, and simply cannot be weighed against one another in the way the proportionalists proposed, that is, by using one's reason but making no use of moral standards in the process of assessing. Human providence and assessment can never soundly conclude that a choice to kill an innocent person or to engage in adultery will result in less harm overall and in the long run than the choice to refrain. Among the reasons blocking such a conclusion is a fact, a truth recalled more than once in *Veritatis Splendor*, and central to *The Acting Person*. The truth is that in choosing to do acts of the kinds identified by the Christian and central philosophical tradition as intrinsically evil, one is *not only* choosing to produce the changes that *Veritatis Splendor* in section 71 calls changes "in the state of affairs outside of" the will of the acting person—the choice's "transitive" effects, achieved by the behavior one chose as a means. One is *also* making what *Veritatis Splendor* in section 65 calls "a *decision about oneself*"—creating thus an "intransitive" effect: constituting oneself the sort of person who does such things. Unless one repents, the

---

63. Ibid., para. 79 (emphases in original).
64. Ibid., para. 49, 79, and 81; see especially *1 Corinthians* 6:9–10.
65. Ibid., para. 77.

consequences of such self-determination continue in this world in-definitely (that is, without limit of time), and into eternity, already now. Even the this-worldly implications and results of forming such a willingness, *and of other persons' approving of it* (and so becoming themselves conditionally willing to act likewise), entirely elude all proportionalist or consequentialist efforts to weigh and—by reason and without decisive appeal to moral principles—assess the balance of "pre-moral" good and bad consequences of the choice.

That is the relevance of such choices and acts to eternal life. And I think that the person a fragment of whose work this lecture has been considering would think this a fitting place at which to finish.

JOHN FINNIS—born in 1940 in Adelaide, South Australia. Jurist, philosopher and scholar, taught Law in the University of Oxford 1965–2010, and is Professor of Law and Legal Philosophy emeritus there and also in the University of Notre Dame, Indiana, where he was a chaired Professor 1995–2020. Author of *Natural Law and Natural Rights* (1980; 2011) elaborating a new approach to classical natural law theory; *Fundamentals of Ethics* (1983); *Moral Absolutes* (1991); *Aquinas: Moral, Political and Legal Theory* (1995); and in five volumes *Collected Essays of John Finnis* (2011).

FAITH IN THE MODERN
AREOPAGUS

Introduction

Paul says on the Areopagus: "What you worship unknowingly, I declare to you plainly" (*Acts of the Apostles* 17:23). He takes it for granted, it seems, that worship is one of the things that human beings do; the task for him is not to persuade anyone that worship is necessary but to bring to light what or who is being worshipped. We ought to be clear at the outset that this is not quite the same as the question, popular in liberal theological circles in the middle of the last century, of what is of "ultimate concern" to people.[1] This is not a discussion about "values," that dangerously vacuous term forever hovering on the frontier between descriptive and prescriptive language; it is about what by definition commands a measure of attention and loyalty strong enough to push the ordinary workings of the self aside and denies that self its normal liberty of definition. Put like that, worship appears, reasonably enough, as an area of some risk or danger within human affairs. To be invited to worship

---

1. The phrase is associated especially with Paul Tillich and was popularised in Britain by the writings of Bishop John Robinson, especially his *Honest to God* (London: SCM Press, 1963).

is to be invited to suspend routine assumptions and allow yourself to be acted upon, indeed to be defined by something outside the self. It may, in other words, be the most dramatic example possible of a claim to power, the kind of power that refuses other agencies or presences the capacity to name themselves and narrate their identity simply in their own terms.

I hope to argue that the contemporary force of Paul's Areopagitic argument is precisely in pressing us to reflect on worship, and more specifically on how and why a secular worldview is bound ultimately to avoid the difficulty of dealing with the danger of worship. In brief, I want to suggest:

1) that a robust concept of the non-negotiable dignity of the human person requires that the only proper object of worship be that which is radically other than the contents of the finite universe,

2) that the phenomenon of human language, and the radical trust involved in addressing a human other with the expectation of being understood, entail a fundamental orientation away from the apparent naturalness of individual self-definition in the usual sense, and

3) that once it is clear that God alone is to be worshipped, the finite agent is freed to stand "in the place" of God without the risk of any Luciferian claim to be the object of another's total devotion: the finite person is "deified" not by the accrual of unimaginable power but by the worshipful embrace of a wholehearted responsiveness.

Central to all these points are two orienting convictions which I have tried to explore in other contexts: the significance of the wholly and necessarily non-rivalrous relationship between finite and infinite, and the understanding of all intelligent perception as involving the awareness of perspectives other than that of the individual ego, that is to say the object that is seen or known is seen and known as *always already seen and known*. Paul intends to declare to the Athenians what they act on but do not know; and so here we seek to direct our thoughts to what we act on but do not acknowledge in some of our central linguistic and ethical practices.

1. Rights, Ethics, and The Origins of Culture

There is vigorous debate in theological circles as to whether the notion of human rights as generally understood these days is fully compatible with a Christian anthropology; a number of influential voices (for instance John Milbank, Oliver O'Donovan, and Nigel Biggar[2]) have been raised to argue that any belief that human beings are endowed with a set of intrinsic claims is hard to reconcile both with the conviction of the absolute priority of *gift* in the work of creation and with the imperative of self-surrender articulated in the gospel. Surely, it is said, the human person in the biblical perspective is so thoroughly dependent and interdependent that the discourse of rights as inalienable endowment is at best a distraction from the central moral and spiritual labor of human responsibility. A persuasive argument, and an important corrective to the increasingly fragmented and forensic approach to rights that has become common in recent decades, it nevertheless perhaps misses the seriousness of the founding impulse of those who first shaped the discourse. This impulse might be summed up as the conviction that there is an *appropriate* set of responses to anything recognized as a human agent, responses whose appropriateness does not depend in any way on the *decision* of a human individual or a human group. Recognizing a "right" is not so much (as is sometimes said) recognizing a simply identifiable duty on my part, but recognizing that the moral standing of another person is not in my possession to give

2. See most recently N. Biggar, *What's Wrong With Rights?* (Oxford: Oxford University Press, 2020).

or withhold. It pre-exists the relation or encounter between us; it holds for those I shall never actually encounter or relate to, in past, present, and future. It is, in sum, to do with accepting that what I meet here is not at my disposal or under my control.

To come at the same point from a slightly different direction, this is a recognition that the moral standing of the human other is not something that has to be or can be *earned*. The "appropriate" response is not a reward for performance. Let us look at an example that can be the subject of much confused thinking: if a person is deprived of normal civic liberties as a punishment for criminal activity, this is not a suspension of the category of appropriate response to their humanity; the way in which we manage the deprivation of certain liberties has to have in view the moral standing of the criminal as someone held responsible for their acts and also held responsible for the possibility of changed behavior as the outcome of the penal process. And the responsibility of the penal process is to acknowledge true culpability where it exists and to support behavioral change; if its workings have the effect of humiliating, disempowering, or stigmatizing, it has failed, and the failure is a failure to see what is appropriate to the offender as a human subject. Or to take another uncomfortably current issue: there has been much discussion recently of the pressure exerted on some pregnant women to abort a fetus which may exhibit signs of Down's Syndrome or is in a category where the risk of this is high; there has been something of a campaign to "eliminate" the condition (national policy in Iceland, for example, has led to a near-total eradication of Down's Syndrome by means of selective abortion). The implication has not been lost on those actually living with Down's and their families: there is a prescribed norm of human capacity which those with Down's fail to exhibit, and so they fail to "earn" what would otherwise be the appropriate moral standing for a human subject. It is a conclusion that ought to be familiar from arguments about supposedly inferior races in the eighteenth and nineteenth centuries, or even from what passed as scientific discussion in the nineteenth and early twentieth centuries of the capacities of women.[3]

At root, a defensible discourse of human rights is one that refuses any suggestion that we need to assess capacity before acknowledging moral standing; the organic, physical recognizability of human identity determines what counts as an appropriate response—a set of facts which we as human others do not determine. To respond with appropriate attention—that is, in a way that grants the other a standing like my own, a proper expectation that their need and well-being will be seen as morally significant in the same way as my own—is to accept that there is a response that is "just," that "does justice," as we like to say, to what is in front of us. And justice cannot be done if I am in any sense claiming ownership of what confronts me. It is why slavery is so regularly presented as a sort of paradigm of the infringement of human rights and dignities; but as we become more alert in identifying modern versions of slavery (such as human trafficking, indentured labor, child labor, child marriage, and child soldiering) we may be able better to grasp what is morally at stake here: the fundamental shape of unjust relation is the situation where one party reduces the other to a function they can define and limit—most damagingly a function that is simply a matter of serving the interest of the first party. Security is won and kept by successfully discharging this function, earning dignity or respect. The real moral energy of human rights language is in its attempt to secure the expectation of respect and nurture *independently of successful performance.*

So far, so good—although the mention of Down's Syndrome and the abortion question reminds us that there is a longish trail of inconsistency in the outworking and direction of this moral energy

---

3. A valuable discussion is in J. Bourke, *What It Means To Be Human: Historical Reflections from the 1800s to the Present* (Berkeley: Counterpoint Press, 2011).

and a frequent slippage towards precisely the correlation of status with capacity that the rights schema is supposed to rule out. But how do we establish a coherent basis for the presumption of inalienable moral standing? Affirming this is already a recognition that there is a problem in the human world with ineradicable conflicts of interest, and that securing one group's or individual's interest at the expense of another is a routine matter; "rights" are asserted as a protection against an unmediated battle between acquisitive interests.

If we are to follow René Girard's analysis of the origins of culture,[4] the neural and cerebral developments that enable us to represent to ourselves the thinking of another human agent are also what make possible the peculiar spirals of rivalry that characterize human culture—not merely the competition for resources that is found in the animal world generally but the development of *desire for what the other desires*. We are socialized by imitation, which is also something that we have in common with other animals, but this socializing entails from the beginning the imagining of another's narrative of wanting and achieving, and this act of imagining prompts the fear that what the other wants is a limit on my own wanting and achieving; so that if I then want and achieve what the other wants, I forestall the possibility of frustration, and secure my own projects. In other words, to be sure of the security or welfare I desire, I must learn to want for myself what the other wants. The treatment of this process by Girard and those who have learned from him (Dumouchel, Palaver) continues to provoke controversy and skepticism (and frequently some fundamental misunderstanding), but it offers an unusually comprehensive account of how and why human beings need protection from the impulse to try and "possess" one another, to abolish the distance between agents and

4. R. Girard, *Things Hidden Since the Foundation of the World* (London: Athlone Press, 1987); see also G. Bailie, *Violence Unveiled: Humanity at the Crossroads* (New York: Crossraod Publishing, 1995) and W. Palaver, *René Girard's Mimetic Theory* (East Lansing: Michigan State University Press, 2013).

absorb the projects of others into those of the ego. Girard takes this still further in his complex discussion of the way in which the ego's desire for the other's desideratum eventually constitutes the other both as an object of unconditional and definitive longing *and* as the supreme obstacle to the ego's attaining its goals—as divine and diabolical at the same time.[5] The other becomes an object of "worship" in the sense of commanding absolute attention and devotion, defining my/our desire. It is emulated and resented. And it is this doubling of reaction that enables the scapegoat mechanism to be activated: a dominant group identifies an individual or sub-group as simultaneously possessed of significant and threatening power and also as alien and vulnerable; and it proceeds to their violent extermination or expulsion. They no longer block my/our desire, they can no longer "own" the good I have learned to want; their removal from the scene allows the dominant and excluding group to celebrate its self-identity and its reconciliation with the longed-for, sacred terminus of desire: the divine.

Girard, like Freud, wants us to think in terms of a literal and historical "founding murder" at the roots of every human culture.[6] Whether the overall theory really requires this is not clear; what is clear is the mechanism by which the "sacred" is generated through the mimetic spiral which eventually demands an act of collective and violent expulsion or exclusion. That which is both adored and dreaded is made the subject of successful negotiation by the sacrificial process. The relevance of this to our thinking about rights and about worship needs some spelling out, but the connection seems to be something like this. Human beings perceive themselves as living precariously, their desires bounded by the insistent rivalry of others. They seek to circumvent that boundedness by making the desire of others their own.

---

5. Palaver, *René Girard's Mimetic Theory*, 129; cf. Girard, *Things Hidden*, 99-104, 290-4, 331-2.
6. Girard, *Things Hidden*, Book I, Chapters 1 and 2.

There is thus at the root of human life together a profound faultline, the threat of an endlessly intensified competition which could issue in a "war of all against all." Cohesion is secured by identifying a candidate for expulsion, the collective bearer of the mimetic fantasies of the group. Archaic religion is the regularizing of this mechanism (since it is never done with once and for all). Thus far Girard; and linking this with our Areopagitic starting-point, we can then say two things. What is *worshipped*, what makes an irresistible claim on the ego, is in Girardian perspective the ego's own alienated desire, mediated by the imagined desire of the other. Our collective life as humans is haunted by the compulsive pressure towards absorbing and (at best) immobilizing or silencing one another; in times of serious social crisis, this pressure leads to the scapegoating and expulsion (often the murder) of those who cannot defend themselves against the projection of frustrated desire. We do not have far to look in the contemporary scene for the rhetoric that combines a picture of the threatening other as both failing or weak and endowed with sinister and elusive powers. Thus, the idea of ascribing to human subjects a moral standing that is outside this mechanism becomes an important aspect of challenging both the mimetic spiral and the scapegoat ritual; we must learn to see the other as more than the model, rival and obstacle to my desires. To put it in condensed form, we must see the other as more than simply other to *me*. But what is it that establishes the other as—in this sense—"turned away" from its relation to my desire or my ego, as living, desiring and acting out of a depth of difference that is inaccessible to me? The genius of Girard is to bring to light the way in which both the classical theological account of the divine nature and the specific narrative of the incarnate life of God the Word provide a decisive and liberating ground for this.

The traditional doctrine of God, including the affirmation of immutabilty and impassibility, is completely misconceived if it is read as a bloodlessly philosophical attempt to deny to the divine life some of the active and positive qualities we prize as finite subjects. By insisting that God is beyond need or lack of any kind and that God is never passive to finite agency, it declares that God is in a fundamentally non-competitive relation with the universe. God is not one of several candidates for successfully filling a space within the universe; God's agency is not, like ours, evolving in a mixture of initiative and reaction. The way in which God sees the world can therefore in no sense be shaped by any kind of self-defense, any kind of *interest*; the divine regard for finite reality is the ground of its very existence and so cannot be dependent or reactive, cannot be conditioned by what happens within the universe. That is a very abstract formulation, but it can be translated immediately into the recognition that the divine regard is never to be *earned*. If God's action is creative action, bringing into being what is other to God and yet is open to God's life-in-act, that divine action is always a bestowal of reality and thus a loving self-communication devoid of self-interest. What therefore we see and encounter in any other human being (and indeed in the finite world as such) is *that which is regarded by God with unconditioned, non-acquisitive affirmation.* What is other to me is always already in relation to God, as a reality willed into being and loved by God. That is what is non-negotiable in the finite other, the ground of "moral standing." But this recognition, in the Jewish and Christian languages of faith, of the non-rivalry between God and the world is not a deduction from general principle; it is anchored in specific narratives in which the relation between God and finite reality is given a decisive shape, narratives in which God's distance from any kind of self-interest is rendered concrete in the form of both justice and mercy. God is encountered as "doing justice" to the world, and doing so by manifesting mercy.

When Abraham in Genesis 18 intercedes with God for the population of Sodom, he casts his appeal in terms of God's consistency with God's own laws: "Shall the judge [*shophet*] of all the world not act according to statute [*mishpat*]?" (*Genesis* 18:25). And that "statute," paradoxically, turns out to be the sparing of the wicked so as to guarantee the life of the righteous. This is an odd and disturbing justice, which appears as inseparable from comprehensive mercy. In the prophetic tradition, God's unwillingness to give up the people that have been chosen simply because compassion is stirred in the divine heart (*Hosea* 11:8) expresses the further paradox that God's consistency in mercy is God's way of "doing justice" to the divine life and nature itself: God cannot cease being merciful without ceasing to be God. God's "self-interest" is precisely the interest of all those who have been created, chosen, and loved. A justice that decrees punishment makes sense only within the context of divine self-consistency in seeking the good of what has been made. These attempts in the texts of Hebrew Scripture to clarify how the apprehension of divine mercy opens up a perspective on a justice that goes beyond simple reward undergird the developed and revolutionary narrative on which a distinctively Christian theology rests. In the life of Jesus of Nazareth, the divine life lives fully within a finite human agent without in any way reducing or compromising the integrity of the finite[7]; returning more directly to Girard's framework, this divine agent becomes the one whose murderous rejection uncovers the lethal nature of the scapegoat mechanism. God becomes unequivocally the victim of human power and violence; no shred remains of a divine power that will fight for its place by subduing hostile human activity. "If my kingly authority derived from this world, then my servants would fight," says Jesus to the Roman governor (*John* 18:36).

What human society, trapped in the patterns of retributive

---

7. See R. Williams, *Christ the Heart of Creation* (London: Bloomsbury, 2018), 1-6, for fuller discussion of this; and cf. K. Tanner, *God and Creation in Christian Theology* (Oxford: Basil Blackwell, 1988), Chapter 2, for an exemplary treatment.

fantasy and rivalrous power, expels and seeks to destroy in Jesus is precisely the wholly guiltless, wholly non-violent affirmation of the other that is God's own life: just *because* it is God's own life, it cannot be ultimately expelled or destroyed, it cannot be denied a place in the world *because it does not seek a place in the world that is won and held at the expense of any reality within the world.* The event of Jesus's crucifixion exposes the contradictory and arbitrary nature of scapegoating, its ultimate toxicity for the human world, its refusal of its own foundational reality, and uncovers the character of the creative act that is beyond rivalry and so universally affirming and compassionate. From the point of view of this narrative of faith, the foundation of an unequivocal and universal valuation of every human organism is this revealing and imagining of a creative act involving eternal commitment to the freedom and well-being of the finite. The doctrinal formulations of incarnation and atonement express in complex and extended terms the conviction of unconditional divine regard as the ground of all finite identity. This in turn entails a comprehensive refusal of any object of worship other than the life revealed in these narratives. There is always a dimension or level of the life of any human subject inaccessible to ownership or control by any other finite subject. No finite agent has the authority to require another to abandon all right to self-definition, to the possibility of shaping the conditions of their life. No finite subject is the embodiment of the ultimate and total good for any other finite subject. No finite subject can be simply the model for another's desire, adored, and feared as the numinous "ideal possessor" of desired goods. The ego and its "other," its mimetic competitor, are alike freed from their mutually destructive compact; and the authority to resist the totalizing claim of any human system is established. The only intelligible terminus of worship—the only reality that can "legitimately" be expected to displace and re-condition the human self—is that which is not in competition for power or control;

surrender to what in this way transcends the economy of rivalry is not victory for one party and defeat for the other, because what is surrendered to is the generative love from which the self's very reality arises. Surrender to this is acceptance of what is already the self's actual and radical identity; or, in the more familiar formulation, "the one who loses their life will save it" (*Mark* 8:35).

2. Language, Recognition and Mutuality

Thus far I have been outlining how the classical grammar of Christian doctrine and Jewish-Christian narrative bears on the question of how we can ground the notion of ineradicable "right" or universal human dignity; if convictions about this are not to be simply the corporate decision of a human majority, if they are to be genuinely something apart from power and choice in the human world, they stand in need of grounding. A Christian and Christocentric anthropology proposes such a grounding, declaring openly what has been hidden, declaring above all the secret toxicity of "worship" in the world of rivalry and destructive competition. We noted earlier the role played in Girardian thinking by questions about the origins of culture and language; in the next part of this reflection, we return to this issue of language and its associated topics of intelligence and self-understanding.

To speak at all is to invite *recognition*: when I say something, I assume that I occupy a world that is not exclusively mine, a world where the criteria for speaking intelligibly are shared with others whom I may never have met, others with whom I have never negotiated any sort of agreed protocol for conversation. I assume that the human stranger, even when speaking what seems a completely alien tongue, can make sense to me. The impulse to *translate* is universal. But in contrast to what some philosophical models—the kind of models decisively challenged both by phenomenologists like Maurice Merleau-Ponty and by Ludwig Wittgenstein in the

Philosophical Investigations—seem to imply, we do not gradually assemble evidence for the conclusion that the human stranger has an interior life comparable to my own, and so deduce that they are making sense on the same basis as myself. I pick up a set of behavioral conventions, patterns of making noise, from my human environment, and sort out in the process a kind of mental map in which I as an agent/speaker am located over against another agent/speaker. As Merleau-Ponty puts it in *Consciousness and the Acquisition of Language*:

> We are no longer in the presence of two entities (expression and meaning), the second of which might be hidden from the first [...] acquisition no longer resembles the decoding of a text for which one possesses the code and key; rather it is a deciphering (where the decipherer does not know the key to the code) [...] The child [...] learns to speak because the surrounding language calls up his [sic] thought.[8]

The notion of being a conscious agent is one that comes into focus as I assimilate the patterns of sound to which I am intensively exposed, patterns that manifestly expect my imitative response. What is more, this is a process that goes in step with acquiring the concept of being a *body*—imagining the bounded physical space from which I speak, including those dimensions to which I cannot have direct sensory access (I cannot see the back of my head, as I cannot walk around my body).

St. Edith Stein, whose 1914 thesis on empathy significantly anticipates a good deal of what was later elaborated by Merleau-Ponty, argues in this work that the registering of the fact that I am physically alive is inseparable from developing the concept of "life" in the world around me, so that I know myself as always already potentially an object to the other;[9] in this process, I form the concept of plural cen-

8. M. Merleau-Ponty, *Consciousness and the Acquisition of Language* (Evanston: Northwestern University Press, 1973), 50-1.
9. E. Stein, *On The Problem of Empathy* (Washington, DC: Institute of Carmelite Studies, 1989).

ters of perspective. It is this recognition of plural center of perspective that allows me to construct the very notion of a physical object and thus of a consistent spatial world. I acknowledge that the idea of a world is a continuous process in which I am one partner among many; and I acquire the notion of the body as intrinsically a center of pattern-making, a "zero-point of orientation" in the collaborative mapping of a coherent environment. In this context, it is equally important to register that self-awareness is necessarily incomplete and that the sensorium of an individual body alone cannot deliver a coherent picture of the world or a coherent account of the body. Stein notes that this also entails the fact that encounter with other embodied selves clarifies in various ways what we are *not*: not simply the boundedness of our own embodiment, but the partial character of our systems of value.[10] Any ethic, in other words, requires corporate labor and the relinquishing of any aspiration to create a moral schema by the exercise of my will. The implication of this is that the search for a human ethical framework is always tied up with the articulating and exploring of a *shared* world: each individual is "preceded" by the continuing life of ethical work, the negotiating of different schemes of value within a shared material environment where we have no option but to seek hopefully for mutual intelligibility. Law and social protocol may accept and manage diversities, often deep diversities, in society, but *argument* manifestly continues, seeking at the very least some possibility of imaginatively penetrating and identifying with other convictions and drawing closer to a picture of the human good that can be "owned" increasingly widely (this is what I have elsewhere called an "interactive pluralism" in society, a situation where the constituent sub-communities of a society are free to argue over unchosen, "absolute" imperatives, but the social and legal order overall does not seek to enforce any system as binding on conscience). But the point in relation to our wider argument

10. Stein, *Empathy*, 116.

is that the entire character of our work in constructing a concept or image of our humanity—its embodiedness, its social nature, its capacity for memory and narrative, its commitment to making sense of, to, and with one another—works on the assumption that something is *accessible* to us as we speak together, an order of coherent communication which puts a certain sort of pressure upon speakers in the direction of convergence. We assume a shared world, not only in the obvious sense of assuming compatible levels of sensory experience in other agents/speakers, but at a more elusive level.

Stein makes a few very tantalizing remarks about how our imagining of other perspectives in the construction of the idea of the embodied self is parallel in some ways to the imagining of past selves, including the imagining of my own past self that we call memory: we experience and understand ourselves as single embodied agents here and now not only because of the network of current others whose perceiving I must imagine, but also because of the recognition of how this network extends back through time. The self is always "embedded," but (more specifically) always engaged by what it has not itself generated, stimulated into coherent and collaborative mental activity by what is—to use the word again—accessible to us in the exchange of language. Linking this to our earlier discussion of the Girardian scheme, we can see how the mimetic spiral of Girard's anthropology is precisely a depiction of the shadow-side of Stein's analysis: to desire the desire of the other is indeed to assume a convergence of human experience, a mutual intelligibility in the form of the recognition of what the other wants or values as something I might intelligibly want for myself. As Terry Eagleton observes, referencing Freud, though he might equally well have cited Girard: "It is possible, Freud considers, that the project of culture or civilization demands more from us than we can properly yield"[11]—that is, the ideal of mutual transparency

---

11. T. Eagleton, *Culture and the Death of God* (New Haven: Yale University Press, 2015), 173.

and coherent intelligibility among human beings has the capacity to become an idolatrous object of worship, demanding sacrifices it cannot rightly claim. Yet that ideal is built into linguistic and social practice, a necessary aspect of any account of human identity that is not destructively and nonsensically individualistic. We should not see Girard as offering a negative picture of the processes of formation in self and society, and neither should we see Stein and other phenomenologists as giving a more positive image of co-operative world-construction. The interdependence of selves in the labor of world—or self-construction—is a mark *both* of the possibilities of convergence and mutual nurture in the human community *and* of the possibilities of murderous competition, precisely because I am able in some degree to understand and imaginatively own my neighbor's desire, and because I come to the recognition of my own desire through the mimetic process. If the Girardian analysis of destructive desire opens up the meaning of the revelation of a God who is entirely beyond the competitive struggle of finite agents sharing a world, Stein's understanding of the "empathic" basis of our awareness of our embodied selves similarly offers a way in to understanding what is meant by seeing the world as the product and the bearer of logos, the active communication of convergent meaning in the unceasing action of God towards creation. The act of trust involved in our speaking, the constant work of making collective sense, fits with the narrative of creation as an unconstrained act of intelligent love, communicating its own generous relationality in and through the ordered relation of finite things.

3. Witness and the Divine Image

The two analyses of culture and knowledge outlined here, Girardian and phenomenological, suggest a reading of the human consciousness as always both addressed or invited and insecure or acquisitive. This does not add up to some contemporary version of the Five Ways or whatever other structure of argument towards the divine that may be thought of as canonical, but it pictures human consciousness in a way that converges strikingly with the implications of the Christian story of creation and incarnation. It is possible to say that *if* the reality of the divine were as Christian doctrine claims, this would make sense of these features of human awareness and agency, and that if these are the salient and distinctive features of human awareness and agency, it is this kind of narrative of divine action that would most comprehensively address the imprisonment and aporia of human imagining and relating. It is what Alister McGrath has called—with reference to C.S. Lewis, though many aspects of Newman's thought would exemplify it also—an "abductive" mode of apologetic reasoning: not a deduction of conclusion from established premises but a kind of heuristic appeal to a framework which connects and grounds various imperfectly articulated assumptions about human intelligence in action.[12]

This takes us into our final area of reflection. If it is the case that the Christian narrative offers a solid framework for understanding the nature of human understanding itself, its "justification" is never going to be some conclusion that makes no difference to the self-understanding of the subject. Wittgenstein notoriously said that he could not believe in the resurrection of Christ without becoming a different kind of person, and this was not said dismissively. The Areopagitic line of thought we have explored here implies that if we test the ultimate foundation of our working assumptions about our human world, we can come to see ourselves as the object of a transcendent and changeless regard, and at the same time as wholly implicated in the interdependence of finite identities. The action of the transcendent source of affirmation upon us and our world is such as to make clear that our interdependence does not have to be violent, toxic, and destructive, if we are enabled to step

---

12. See A. McGrath, *The Intellectual World of C.S. Lewis* (Chichester: Wiley-Blackwell, 2013).

back from perpetuating the mimetic spiral. To identify with the act that breaks the mimetic spiral—in Christian doctrine, the Creator's self-identification in the Incarnation of the Eternal Word with the guilty and suffering creature—is the way in which the hidden truth of our humanity is allowed to come to light, both its destructiveness and its intrinsic relational connectedness.

It is a significant fact that such an identification can be seen at times in those who do not overtly profess belief in the Christian narrative but believe that it is possible to embody the refusal of a mimetic and violent destiny. Interest continues to grow in the figure of Etty Hillesum, whose notes and journals from the era of the Second World War and the German occupation of the Netherlands chronicle her journey from a sympathetic agnosticism to something like religious faith—though there is no sensible way of assigning her to any one religious community. She never abandoned her Jewish roots, though her vocabulary and reading became increasingly shaped by Christian sources. But what is most salient for our discussion here is the theme that recurs with increasing intensity in her writing about and from Westerbork, the holding camp for those who were to be transferred to Auschwitz (where Etty would be killed in November 1943; it is an extraordinary coincidence that she met Edith Stein and her sister in Westerbork in 1942). She expresses it in her wartime letters and diaries as "safeguarding" God[13] or as "clearing the path" to God for others in oneself[14] and being a "mediator" for the encounter with God,[15] a means by which direct encounter with God can be opened up; most strikingly,[16] she declares that there must be "someone to live through it all and bear witness to the fact that God lived, even in these times," and asks why she should not be that witness,

---

13. *Etty. The Letters and Diaries of Etty Hillesum 1941–1943* (Grand Rapids, MI: Eerdmans, 2002), 488–9.
14. Ibid., 519.
15. Ibid., 516.
16. Ibid., 506.

"saving" God in herself, taking responsibility for "shepherding" the "great and beautiful feeling of life" that she carries.[17]

It is a very distinctive theme; she does not attempt to systematize it theologically in any way, but it is clearly grounded in her overwhelming sense that something had opened up within her that was quite beyond her comprehension, and that this gave her the resource to approach the appalling squalor and suffering of the transit camp and the casual cruelty of those administering it with a clear perception of comparable depths in every other she encountered, including camp guards—although she can record poignantly that, after one night of watching the guards rounding up people for transport to the death camps, she struggles with relating the guards' faces to the biblical declaration of our creation after God's likeness; "That passage spent a difficult morning with me."[18] The central point is that her awareness of a persistent and never fully accessible depth in her selfhood—her belief in God—is strictly inseparable from the imperative to *become a means* of opening up that depth for others. If the existence of God is debatable, incredible, unintelligible for those around, her responsibility is to live in such a way that it would make sense to say "God lived, even in these times." Connecting this to our earlier discussion, we could say that if language about God is language about (among other things) the actuality of non-competitive, non-revengeful, non-violent engagement with otherness, including violent and threatening otherness, that actuality becomes believable when it is actual in finite acts and lives. It is actualized in those lives through *surrender*—in worship of what alone is worthy of worship, which is the generative reality of the non-worldly act of God, the act that does not contend with or displace finite action but lives in the depth of finite reality and is able to work through that reality as and when it is radically opened

17. Ibid., 498.
18. Ibid., 644.

up to be more completely a vehicle for the eternal act of gift. Etty Hillesum's language about "shepherding" and "safeguarding" the divine, so far from making the divine dependent on created agents, is about witnessing to the persistence of an agency that is not vulnerable to defeat or extinction.

The believer's act of faith is a "stepping aside" from the self-sufficiency that blocks the access of others to God—a self-forgetting that is also an alignment with what gives the self its life in the first place. The believer can thus be said to "stand in" for God, to take on the responsibility of representing God by the radicality of their standing *aside*. Etty Hillesum sees her calling in the Westerbork transit camp as a letting go of whatever in her might stand in the way of God being credible and palpable to her neighbor, and this is the essence of the worship she offers. There is no gap between the act of self-surrender to God and the denial of private and protective self-interest in order to clear the way of the neighbor to God and God to the neighbor.

4. Conclusion

It is not difficult to see how the life of faith understood in these terms embodies the insights from Girard, Stein and others summarized earlier. The life of faith sets out to realize in the created order the non-defensive, non-interest-dominated life that is God's, the life whose manifestation in our history releases us from the lethal mythology of mimetic struggle and sacrificial exclusion. It implies a reimagining of "human rights" in terms of the perception of the other as one who needs me as an acquisitive or self-defended individual to step out of the light and allow God to be visible to them—a particularly focused form of attentiveness and service. It also assumes that my own growth into humanity needs always to be nurtured by the divine act and image in the neighbor, and that my receptivity to this is the key to my own release.

That all of this is realized not by unaided imagination and human effort but by the gift that is bestowed in the events of biblical history, culminating in the paschal mystery of the rejection and killing of the Word Incarnate and the overcoming of that rejection by God is not to be established by argument; its evidences are to be found in the persistence of lives characterized by the mutual 'standing-aside for the sake of God' that are to be found in the community of Christ's Body. The ongoing life of that Body is centered upon the act of surrender and adoration that is the sacramental enactment of Christ's own life-giving surrender to the Father—the Eucharist. In our own recognition that we come to "stand in" for God in faith, a somewhat terrifying realization, we accept that this happens only in an unqualified embrace of our complete dependence on divine gift as the source of our being; and so the divinity we come to embody in the life of faith is always the divinity of the Word, the Son, eternally dependent on gift, eternally pointing to its source, standing in and standing aside.

Paul's Athenian audience appear to have lost interest when he began to speak about Jesus and the resurrection; and the contemporary Areopagus is not likely to be any more receptive.

What these reflections have sought to do is to suggest the need for human society to understand something about true and false worship. To know that God alone is to be worshipped because God alone has no desired goal to pursue, no interest to defend and no coercive power to reinforce is to know that no other claimant to worship is to be taken seriously, whether the external tyrant or the internal systems of desire. If God is to be worshipped, *nothing else is*. God's transcendence of the economy of negotiating and warring egos is the ground of that human transcendence of the claims of power that is seen in the confessors and martyrs—including those who, like Etty Hillesum, might not have made anything remotely like an orthodox confession but yet understood the imperative of

resisting both idolatrous power and revengeful violence. The liberty
of human beings from the economies of coercion and competition,
as also from the anxieties of earning worth and security, is linked
inseparably to the acknowledgment of a self-imparting divine action, embodied in the drastic non-violence of Jesus: the bearer of
the plenitude of divine meaning who is excluded by the exercise of
human coercive power and manifests in his resurrection that coercive power can have no hold on the divine.

The question of faith in the context of a modern Areopagus is
still to do with that opening question: what do humans worship?
And how does worship become life-giving rather than the ultimate
tyranny? If God is not as manifested in the scriptural narrative,
God's claim to worship is indeed no more than another case of the
destructive pattern by which some are disenfranchised, silenced or
annihilated by others within the world. Any apologetic inspired by
Paul in Athens needs to attend to two interrelated tasks: it must
return again and again to the clarifying of the underlying grammar
of what the Jewish and Christian tradition says about God; and it
must find ways of displaying how that tradition charts the way of
liberation from a world in which the non-negotiable worth of human subjects is repeatedly eroded. This entails some close tracking
of how we speak about ethics and language; perhaps it is ultimately
most engaging when it takes us back to story and practice, to the
not always articulate witness of the person who offers their body
as a place where God may become credible, and to the collective
practice of Christ's Body in its performance of the transforming
"anti-sacrificial" sacrifice of the Eucharist. After all, one of those
who did linger to listen further at the Areopagus was the Dionysius
to whom the entirely unreliable tradition ascribes those classical
works on liturgy and on self-forgetting inarticulacy.

BISHOP ROWAN WILLIAMS—born in Swansea, Wales, in 1950. Anglican bishop, scholar, theologian and poet. Master of Magdalene College Cambridge in the years 2013–2020 and honorary professor at the Department of Modern Christian Thought at the University of Cambridge. Chancellor of the University of South Wales since 2013. He was Archbishop of Wales (2000–2002) and Archbishop of Canterbury (2002–2012). Appointed life peer in the House of Lords in 2013, he served as Baron Williams of Oystermouth from 2013 until his retirement on August 31, 2020.

MAREK A. CICHOCKI

EUROPEAN IDENTITY: NORTH AND SOUTH, EAST AND WEST— THE MAIN DIVIDING LINES

1. Distance and closeness: John Paul II and his first address

"He was called from a distant country, distant but always so close through communion in the Christian faith and tradition." Those were the words with which Pope John Paul II referred to himself in his first address to the Christians gathered at St. Peter's Square in October 1978, just after the conclave's decision. These words, along with the Pope's appeal at the Holy Mass held at Victory Square in the center of Warsaw in 1979, "Let Your Spirit descend! And renew the face of the earth, the face of this land," became the symbol of an overturn in history for every Pole of my generation. The same change of course later took place in Europe, leading to the end of the Cold War, the collapse of communism, and the transformation of the whole world. With four decades' perspective, I recall these words spoken in 1978 and 1979 when considering the current problem of European identity and the ongoing cultural wars. I will identify the meanings of *distance* and *closeness* in this context, as they are crucial in understanding the main dividing lines in the current dispute about the foundations of European identity. These lines, deeply rooted in our European history, are mainly geocultural and they have profound consequences for the current cultural wars. I mean here, first, the older and basic line between North and South, which was decisive in forming the Christian European culture and, secondly, the divide between West and East, which is closely related to the subsequent concept of modern European civilization. According to the latter, a closer consideration of the relationship between civilization and culture seems essential to understanding the problem of *distance* and *closeness* at the center of the current cultural wars over European identity.

Moreover, I would argue that the intersection of these two main lines dividing Europe, East vs. West and North vs. South, is the key factor in understanding the current European identity crisis and in the unfolding of Europe's future.

2. Distance of the bipolar world

It is important to consider the circumstances of the years 1978 and 1979, which I suppose were obvious to everyone who heard the Pope's first speech at St. Peter's Square or his later appeal at the Holy Mass in Warsaw. These circumstances in Europe were vividly symbolized by the Iron Curtain, materialized (among others) in the Berlin Wall, and were implemented generally through the military, ideological, and political conquest of half of Europe by the Soviets. From that perspective, the unexpected election of a pope from behind the Iron Curtain ensured the universality of Christianity and the Catholic Church by undermining the bipolar, Cold War-era East-West division. It also foreshadowed the upcoming collapse of communism and the reunification of Europe. Hence, the pontificate of Pope John Paul II established a bridge over the Cold War borders and enabled the intrusion of long-awaited European closeness into the reality of ideological and political divisions that were responsible for growing feelings of distance in post-war Europe. This context of closeness and distance was clear for everyone during those days at St. Peter's Square and contributed to the awareness of the greatness of that historical moment. The existence of two different worlds and of what was described as the East-West divide and the bipolar Cold War struggle among powers suddenly disappeared at that moment, showing the prospects of making irrelevant the hard and often dangerous realities of divided Europe and paving the way to a restored closeness among Europeans. This development was fulfilled throughout the 1980s, leading to the new reality of the post-Cold War world. The struggle to overcome the East-West divide of the Cold War based on cultural and spiritual closeness was then often depicted in a naive but influential manner: as the liberal "arc of history" or simply as the "end of history." These two politically serviceable views on the meaning and consequences of the end of the Cold War were dominant during the last three decades and representative of the new liberal globalization ideologies, which have completely ignored or even purposely rejected any other possible insight into the meaning of the events that changed Europe in the late 1980s and early 1990s. In this context, Pope John Paul II's first remarks are worth remembering because they stress the experience of closeness and distance in Europe and restore the true meaning of overcoming the East-West divide, which was possible due to cultural and spiritual closeness and the clear awareness of the peril of communism as the real source of distance and alienation in Europe.[1]

---

1. G. Weigel, *The Final Revolution: The Resistance Church and the Collapse of Communism* (Oxford: Oxford University Press, 2003).

3. Distance and the Western concept of European civilization

The distance and alienation created by communism—as opposed to cultural and spiritual closeness—reveal some deeper layers of the historical division between East and West that were related to the "project of modernity" and its chain of unfinished revolutions. This makes the distance the pope was referring to much older and deeper than one would assume based on the realities of the Cold War in Europe, which were the direct outcome of the situation following World War II. Distance created in Europe through communism, along with other powerful modernity ideologies of the 20th century, including German Nazism and Italian fascism, resulted from the events in Europe in the late 1700s and early 1800s, specifically the events in Europe in the decisive period between the years of 1789 and 1814–1815, which in turn were the product of the whole mental, revolutionary transgression of Europeans that had taken place in philosophy, theology, and science earlier, in the 16th, 17th, and 18th centuries. As the product of this longstanding process of fundamental changes mounted in the Enlightenment, Europe altered completely during the turn of the 19th century, and the new modernization logic of the East-West divide (distance and alienation) was triggered, determining the two last centuries, and it still exists. Consequently, these events influenced the new idea of European civilization, shaped on the concept of modernization (the project of modern man as opposed to the ancient and traditional one), on historical progress based on the concept of historical and scientific mind (truth), and finally on the utilitarian ethics of an individual or group's interests. All this together decisively influenced the new understanding of Europe and the West as the center of the project of modernity, while in this context the East became distant, unfamiliar, and extraneous. This enabled the special role of tsarist

Russia for the enlightened West. Considering the tsar's rule extremely cruel and tyrannical, the Westerner modernizers started to perceive Russia as the only power capable of projecting a new, enlightened modern order over the territories and populations in eastern Europe, which had become viewed as eccentric, oriental, and wild. Even more profoundly, it revealed another consequence of the modernization project: the idea of post-Christianity. It is important to stress that this change, which was caused by modernization, happened fully at the expense of Christianity through a rejection of Europe's entire Christian culture, including the Christian concept of truth, the Christian concept of the universe and of human life. Europe's longstanding Christian culture started to be considered the chief obstacle to modern European civilization, one that had to be eliminated for the sake of the project of modern progress. So at the turn of the 19th century, Christian culture and modern civilization started to be perceived and understood as two completely distant and hostile realities within Europe—a situation that Friedrich Nietzsche explicitly named at the end of the 19th century, at a time in Europe's history that was influential on the preparation of the powerful and disastrous modernity ideologies of the 20th century.

4. Enlightenment or Enlightenments?

Many prominent authors such as Leo Strauss, Eric Voegelin, and Karl Löwith[2] tried to examine the evolution of the modernity project taking place at the expense and to the detriment of the traditional divide and the metaphysical context of the human world. The intriguing question remains of whether the hostility between the modern mind and the Christian faith was inevitable and necessarily led to the clash with the divine and metaphysical context, and

2. L. Strauss, *What is Political Philosophy? And Other Studies* (Chicago: University of Chicago Press, 1988); E. Voegelin, *From Enlightenment to Revolution* (Durham, NC: Duke University Press, 1982); K. Löwith, *From Hegel to Nietzsche: The Revolution in Nineteenth-Century Thought* (New York: Columbia University Press, 1991).

consequently to its complete abandonment, which many rational-
ists saw as the only acceptable foundation for the further progress
of modernity. This question refers directly to judgments about the
meaning and the consequences of the Enlightenment and about the
probably unreconciled relationship between the enlightened mind
and religion. Some inspiring debates occurred in the late 20th century on this issue, such as, for instance, the intellectual exchange
between Jürgen Habermas and Joseph Ratzinger about modern
rationalism and Christianity in the post-enlightened age.[3] Pope
John Paul II gave us another indication of this in his book *Memory
and Identity*,[4] in which he recalls the alternative path of the Polish
Enlightenment, which at the time of the reign of Stanisław August
Poniatowski made efforts to reunite Christian faith with modern rationality. Regarding the possible alternative developments
of modernity, Gertrude Himmelfarb aptly explained her strong
reservations about the concept of what is called the European
Enlightenment, which in her view was incorrectly established as
the model of the common experience constituting the main conceptual images of the current modern West.[5] For her, the European
Enlightenment usually means the unique experience of French radical rationalism and laicity, which in modern history profoundly
differed from the logic of modernization that took place in North
America, England, and even Germany, where the relationship between the modern mind and religion went in different, more rec-
onciled directions. Even if we recognize the existence of different
types of European modernity framed differently in different cultural contexts, however, and we realize the specific French case of

3. J. Habermas, J. Ratzinger, *The Dialectics of Secularization: On Reason and Religion* (San Francisco: Ignatius Press, 2007).

4. Pope John Paul II, *Memory and Identity: Conversations at the Dawn of a Millennium* (New York: Rizzoli, 2005).

5. G. Himmelfarb, *The Roads to Modernity: The British, French, and American Enlightenments* (New York: Vintage Books, 2005).

modernization to be only one among many others, we have to admit that in the end the radical forms of rationalism and materialism dominated the Western project of modernity identifying modern civilization through a complete opposition and hostility to religion and culture. It is also disturbing how the growing radicalism of the modernity project during the 19th century was linked to the powerful and destructive modern ideologies of the 20th century. Hence, the discussion of distance and alienation during the Cold War was only partly related to the geopolitical realities of a Europe divided into West and East. In a much more profound sense, it touched on the general consequences of the increasingly radical face of modernity, which has been replacing cultural and spiritual closeness with the realities of the civilizational distance. The radicalism of the modernity project, nurtured and growing during the 19th and 20th centuries, did not halt with the end of the Cold War and is still affecting the West and the Western approach to Eastern Europe.

5. North and South divide— closeness to the sources

It is worth noting the time when American historian Larry Wolff published his excellent book, *Inventing Eastern Europe: The Map of Civilization on the Mind of the Enlightenment.*[6] It was the year 1994, and as the author of the book declared once to me personally, it was exactly the time, at the peak of the events leading Europeans to the new post-Cold War world, when he felt that Europe was on its way to restoring its unity and cultural closeness. He realized, too, that it is vital to inquire into the reasons for the distances that divided Europe in the last two centuries, including the most important division between West and East. The title of his book includes the key problems: the invention of the East, the shape of the

6. L. Wolff, *Inventing Eastern Europe: The Map of Civilization on the Mind of the Enlightenment* (Stanford: Stanford University Press, 1994).

new civilization, and the enlightened mind. His main argument in the book was that the East-West divide was an ideological design created for the purpose of the new self-identification of the West recreated around the new ideas of the Enlightenment and rationality. By legitimizing the foundations of the new European civilization, the key invention of the East-West divide aimed at a complete rejection of the foundations of the "old" Europe, which for many centuries, specifically from the second half of the first millennium, when Europe erected its geographical and cultural outlines, was designed along the continent's main geocultural line between North and South.

Let us now focus on another important line, the prior one in Europe's history and identity, which for centuries organized the geocultural and spiritual order of Europe along the North and South axis. It was decisive in forming European identity, European culture, and the spirit of Europe in general. This line is much deeper and older than the modern East-West divide modeled on the secular concept of modernity and progress. It was, after all, rooted in Christianity and its impact on Europe. It revolved around the divine Revelation, human openness, and conversion to the Christian Truth. At the same time, it was framed by the recurring attraction of the old world of Romanitas and its ancient traditions and achievements, which were Christianized and later became the chief spiritual and cultural inspiration for European nations during Europe's history. Geographically, this line between the South and North followed the Rhine and Danube rivers and the Alps, which for a long time remained a real and mental boundary of Roman civilization on our continent.

This key line has disappeared slowly but was replaced during the 19th and 20th centuries by new, progressive modernity ideologies at the expense of Christianity and ancient traditions. In unexpected and intriguing ways, however, it has been recalled recently by some crises that shook the European Union profoundly in the last decade, making many aware of the existence and impact of the North-South divide. Although these crises have been of a pragmatic character and primarily of a financial, economic, and social nature, they displayed and recalled the whole cultural and historical complexity of the old, abandoned division between Southern and Northern Europe.

This previously appeared in different forms as the Renaissance and the Reformation, which were powerful forms of pre-Enlightenment change and progress in Europe. As recurring ruptures and reunions, they helped each time to restore and redefine the central sources of European identity and culture existing in the heritage of Christianized Romanitas and the ancient Mediterranean South. The Renaissance, as the opposite of the progress that was a pillar of the modern concept of post-Enlightenment Europe, rested on an entirely different understanding of change. It understood the key North-South axis not in terms of distance, of civilization's dividing lines, but as the constant tension within Europe with ways of restoring spiritual and cultural closeness and re-unity based on their common sources. It recurrently enabled Europeans to restore the bridges between the past and the present. It was like the story of passing away, of vanishing and resurrection and reunion, of Persephone and Demeter: the fall and rise of Europe along common lines of cultural and spiritual continuity. This fruitful dynamic of the cultural closeness enshrined in the South and North relationship started with the clash between the barbaric tribes from the North and Roman civilization at the very beginning of what we call European history. This relationship, at first hostile and violent, has been transformed into the adoption, assimilation, and overtaking of the passing civilization as the form and source for the new, beginning European reality. Christianity, the Christian message, the Gospel, and the conversion to the Christian truth played the key role for centuries in this process of adoption, fruitful translation, and establishing closeness between the North and the Southern sources.

6. The self-conscious barbarian who converts

Rémi Brague drew attention to one fundamental aspect of this translation process, which took place between the South and North in Europe's pre-Enlightenment history. Describing it in his excellent book *The Eccentric Culture: A Theory of Western Civilization*, originally titled *Europe, la voie romaine*,[7] he emphasized that the specific closeness, restored thanks to Christianity through adoption and translation of the ancient, Southern sources, did not mean identity or replacement by an entirely new civilization. It established a specific relationship between South and North, which Brague calls "secondarity" and "intermediation" and which he puts at the very heart of the European, pre-Enlightenment cultural and spiritual identity. According to that secondary of Europe, the normative and formative impact of the ancient civilization was transmitted by Christianity into the barbarian souls. Hence, the converted barbarian from the North, who is constantly conscious of his own dark origins and his hidden, unformed, and dangerous might, struggling recurrently against this dark heritage of his own barbarism and drawing from ancient sources transmitted to him by Christianity—such a "barbarian" becomes the very essence and the permanent symbol of Europe and European culture. He is the historical and spiritual product of the clash and closeness between the North and South. This leads Brague to one important and practical conclusion: the lack of consciousness about the secondary nature of European culture indicated through the lack of consciousness about its own inherent barbarianism and the need for conversion as the only way to calm it, this lacking consciousness or the hope of overcoming

---

7. R. Brague, *Eccentric Culture: A Theory of Western Civilization* (South Bend, IN: St. Augustine's Press, 2009).

it, which was and still is the main promise of modernization and progress, each time in Europe's history led us, Europeans, to amoral acceptance of pure force, violence, and dehumanization.

7. *Translatio imperi* or lost in translation

The best known historical example of that kind of translation and adoption in the relationship between the North and South, was, of course, the Holy Roman Empire, later renamed the Holy Roman Empire of the German Nation. For centuries the German Medieval emperors claimed to be the only true vicars of Christ on earth and so to be the only legitimate head of the universal Christian spiritual and political order. This, of course, led recurrently to conflicts with the papacy and Rome about its supremacy. This political and historiosophical universal concept of the Holy German Empire was based on the specific idea of *transatio imperi*, which was the key political idea of pre-modern Europe. According to this, Europe was founded politically on the Roman myth of the golden city on a hill, Rome, erected as the fulfillment of the divine mission by the first European pioneer, Aeneas. This mission is continued and repeatedly fulfilled in Europe's history by establishing new centers of universal power in other places of the continent. The Holy Roman Empire claimed its legitimacy from being the most powerful representation of this transmission between the South and North.[8]

Translation can ensure transmission and connection, but it can also keep us lost in translation. This was the main reason for the failure of the imperial German project, which became focused on exercising pure secular power in Europe, and was then due to reformation, aimed at decoupling the powerful North from the South. Finally, the idea started to prevail that the North, liberated

8. J. Le Goff, *Medieval Civilization* (Oxford: Blackwell Publishing, 1991), Part II, Chapter VI; and A. Latowsky, *Emperor of the World: Charlemagne and the Construction of Imperial Authority* (Ithaca, NY: Cornell University Press, 2013), 800–1229.

from Southern patronage, which was seen as obsolete and depraved, should entirely replace the South in Europe and provide itself with its own sources. The whole relationship between the North and South was questioned, and so were the primacy of Christian culture and ancient traditions along with the secondary nature of Europeans. The path to establishing the concept of a new modern European civilization was open. Hegel was right, indeed, seeing in German reformation the first powerful step toward the entirely new project of modernity in Europe.

8. The Polish case and the South-North transmission

Pre-modern Europe was constituted in consequence of many different attempts to fulfill the South-North transmission. Let me make some remarks about the Polish case regarding this, as it differed substantively from the German *translatio imperi*. The Polish *translatio*, however, remains pivotal for Poland's place in Europe as well as for the evolution of its culture and identity. The importance of the transmission between South and North seems obvious in the Polish case if we consider that the political and cultural statehood of Poland in Europe, which started in the 10th century, rested directly on the act of Christianizing the Poles. Although having its own pre-Christian history, albeit drowned in darkness, the foundation of the Polish state was not an act of conquest or an establishment of a new dynasty but an act of conversion, adoption, and transmission and coupling to the Southern sources of medieval Europe—an act that cannot be perceived purely in terms of a geopolitical decision. It was a strong commitment and a declaration of faith. As an independent and conscious act of faith, Christianization was the foundation of the Polish political and cultural community at its inception. It also lay in the open tension with the universalistic idea of the Holy German Empire and its *translatio imperi*, but in turn, in direct connection to Rome. This was the crucial point for further developments in Poland's history.

At the end of the 12th century, at the peak of the Medieval Renaissance, the Polish transmission evolved into a full-fledged political and cultural European self-identification intellectually and literarily worked out by the Cistercian monk Blessed Wincenty Kadłubek, Bishop of Cracow, whom Pope John Paul II once aptly called "the father of Polish culture." His main work, *Chronicles of the Kings and Princes of Poland*, is much more than a typical chronicle enumerating rulers and historical events. Its four volumes contain several important political and philosophical tracts containing many references to antiquity and recalling some concepts of political philosophy drawn from Cicero and John of Salisbury. Wincenty was an intellectual and a prelate of the Polish Church who represented the European Medieval Renaissance of the 12th century in Polish thought and contributed substantively to the creation of Polish political culture and Polish political language (expressed, of course, in Latin). Thanks to him, they were permanently bound with the ideas of *res publica* and of equal and free citizens directly constituting a republican community, both drawn from the Aristotelian and Roman tradition transmitted to Poland in the strong context of Christianity. This kind of republicanism in the form of political constitution and at the same time as a kind of public ethics and a vision of republican history with its roots in antiquity deviated, of course, completely from the Medieval political realities of the Polish Kingdom and the Polish Principality. As a political and philosophical idea, however, it contained an immense and powerful potential for further intellectual and political reception and continuity in Polish political life. It shaped the political culture, political vocabulary, political practices, and self-perception of many Polish generations in the following centuries, forming the strong foundations of the Polish *Rzeczpospolita* from the 15th to the 18th century. It also positioned Poles against the concept of the Holy Empire in Europe and the universalism enshrined in *translatio imperi*, making them convinced and devoted Christian republicans for generations.[9]

9. The golden age of 16th century— Cicero in Poland

The 16th century is the peak, the Golden Age, of the evolution of spiritual and cultural closeness between North and South in the Polish case. Neo-Roman republicanism, with a strong and unique reception of Cicero and Aristotle, special diplomatic, political, economic, and academic relations with the republic of Venice, a huge number of Polish students at Italian universities, mainly in Padua—all this contributed to the rise and flowering of the Polish Commonwealth in the North. It is worth noting that this spread of the idea of neo-Roman Ciceronian-based republicanism at that time also involved some other countries in the North of Europe as well, like the Dutch Republic or England, and, as comprehensively shown by Quentin Skinner in his historical analyses of the evolution of freedom before liberalism, it contributed decisively to rebalancing the political absolutism in Europe.[10]

The Polish case shows vividly how the North-South line, so essential for the evolution of European culture and identity, through Christianity and republicanism, enabled the closeness of the cultural and spiritual sources of the South to the distant countries from the North for centuries.

---

9. M. Cichocki, *Nord und Süd. Texte über die polnische Geschichtskultur* (Wiesbaden: Harrassowitz Verlag, 2020).

10. Q. Skinner, *Liberty Before Liberalism* (Cambridge: Cambridge University Press, 2012).

10. How the West was reshaped and replaced the North and South axis

Coming back to the East-West distance created by the new post-Christian European civilization, the Reformation had a remarkable impact as an originally religious, Christian movement of the North, which decoupled Europeans from the sources of the South (through the anti-Rome affects). It gave rise to religious and anthropological individualism and laid the foundations for the existential loneliness of the void secular world (Kierkegaard) by questioning European Christian universalism and establishing absolutism in politics. This change, however, was revealed to be only a preparation for further revolutionary spiritual, scientific, theological, and philosophical changes that took place in the 17th and 18th centuries in Europe and finally led to the establishment of the modernity project. The appearance of that project was associated with the real change in the basic geopolitical and geocultural directions, which completely altered European self-identification and replaced the old North-South axis with the East-West divide. What one usually calls the European Enlightenment was a reintegration of the old concept of *L'Occidence* or *das Abendland* around new rational ideas, openly critical of or even hostile to the theological and philosophical Christian world view, in order to establish the new West as an enlightened and post-Christian modern civilization. This reintegration and creation of the new West mainly took place in France and was to be massively strengthened in its effects and intensity by the French revolution, although the processes that simultaneously took place in England were no less important for the formation of a modern West of a different nature (there, it was related chiefly to the formation of capitalism). While the idea of the new West was modelled on modern rationalism and new, post-Christian values, at the same time the new concept of the East, as the Oriental opposite to the rational West, was invented.

11. Napoleonic modern pan-Europeanism

Certainly, the French revolution made this whole change in Europe irreversible, despite all attempts by traditionalists and conservatives—from de Maistre to Chateaubriand. What might have been the outcome and impact of this revolution without the emergence of Napoleonian Caesarism? One could even argue that without Napoleon the French revolution would have remained a marginal, local historical event. Historical fiction? Not at all. Napoleon transformed the French revolution into a pan-European civilization project and universalized its political and legal consequences. By doing this, he contributed to the final collapse of the old cultural and spiritual transmission and closeness between North and South, replacing it through his powerful project of the French Empire as the center of the new European civilization, which marked the historical and irreversible transgression of old boundaries. Paris as the capital of the new, enlightened West was supposed to replace Rome, which was the center from the past. Later, already imprisoned on St. Helena Island, Napoleon recalled his ideas as follows:

The Western world should be enlightened, in the new era all nations should be equal, but the spiritual and civilization level on which they will be equal was to be determined by the spirit of the French Revolution,[11]

and further he added:

All united countries must be similar to France, and if they are united from the Pillars of Hercules to Kamchatka, French laws must extend throughout this area.[12]

Europeans who faced this modern, post-Christian hegemonic universalism of the reintegrated French West very often reacted to this using old, well known and deep-seated symbols and ideas. So, for

---

11. *Au Conseil d'Etat , Juillet 1805*, in: Napoléon, *Vues Politiques. Avant-Propos de Adrien Dansette* (Rio de Janeiro: Améric-Edit, 1939), 341.

12. Ibid.

example, many in German countries who initially welcomed the ideals of the French revolution as the new republican freedom were later disappointed by the French occupation and started to see in Napoleonic universalism (Hegel) the pure incarnation of Roman violence and quest for hegemony. They tried to oppose this by referring to Greek ancient traditions and by interpreting the central role of culture in the classical Weimarian vein. As one of the disappointed German Romantic poets, Joseph Görres, said about Napoleon:

We believed we were in Rome, but we found ourselves in Paris.[13]

It was likewise with Russia and the great opponent to Napoleon, Tsar Aleksander. The new post-Christian universalism revived the reaction in the form of old sentiments about the special relations and ties between tsarist Russia and the heritage of Byzantium, and along with that the mystical idea of Russia as the Third Rome.

But under the surface of these old symbols and ideas rooted in the past South and North relation, now reactivated in reaction to modern, enlightened French universalism, it became crystal clear, especially after 1815 and the Vienna Congress, that with the defeat of Napoleon a new kind of civilization dividing line in Europe was decided on and established. From then on, the West and East divide began to prevail in determining European self-identification and European politics.

12. Historical, scientific mind and utilitarianism

One could explain what this modern divide of Europe means in a deeper sense using the terms of distance and alienation in their cultural and anthropological meanings, both of which became the foundation of the modern Western world. Instead of recurrence and closeness of the sources and the Renaissance enabling

---

13. G.P. Gooch, *Germany and the French Revolution* (London and New York: Longmans, Green, and Company, 1920), 485.

redefinition of the sources through transmission, the radical transgression was placed at the center of the new civilization to pave the way for the final emancipation of individuals and mankind as a whole from the transcendent and metaphysical context. This new ideal of individual freedom, ultimately achieved by the fulfillment of the modernity project and the unhalted progress of modernization, completely redefined the meaning of humanism, human values, and Europe's self-identification. It gave rise to the new, modern European civilization, which is still our home, although the German philosopher Peter Sloterdijk more appropriately calls this civilization the "European greenhouse," "glasshouse," or "Crystal Palace," emphasizing the protection and alienation which simultaneously characterize the process of modernization.[14]

The concept of the new post-Christian civilization in Europe rested principally on two modern ideas that were elaborated in the 19th century, ones that must be stressed here, especially in the context of replacing the old transmission with the new transgression. The first idea was, on the one hand, modern utilitarianism, which should be perceived as a kind of radical ethical revolution resulting from rationalism, and on the other hand, the social, political, and economic consequences of the forceful and rapid evolution of capitalism. Using the radical concept of individual interests and happiness, Jeremy Bentham proposed his famous rational calculation of pleasure and pain as the only possible ethical foundation of human actions and decisions. He went further and used his calculations to design a detailed plan for a perfect, totally functional modern society in the form of his Panopticon—the perfect system of control, steering, and stimulation of humans confined to being merely behavioral objects. This monstrous project very quickly became the symbol of the modern industrial society managed by the narrow

14. P. Sloterdijk, *In the World Interior of Capital: Towards a Philosophical Theory of Globalization* (Cambridge: Polity Press, 2013).

group of entrepreneurs and scientific specialists who replaced the old group of clergy. The Panopticon was originally invented as the ideal prison, but as Bentham stated later:

> It will be found applicable, I think, without exception to all establishments whatsoever, in which within a space not too large to be covered or commanded by buildings, a number of persons are meant to be kept under inspections. No matter how different or even opposite the purpose.[15]

In consequence, the radical ethical revolution of utilitarianism, proposed by Bentham and modified later by other thinkers in the 19th century like John Mill and Henry Spencer, utterly undermined the ancient republican and Christian concept of justice and its applicability to modern political, social, and economic life. This ethical revolution contributed decisively to establishing the modern post-Christian European civilization.

The second idea was the new concept of history enshrined in Hegel's philosophy and resulting from the appearance of a new kind of modern historical consciousness, which during the 19th century was transformed into a completely secular, positive scientific mind and into the concept of the scientific and objective history of mankind. In his famous *Untimely Meditations* series, Friedrich Nietzsche revealed the consequences of this entirely new understanding of human history and of human understanding of time. The scientific mind as the product of a secularized philosophy of history utterly expelled God, freedom, theology, and metaphysics in the name of positive, objective, scientific truth, as thinkers like August Comte, Ernest Renan, and David Strauss showed vividly in the 19th century.

---

15. J. Bentham, *Panopticon or the Inspection-House*, in: *The Panopticon Writings*, ed. Miran Božovič (London: Verso, 1995), 29–95, Letter I. Idea of the Inspection Principle.

13. Final remarks

The effect of this process was the ultimate replacement of the North-South transmission by the East-West transgression in Europe, and furthermore the enhancement of the open contrast between the new European civilization, the European glasshouse or Panopticon on the one hand, and cultural and spiritual closeness on the other. Looking at this effect from the perspective of the changes that occurred in Europe in 1989 and 1990, one could argue that they were the great and unfulfilled hope to bridge this modern antagonism between civilization and culture. The collapse of Communism and the reunification of Europe substantively contributed to the awakening of hopes for a possible correction of the Western path of modernity by reconciling the clashes between modern European civilization and Christian cultural and spiritual context. It turned out that this kind of closeness, however, was not restored during the last three decades. Moreover, what we are now witnessing in Europe is the acceleration of alienation instead of closeness. Modern civilization has radicalized its hostile stance to Christian culture, strengthening the quest for the ultimate transgression and justifying it, alongside the well-known ideological modes of thinking about modernity and progress from the 19th and 20th century, as a historical and scientific necessity. The project of emancipation must be completed at any cost. Even the slightest compromise between progressive liberalism and conservative reservations is not on the horizon. The modern mind, once set free from any context (transgression instead of transmission), will never stop on its own and will never again recognize any boundaries where it has to halt. The project of modernization certainly does not allow any self-limitations, so it always leads to efforts to establish a new civilization without culture, which is the ideal of transgressed modernity.

This paper sought to explain the meaning of closeness and distance in the context of the evolution of the European identity. It is no secret that this identity is currently undergoing a very deep crisis. To understand the reasons for this and to look for remedies, we need better knowledge of Europe's evolution in history. South and North versus West and East enables us to recognize the main directions and paradoxes of this evolution. We are actually at the crossroads of both: on the one side is the deep-seated tradition of Christian European culture that transmitted the ancient sources for us; on the other side is the concept of modern post-Christianity and transgressing civilization that is now under unprecedented strain and uncertainty. How we get through this crossroads will be determinative for Europe's future.

MAREK A. CICHOCKI—born in Warsaw, Poland, in 1966. Professor at Collegium Civitas in Warsaw and visiting professor at the College of Europe Natolin, co-founder of the Polish yearly "Teologia Polityczna" [Political Theology] and editor-in-chief of the journal "Nowa Europa. Przegląd Natoliński" [New Europe. Natolin Review]. He was program director of the Center for International Relations in Warsaw (2000–2003) and also an advisor to the late President of Poland Lech Kaczyński (2007–2010). Author of awarded books: *Porwanie Europy* [Kidnapping Europe] (2004) and *Północ i Południe. Teksty o polskiej kulturze i historii* [North and South. Essays on Polish culture and history] (2018).

JOHN CAVADINI

POPE ST. JOHN PAUL II, THE SECOND VATICAN COUNCIL, AND THE CRISIS OF MODERNITY.

What is the "crisis of modernity?" To put it in terms of the Second Vatican Council, we can look specifically at *Gaudium et Spes,* which has the subtitle *De Ecclesia in Mundo Huius Temporis,* commonly translated into English as "concerning the Church in the modern world." If we take our cue from *Gaudium et Spes,* then we would say that the crisis of modernity is a "crisis of the human being" or of the human "person." The pastoral constitution identifies the "human person" as the key to its whole discussion, the "hinge" (*cardo*) of its exposition, that very human person (*hominis persona*) who is to be "saved" and whose society is to be "renewed" (*instauranda*).[1]

More specifically, the 1965 pastoral constitution calls us to discern the "signs of the times" in this "modern world" which is a "new age in history" (*mundi hodierni; in nova historiae […] aetate*).[2] It

---

1. Second Vatican Ecumenical Council, Pastoral Constitution on the Church in the Modern World *Gaudium et Spes* (Vatican City, 7 December 1965), para. 3. The Latin text is available online at: https://www.vatican.va/archive/hist_councils/ii_vatican_council/documents/vat-ii_const_19651207_gaudium-et-spes_lt.html.

2. Ibid., para. 4.

finds as one of the principal signs of these modern times a "spiritual turbulence" or "uneasiness" (*hodierna animorum commotio*),[3] which stems, on the one hand, from a growing technical ability to achieve practical mastery over the natural world and, on the other, a disproportionate lack of moral and theoretical apparatus to make sure that the human being is able to control the forces unleashed by our growing technical mastery rather than being, paradoxically, enslaved to them. The modern world displays itself as one that is "at once powerful and weak, capable of doing what is noble and what is base, disposed to freedom and slavery, progress and decline, amity and hatred."[4] There is, on the one hand, "a growing conviction that the human being is able and has the duty to strengthen its mastery over nature" and that the benefits of this mastery should be widely available, and, on the other hand, that these benefits are actually available only to the few and that many are unjustly deprived of them, and that this is an affront to "the dignity proper to individuals and to societies."[5] Aware of these conflicting tendencies, modern "man questions himself" (*Unde [homo] seipsum interrogat*).[6] The questions are age-old questions but with a modern inflection:

In the face of modern developments [*coram hodierna mundi evolutione*], there is a growing body of people who are asking the most fundamental of all questions or are glimpsing them with a keener insight: What is man [*homo*]? What is the meaning of suffering, evil, death, which have not been eliminated by all this progress? What is the purpose of these achievements, purchased at so high a price? What can people contribute to society? What can they expect from it? What happens after this earthly life is ended?[7]

In the same paragraph, the Council gives the Church's fundamental answer to these questions which is able to "illuminate the mystery of man" (*ad mysterium hominis illustrandum*): "The church

3. Ibid., para. 5.
4. Ibid., para. 9.
5. Ibid.
6. Ibid.
7. Ibid., para. 10.

believes that the key, the center and the purpose of the whole of human history is to be found in its Lord and Master […] Christ, who is the same yesterday, and today, and forever" (cf. *Hebrews* 13:8).

After this introduction, which lays out the basic problem and the basic approach to addressing it, the first chapter of *Gaudium et Spes* specifies the Church's answer more fully, this time focusing the question of the human being on the question of human dignity: "Enlightened by divine revelation, the Church can offer a solution to [these problems] by which the true state of man may be described, his weakness explained in such a way that at the same time his dignity and vocation may be perceived in their true light."[8] The dignity and vocation of human beings comes from their creation in the image of God[9] and possession of an immortal soul,[10] and are thereby called to communion with God.[11] But also, this dignity is obscured by sin and the proper freedom attaching to it has been diminished by sin, which hampers human beings in fulfilling their vocation to communion with God and with each other.

When people "look into their own hearts they find that they are drawn towards what is wrong and are sunk in many evils which cannot have come from their good creator."[12] Though atheism seems to exalt man, who is thereby seen to "constitute his own end and as his own sole maker, in total control of his own history," encouraged in this view by the technical mastery of nature made possible by modern science,[13] it detracts, in fact, from human dignity, which is impaired by loss of hope in eternal life and which is not diminished by the acknowledgement of the Creator but rather is "grounded and brought to perfection in God."[14] The Church

---

8. Ibid., para. 12.
9. Ibid.
10. Ibid., para. 14.
11. Ibid., para. 19.
12. Ibid., para. 13.
13. Ibid., para. 20.
14. Ibid., para. 21.

"knows full well that its message is in harmony with the most secret desires of the human heart, since she champions the dignity of the human being's calling, giving hope once more to those who already despair of their higher destiny."[15]

It is in the famous paragraph 22 that the Church's answer is more fully revealed: "In reality it is only in the mystery of the Word made flesh that the mystery of man [*mysterium hominis*] truly becomes clear." It is in Christ "the new Adam" that we see the fullness of human being and dignity, for He "in the very revelation of the mystery of the Father and of His love, fully reveals man to himself and brings to light his high calling" (*Christus, novissimus Adam, in ipsa revelatione mysterii Patris Eiusque amoris, hominem ipsi homini plene manifestat eique altissimam eius vocationem patefacit*). Because He is the Son of the eternal Father who united to Himself human nature and thus each and every one of us, because now each one of us can say, with Paul, "the Son of God loved me and gave Himself for me" (cf. *Galatians* 2:20), human dignity has been elevated "to a dignity beyond compare."

It could be said, I think, that in its elevation, human dignity is fully clarified and, to use an Irenaean word, "recapitulated. " It is "summed up" in the last Adam, the new Adam and new head of the human race. Those conformed to His image are able to fulfill the "new law of love," that is, they are enabled to act more and more with the dignity proper to humanity and, more and more, to fulfill the human vocation of communion with God and with others, in that very love which was revealed in the Paschal mystery. "Such is the nature and the greatness of the mystery of man as enlightened for the faithful by the Christian revelation," and this includes "the mystery of suffering and death which, apart from His Gospel, overwhelms us."[16]

15. Ibid.
16. Ibid., para. 22.

The light shed by Christ on the mystery of human being is also thereby shed on the social aspects of human life, "for the Word made flesh willed to take his place in human society", and in so doing "he sanctified those human ties, above all family ties, which are the basis of social structures."[17] The communion of the Church is invoked here as *Lumen Gentium* describes it in paragraph 9, as a reflection and accomplishment of God's creative will. God "did not create people to live as individuals but to come together in social unity," and therefore, as *Lumen Gentium* says, "he willed to [...] save human beings not as individuals without any bond between them, but rather to make them into a people."[18] The social character of human nature is "perfected and fulfilled in the work of Jesus Christ, who, by His incarnation willed to take his place in human society," and to sanctify its ordinary interpersonal bonds such as those of the family.

The Church, one could say, recapitulates and in doing that fully reveals God's intentions for the communal character of human life, not because the Church is without corruption or has a perfect governmental structure, but because it is established by "the gift of [Christ's] Spirit [...] a new fraternal communion among all who received him in faith and love, his own Body, the Church."[19] Christ's Spirit binding the Church into communion or solidarity recapitulates the solidarity that is part of God's intentions for human creatures in the first place, and therefore provides perspective on all other claims to solidarity. From the perspective of this recapitulation, the solidarity already glimpsed in various forms of human community as an aspiration can be recognized as something which must be nurtured: "This solidarity must be constantly increased until that day when it will be brought to fulfillment."[20]

17. Ibid., para. 32.

18. Paul VI, *Lumen Gentium* (Vatican City, 21 November 1964), para. 9. The Latin text is available online at: http://www.vatican.va/archive/hist_councils/ii_vatican_council/documents/vat-ii_const_19641121_lumen-gentium_lt.html.

19. *Gaudium et Spes*, para. 32.

20. Ibid.

Until the eschatological fulfillment of human solidarity, the
Church provides an anticipatory vision of human community and
social life, and this is found in the principles of what is usually
called "Catholic social teaching". The Council draws attention to
features of Catholic social teaching especially relevant to the problems of the modern world, namely, the increasing global interdependence of peoples and thus an expanded sense of the common
good,[21] the essential equality of all human beings,[22] the need to
transcend a morality that is narrowly individualistic,[23] and above
all, and included as an element in all of these principles: respect for
the dignity of the human person. There is in the modern world "a
growing awareness of the sublime dignity of human persons, who
stand above all things and whose rights and duties are universal and
inviolable."[24]

1. Recapitulation and Dialogue

It is from this perspective of the recapitulation of man, of *homo,*
of the human being in Christ, that the Church wishes to engage
in dialogue with the modern world. Although it is a common-
place to note that the Council wanted to foster dialogue between
the Church and the "world of today," or as we have been talking
about it, the "modern world," it is less commonly noted that each
of the four Chapters that constitute Part I of the document ends
on different aspects of the way in which Christ has recapitulated
human being and human history in Himself and is therefore the
starting point for any contribution the Church can make to dialogue. This dynamic is not confined to paragraph 22. In fact, it is
explicitly named in the closing section of Chapter 3: "The Word
of God, through whom all things were made, became human and

21. Ibid., para. 25-6.
22. Ibid., para. 29.
23. Ibid., para. 30.
24. Ibid., para. 26.

dwelt among us, a perfect human being, he entered world history, taking that history into himself and recapitulating it."[25]

It is actually in Chapter 4 that this recapitulatory dynamic and its connection to dialogue rises to a kind of crescendo. "All we have said up to now about the dignity of the human person, the community of human beings, and the deep significance of human activity provides a basis for discussing the relationship between the Church and the world and the dialogue between them."[26] The perspective is drawn from *Lumen Gentium* and is frankly Augustinian, with overt reference to the dynamic of the two cities, the way that members of the earthly city are called forth to form "the family of the sons of God in the midst of history," and the way the two cities are intermixed, or "penetrate one another." The Church is at once "'a visible organization and a spiritual community'"[27]—could we say, the sacrament of the Heavenly City?

In pursuing its own salvific purpose not only does the Church communicate divine life to man [*homine*] but in a certain sense it casts the reflected light of that divine life over all the earth, notably in the way it heals and elevates the dignity of the human person, strengthens the social bond, and endows daily activity with a deeper meaning."[28]

It can only cast this light of divine life because that life is its constitution in the Spirit, so that the Church, as a visible society constituted by a communion in a "life" it did not and could not give itself, is the presence of this life in the city of this world. It elevates the dignity of the human person (and so forth) not simply by its teaching or by the example of some of its members but by its very presence within the world.[29] It provides perspective on the unmitigated claims of the earthly city on the human being insofar as it elevates

25. Ibid., para 38.
26. Ibid., para 40.
27. Ibid., para. 40 (citing *Lumen Gentium*, para. 8).
28. Ibid.
29. Ibid., para. 41.

human beings into a communion, "proceed[ing] from the love of the eternal Father,"[30] that relativizes all worldly claims to defining the ideal community and so serves as the "soul of human society *in its renewal by Christ.*"[31] The recapitulatory dynamic means that, ironically, simply by being Church and by teaching from its identity as such, the Church, "through each of her members and her community as a whole [...] can help to make the human family and its history *still more human.*"[32]

Chapter 4 is very emphatic on this point. It goes on to mention that: "The Church is entrusted with the task of manifesting to [contemporaries] the mystery of God, who is their final destiny; in doing so it discloses to them the meaning of their own existence, the innermost truth about themselves."[33] This is the solution to the crisis of modernity, namely, dialogue with the world on the basis of the mystery of the recapitulation of human being in Christ, both individually and communally. "To follow Christ the perfect human is to become more human oneself."[34] This dynamic of dialogue based in recapitulation is magnificently recalled in the closing section of Chapter 4:

Every benefit the people of God can confer on humanity during its earthly pilgrimage is rooted in the Church's being 'the universal sacrament of salvation', at once manifesting and actualizing the mystery of God's love for humanity. The Word of God, through whom all things were made, was made flesh, so that as a perfect man he could save all human beings and *sum up (recapitulare) all things in Himself.*[35]

Thus to engage in dialogue from the heart of the Gospel is, ironically, to engage in dialogue from the heart of the human being and so to address the crisis of modernity concerning the status of the

30. Ibid.
31. Ibid. (citing *Lumen Gentium*, para. 38) (emphasis mine).
32. Ibid., (emphasis mine).
33. Ibid.
34. Ibid., (emphasis mine).
35. Ibid., para. 45 (citing *Lumen Gentium,* para. 7) (emphasis mine).

human being in terms that have an echo in every human heart regardless of their faith.

2. Pope St. John Paul II and *Evangelium Vitae*

Now I would like to turn to the work of Pope St. John Paul II to demonstrate his use and development of this paradigm for dialogue. To this end, I would like to give some extended consideration to one of his greatest encyclical letters, the 1995 *Evangelium Vitae*, concerning one of the most contentious issues of the modern world: abortion (and related concerns). This letter operates in the tension between a doctrine that is accessible to reason, part of the natural law and so something that could be discussed in civil society without appealing to religion, and yet one that can only be articulated with full force and clarity from the perspective of revelation. Yet the conviction that speaking from revelation is also speaking from the heart of humanity at its best undergirds the confidence with which John Paul II regards the possibility of believers animating a conversation and renewing social life drawing on the terms of revelation, without at the same time insisting on imposing these terms as the only acceptable ones in which the issue can be discussed even in a secular society.

Having laid out the terms of the recapitulatory dynamic in *Gaudium et Spes,* we can immediately notice it in *Evangelium Vitae,* where it is quite prominent. For instance we read:

In Jesus, the "Word of life," God's eternal life is [...] proclaimed and given. Thanks to this proclamation and gift, our physical and spiritual life, also in its earthly phase, acquires its full value and meaning [...]. In this way the *Gospel of life* includes everything that human experience and reason tell us about the value of human life, accepting it, purifying it, exalting it and bringing it to fulfillment."[36]

---

36. John Paul II, *Evangelium Vitae* (Vatican City, 25 March 1995), para. 30 (emphasis original, see the Latin text). The English version is available online at: http://www.vatican.va/content/john-paul-ii/en/encyclicals/documents/hf_jp-ii_enc_25031995_evangelium-vitae.html. Latin text at:

Again, a little earlier the text states: "The Gospel of life is something concrete and personal, for it consists in the proclamation of *the very person of Jesus*," through whom human beings are "given the possibility of 'knowing' *the complete truth* concerning the value of human life."[37]

It can be shocking to read in the same paragraph that, nonetheless, "it [i.e., the Gospel of life] can also be known in its essential traits by human reason," since this might seem to make revelation superfluous. But this is not a zero sum, competitive dynamic between revelation and reason, but rather it fits into the recapitulatory dynamic we have seen from *GS*, meaning that, though the essentials of the doctrine are part of natural law and so can at least in theory be known by reason alone, the mystery of the person of Christ includes everything reason can know and further uplifts, fulfills, and purifies it: "This is the Gospel which already present in the Revelation of the Old Testament, and indeed written in the heart of every man and woman, has echoed in every conscience 'from the beginning.'"[38] To preach the Gospel of Life strictly speaking means at the same time to evoke its "echo" in the human heart where it is to some extent already present in reason alone. It is to recapitulate that echo, which does not mean to erase it or drown it out, but to uplift it precisely as the locus or plane of dialogue with modern secular man.

This dynamic is even more evident in paragraph 2 of *Evangelium Vitae*. God reveals the supernatural vocation of the human being to a "fullness of life" which extends into eternity. And yet the Church knows "that this *Gospel of life*, which she has received from her Lord, has a profound and pervasive echo in the heart of every person—believer and non-believer alike—because it marvelously

http://www.vatican.va/content/john-paul-ii/la/encyclicals/documents/hf_jp-ii_enc_25031995_evangelium-vitae.html.

37. Ibid., para. 29 (emphasis original, see the Latin text).

38. Ibid. (emphasis original).

fulfils all the heart's expectations while infinitely surpassing them."³⁹ Everyone sincerely open to truth and goodness, the Pope says, can "come to recognize in the natural law written in the human heart (cf. *Romans* 2:14-15) the sacred value of human life from its very beginning until its end, and can affirm the right of every human being to have this primary good respected to the highest degree.⁴⁰

Recognition of this right is, in fact, the foundation of human and political community. Believers are even more aware of this right because it is recapitulated in the proclamation of the Incarnation. Recalling and actually citing *Gaudium et Spes* 22, John Paul II notes that "'By his incarnation the Son of God has united himself in some fashion with every human being.' This saving event reveals to humanity not only the boundless love of God who 'so loved the world that he gave his only Son' (*John* 3:16), but also the *incomparable value of every human person.*"⁴¹ Again, far from the erasure of what reason can see in the natural law, the Church is able to invest this universal starting point with a new sense of "wonder" as she contemplates the mystery of the Redemption.

And yet there is a crisis. It is the same one acknowledged by *Gaudium et Spes*; paragraph 11 of *Evangelium Vitae* underlines that: "In the background there is the profound crisis of culture, which generates skepticism in relation to the very foundations of knowledge and ethics, and which makes it increasingly difficult to grasp clearly the meaning of what man is [...]." This is an echo of *Gaudium et Spes* focusing on the crisis of the meaning and value of the human being. We also see the exact same crimes against life and human dignity—from abortion to torture to slavery, the selling of women and children, to disgraceful working conditions, and so forth—pointed out in *Gaudium et Spes* 27 repeated and cited in

---

39. Ibid., para. 2 (emphasis original).
40. Ibid.
41. Ibid. (emphasis original).

Evangelium Vitae 3. According to *Gaudium et Spes*, these crimes "poison human society," and the Church can proclaim this because the revelation in Christ of the sublime dignity of the human person, injured and clouded by sin but restored and elevated as recapitulated in Christ, can explain modern man to himself, can explain how these poisons can arise even though there is a "natural knowledge" available regarding the dignity of the human person and the sacredness of life, and can explain how "conscience itself, darkened as it were by [...] widespread conditioning, is finding it increasingly difficult to distinguish between good and evil in what concerns the basic value of human life."[42]

In a situation where, as paragraph 28 of *Evangelium Vitae* illustrates, the crisis of modernity has become "an enormous and dramatic clash between good and evil, death and life, the 'culture of death' and the 'culture of life,'" it is the revelation of man to himself in Christ that clarifies the situation. It is the blood of Christ, specifically, that reveals man to himself. Poured out on account of sin, and so revealing the depth of human depravity, it also "reveals the grandeur of the Father's love, *shows how precious man is in God's eyes and how priceless the value of his life.*"[43] It is in contemplating the precious blood of Christ, "the sign of his self-giving love (cf. *John* 13:1)," that "the believer learns to recognize and appreciate the almost divine dignity of every human being."[44] Christ's blood is, the text continues, truly the key to the riddle of human being, modern or otherwise, since "Christ's blood reveals to man that his greatness and therefore his vocation, consists in the *sincere gift of self.*" This is a direct echo and development of *Gaudium et Spes* 24, which talks about how the revelation of the Trinity through the Incarnate Word's teaching "has opened up new horizons closed to human

---

42. Ibid., para. 4.
43. Ibid., para. 25 (emphasis original); cf. para. 49 and 86.
44. Ibid.

reasoning by indicating that there is a certain similarity between the union existing among the divine persons and the union of God's children in truth and love. It follows that […] human beings […] can fully discover their true selves only in sincere self-giving."

3. The Sources of Dialogue and Renewal

So then, what is the point? Though it seems an irony, the fact that the recapitulation of human being and solidarity in Christ grounds the conviction of human dignity more firmly in specifically Christian faith, which might seem to narrow the possibilities for dialogue with an unbelieving world, in fact, following the pattern laid out in *Gaudium et Spes*, it actually increases those possibilities. This is precisely because revelation is recapitulatory: it does not erase the primordial common ground that human reason can see on its own, but strengthens it, clarifies it, purifies it, and uplifts it. It does not take away the common territory, as it were, in which dialogue in a secular or modern culture can take place, but increases the possibilities for dialogue in just that space. Christian conviction does not shut down dialogue with a "my way or the highway" insistence on the acceptance of revelation as the only acceptable terms of discussion, but, as John Paul II says, it is in fact "capable of bringing about a serious and courageous cultural dialogue among all parties" towards the end of a "*general mobilization of consciences* and a *united ethical effort.*"[45]

How does this work? Revelation enables us to see more deeply into the sacredness of human life, something that all people have and have had access to "from the beginning."[46] Contemplating the offer of sharing the life of God eternally which we receive in Christ, "believers cannot fail to be filled with ever new wonder and unbounded gratitude,"[47] and the recapitulatory effect means that this wonder and gratitude draws into its orbit the natural life which is

45. Ibid., para. 95 (emphasis original).
46. Ibid., para. 40.
47. Ibid., para. 38.

the seed of the eternal life won in Christ's victory. Let us emphasize and extend a passage previously quoted:

Precisely by contemplating the precious blood of Christ, the sign of his self-giving love (cf. *John* 13:1), the believer learns to recognize and appreciate the almost divine dignity of every human being and can exclaim with ever renewed wonder: "How precious must man be in the eyes of the Creator, if he 'gained so great a Redeemer!'"[48]

The believer is filled with "awe and wonder" at the genesis of life in procreation,[49] which extend even to the whole natural world,[50] our "common home" as Pope Francis has recently put it, in which our bodily human life takes its place. Our meditation on the Pierced One draws forth "praise and thanksgiving" for the sacrifice of Christ and thereby the humanity that He took up—*our* humanity—is drawn within the orbit of this thanksgiving. At the outset of the encyclical, we read that: "The Church, *faithfully contemplating the mystery of the Redemption*, acknowledges *the incomparable value of every human person* with ever new wonder."[51]

The renewed appreciation of the dignity of the human person as recapitulated in Revelation also casts light, and helps to define, the characteristic offense of that dignity prevalent in modern culture. It is one that "denies solidarity," the very solidarity we have seen uplifted in *Gaudium et Spes*, and in many cases this denial "takes the form of a veritable 'culture of death.'"[52] Although this is a rather dramatic way of putting it, we can analyze the essential features of this culture of death. It is, the encyclical says in paragraph 12, "actively fostered by powerful cultural, economic and political currents which encourage an idea of society excessively concerned with efficiency," which turns out to be one excessively concerned with

---

48. Ibid., para. 25 (citing the *Exsultet*).
49. Ibid., para. 44.
50. Ibid., para. 42.
51. Ibid., para. 2 (first emphasis added, second is original).
52. Ibid., para. 12.

power, one that therefore victimizes the weak, the vulnerable, and those who lack autonomy. This in turn attacks the basis of democracy and democratic freedom, since freedom is degraded to an individualism, the "freedom of 'the strong' against the weak who have no choice but to submit."[53] This is a threat "jeopardizing the very meaning of democratic coexistence"[54] and dissolving its solidarity because it becomes a benefit extended only to the powerful.

Another way of characterizing the culture of death is that it prioritizes *having over being*, which echoes *Gaudium et Spes* 35: "People are of greater value for what they are than for what they have." And this in turn goes hand in hand with prioritizing *efficiency over persons*: "The values of *being* are replaced by those of *having* [...]. The so-called 'quality of life' is interpreted primarily or exclusively as economic efficiency [...]."[55] Or, even more forcefully, in the same passage we find: "The criterion of personal dignity—which demands respect, generosity and service—is replaced by the criterion of efficiency, functionality and usefulness: others are considered not for what they 'are,' but for what they 'have, do and produce.' This is the supremacy of the strong over the weak." This includes, especially, and "above all," the "poor."

There is provided here the basis for cultural renewal through dialogue because the cultivation of wonder and gratitude for human life, correlated with the philosophically articulated values prioritizing being over having and person over efficiency, can be engaged without overt reference to revelation, even if revelation is the source of the believer's ever new wonder and gratitude and of his or her clearer seeing of the priority of being over having and person over efficiency. In the last chapter, calling for cultural renewal and dialogue, in paragraph 98 the encyclical notes:

53. Ibid., para. 19; cf. para. 20.
54. Ibid., para. 18.
55. Ibid., para. 23 (emphasis original).

We can say that the cultural change which we are calling for demands from everyone the courage to *adopt a new life-style,* consisting in making practical choices—at the personal, family, social and international level—on the basis of a correct scale of values: *the primacy of being over having, of the person over things.*[56]

Note that this is demanded "from everyone," and it is assumed that "everyone" regardless of faith can understand the values named here. That is because these values are written in the human heart, however obscured by sin and by cultures formed in sinful practices. There is nothing in them that depends on accepting revelation. A modern, pluralistic secular culture can understand wonder and gratitude, even if the culture on its own is not enough to sustain it (the question must arise, gratitude to whom?) but requires the "leaven" of the Church, the sacrament of the city of God, to diagnose the problem, and to illuminate and activate a persuasive dialogue about these values in order to awaken consciences.

We find Pope Francis calling for the same thing some thirty years later in *Laudato Si'.* A democratic society has the ability and resources to engage in thinking about its own foundations in respect for persons, even if the ultimate grounding for that respect is not fully available to reason alone, and yet the terms can be understood, and what is at stake can be grasped, while the democratic values and practices of wonder and gratitude, of preferring being over having and persons over efficiency, can be taken up in partnership with believers.

It will be possible for believers to engage in this way precisely because they are not relying only on the resources of reason alone, but on the renewal and recapitulation of human being accomplished in Christ. From there flows a clear-sighted diagnosis of the problem and, even more importantly, a ready flowing gratitude and wonder which is ready, precisely out of gratitude, to be conformed to the

---

56. Ibid., para. 98 (citing *Gaudium et Spes* 35) (emphasis original).

self-giving love of Christ and to undertake the kinds of sacrifices that will be necessary to inspire a dialogue that is more than words. In Jesus, the law, available to reason, but which on its own can seem to dwindle to an obligation imposed externally and so to invite limitation and mitigation,[57] "becomes once and for all the 'gospel,' the good news of God's lordship over the world," and through the figure of the Servant of the Lord, fulfilled in Jesus, we are given "a 'new heart,'" which "will make it possible to appreciate and achieve the deepest and most authentic meaning of life: namely, that of being *a gift which is fully realized in the giving of self.*"[58]

More emphatically, the same contemplation of the Precious Blood of Christ that prompts us to grateful wonder, also, because it reveals to man in a recapitulatory way that "his greatness, and therefore his vocation, consists in *the sincere gift of self*"—it is precisely from the blood of Christ "that all draw *the strength to commit themselves to promoting life.*"[59] There is no cultural renewal without sacrificial witness, but this is part of the priestly, prophetic and royal vocation of the baptized. Promoting a culture of dialogue means encouraging among believers a culture of self-giving sacrifice, and not necessarily in big ways but in "all those daily gestures of openness, sacrifice and unselfish care which countless people lovingly make in families, hospitals, orphanages, homes for the elderly and other centers or communities which defend life."[60] There is no cultural renewal on the cheap, and no dialogue on the cheap. Yet out of a truly self-giving witness, which is consistent and thick in its many manifestations and venues, engagement in a dialogue about the democratic values of being over having and persons over efficiency can emerge and touch consciences, and has the potential of renewing

57. Ibid., para. 48.
58. Ibid., para. 49 (emphasis original).
59. Ibid., para. 25.
60. Ibid., para. 27.

democracy itself in the awe and wonder at the gift of human life and the dignity of the human person.

4. *Veritatis Splendor*

In conclusion, it is worth mentioning that this recapitulatory dynamic, and its power to engender witness that can serve as a wellspring for dialogue which operates within terms accessible to reason alone, is rather movingly present in the 1993 encyclical *Veritatis Splendor,* which begins in paragraph 2 with a citation of *Gaudium et Spes* 22 (and we have seen that the recapitulatory dynamic is by no means confined to that one section). After its introduction, we find it operative throughout *Veritatis Splendor.* But when the discussion turns to martyrdom, we are confronted with a particularly sublime version of this dynamic. Christ's witness to the truth that human freedom is lived most deeply in the "gift of self, *even to the total gift of self,* like that of Jesus" is the "source, model and means for the witness of the disciples,"[61] which from the earliest times until today has borne fruit in martyrdom. Christ's martyrdom, and the martyrdom of His disciples who, in a way, make Christ's martyrdom present, cast light on the natural law that is part and parcel of human nature and accessible to reason alone. The relationship between faith and morality, John Paul II says, "shines forth with all its brilliance in the *unconditional respect due to the insistent demands of the personal dignity of every man.*" He continues: "the universality and the immutability of the moral norm make manifest and at the same time serve to protect the personal dignity and inviolability of man [...]." He then argues that the "unacceptability" of ethical theories that deny the existence of negative moral norms that are universally binding is "confirmed in a particularly eloquent way by Christian martyrdom,

---

61. John Paul II, *Veritatis Splendor* (Vatican City, 6 August 1993), para. 89 (emphasis original). The English version is available online at: https://www.vatican.va/content/john-paul-ii/en/encyclicals/documents/hf_jp-ii_enc_06081993_veritatis-splendor.html.

which has always accompanied and continues to accompany the life of the Church today."[62]

We recognize what we have been calling the recapitulatory uplifting and purification of that which is most human, that which all human beings share, including here the natural law itself. Perhaps an unexpected result is that Christ's martyrdom, and Christian martyrdom formed in its pattern, shines a light on the heroism of others who are not Christian and who come from various traditions and cultures. John Paul II continues: "In this witness to the absoluteness of the moral good *Christians are not alone:* they are supported by the moral sense present in peoples and by the great religious and sapiential traditions of East and West, from which the interior workings of God's Spirit are not absent."[63] The recapitulatory character of this recognition of the heroism of non-Christians is absolutely clear here: "In an individual's words and above all in the sacrifice of his life for a moral value, the Church sees a single testimony to that truth which, already present in creation, shines forth in its fullness on the face of Christ," and invokes Justin Martyr's characterization of the hatred and destruction some of the Stoics faced for their teaching.

Thus the heroic witness to the moral law by persons of different religions and cultures offers a way for dialogue to take place about that law, dialogue which helps to reveal its meaning and its appeal to those without the benefit of Christ's revelation—in other words, to a secular modern world. It can take the form of dialogue precisely about this heroism. And, most interestingly, the natural law itself is revealed, in this way, as offering a theorization of inter-cultural and inter-religious admiration. Surely that is a wonderful path for communication and dialogue in the modern world, a world which seems so closed off to something seemingly so narrow and

62. Ibid., para. 90.
63. Ibid., para. 94 (emphasis original).

intransigent as the "universally binding character of the negative precepts of the moral law!"

All of a sudden dialogue means leveraging the admiration for human heroism that we do all feel. It is not so hidden in the human heart and it occurs, we know, even across the boundaries of cultures that are sometimes portrayed in a *post*-modern world as incommensurable barriers to human understanding. In this light, John Paul II appears as a faithful and brilliantly creative interpreter of the dialogical imperative of the Second Vatican Council and its grounding in the "light of the nations" that is Christ and that shines on the Church as the seed of the new humanity, and from there on the whole world.[64]

JOHN CAVADINI—Professor of Theology at the University of Notre Dame and Director of McGrath Institute for Church Life. A member of the Notre Dame Department of Theology since 1990, he teaches, studies and publishes in patristic and early medieval theology, and the history of biblical and patristic exegesis. He was appointed by Pope Benedict XVI to a five-year term on the International Theological Commission in 2009. He is the recipient of the Monika Hellwig Award for Outstanding Contributions to Catholic Intellectual Life and is the author of *Visioning Augustine* (2019).

64. Paul VI, *Lumen Gentium*, para. 1.

François Daguet, O.P.

POLITICAL THEOLOGY FROM ST. THOMAS AQUINAS TO JOHN PAUL II AND BENEDICT XVI

The notion of political theology effectively emerged in the twentieth century in a rather special context, that of the "rise of totalitarianism" and the controversy between Carl Schmitt and Erik Peterson. In his *Political Theology* (1922), Carl Schmitt transposes theological and political concepts: "the dominant concepts of modern theory are secularized theological concepts."[1] At the same time, in France, Charles Maurras follows a similar thought process, justifying the monarchic principle according to theological ideas. These "political theologies" of the interwar period, which are better described as political philosophies which invoke principles taken from Christianity, can to some extent be considered Christian ideologies when they treat Christianity as the religious substratum of

---

[1]. C. Schmitt, *Théologie Politique I, Quatre Chapitres sur la Théorie de la Souveraineté* (Paris: Gallimard, 1988). Carl Schmitt would come back to the question much later, in 1969, with his *Théologie Politique II* [Political Theology II], which has been published in French in the same volume.

the political organization, even if they are sometimes radically opposed to it. As Schmitt says, these political theologies are in fact the product of a secularization of theological notions emerging form Christianity, which then become instruments in service of something completely different.

Erik Peterson, a laic theologian who moved from Protestantism to Catholicism in 1930, published several works during the 1930s, without directly critiquing Schmitt. In the guise of being historical studies, they target Nazism and the number of Christians colluding with the regime. All these works address political theology.[2] In *Monotheism, a Political Problem,*[3] Peterson alludes to—and criticizes—the political ideas of Carl Schmitt, that is, his political theology understood as a justification of a political order using theological arguments.[4]

In this obviously dated approach, political theology is understood as the justification of a given political order by theological means; it is therefore a very specific perspective which is not, at its heart, theological, but rather philosophical. Consequently, there is a great risk of removing politics from the profane order by making it

---

2. In *Monotheism: A Political Problem* (1935), Peterson first refers to Eusebius of Caesarea who saw in the Roman Empire a providential preparation for the advent of Christianity, and a connection between the affirmation of monotheism with the establishment of a regime with a single sovereign. From this perspective, the *Pax Augusta*, during which the Savior was born, was the realization of prophetic oracles. Erik Peterson refutes this idea, in the name of the Trinitarian dogma which characterizes Christian monotheism, and in the name of the inherent eschatological character of Christian dogma. According to him, these aspects preclude any confusion or association between the belief in a single God and that of a single political power. See E. Peterson, *Theological Tractates*, trans. Michael J. Hollerich (Stanford, CT: Stanford University Press, 2011). The essay under discussion here, entitled "Monotheism as a Political Problem", is contained in this volume.

3. E. Peterson, *Le monothéisme: un problème politique et autres traités* (Paris: Bayard, 2007).

4. Ibid., 124: "Le concept de 'théologie politique' a été introduit en littérature par les travaux de Carl Schmitt, *Théologie politique*, Munich, 1922. Ses considérations, à l'époque, n'ont pas été exposées de façon systématique. Nous avons tenté ici de démontrer à partir d'un exemple concret l'impossibilité d'une telle 'théologie politique.'" [English translation: "the concept of 'political theology' was introduced into the literature in the work of Carl Schmitt, *Political Theology*, Munich, 1922. His arguments were not at that time explored systematically. Here I have tried to demonstrate with a concrete example the impossibility of such a 'political theology.'"] It is this note which justifies the subtitle Schmitt gave to his *Political Theology II*: "The Myth of the Closure of any Political Theology."

a sacred object.[5] This fits with the trend identified by Eric Voegelin who saw the rise of "political religions" in the first half of the twentieth century. In fact, the totalitarian movements of the twentieth century all sought, in one way or another, to confer a religious character—which they otherwise rejected—on the political order.

Contemporary political thought thus inherits the notion of political theology, but we will understand it differently here, that is, not in the sense of drawing political applications from Christian theological principles in order to shape a communal order, but as deriving from the idea in Christian theology of taking into account the community aspects of human life. This is a strict theological perspective. Since nothing that falls under the category of the created order is outside the field of theology, it is natural to consider the communal nature of man and the existence of human communities. For that matter, the communal character of God's design itself justifies the elaboration of a theology *of* politics, that is, of the communal. This is, in my view, the only legitimate meaning of the expression, even if certain contemporary authors have sought to orient it in a different direction.[6]

5. This is the criticism that Jacques Maritain makes of Carl Schmitt in 1936 in *Humanisme intégral*: "M. Carl Schmitt, qui fut un des inspirateurs et des conseillers intellectuels du régime nazi, avait cherché jadis à montrer dans les grandes idées politiques et juridiques modernes une transposition de thèmes essentiellement théologiques. De là, si l'on se place, pour spéculer, à un point de vue pratique et concret, sans tenir compte de la distinction des objets formels, on viendra très aisément à dire que les réalités politiques sont elles-mêmes de l'ordre divin et sacré. Tel est le sens que les théoriciens allemands contemporains du 'Sacrum Imperium' donnent au mot *politishe Theologie*. Ils se réfèrent ainsi à l'idée messianique et évangélique du Royaume de Dieu dont ils veulent trouver une réalisation dans le temps et dans l'histoire." [English translation: "Carl Schmitt, who was an inspiration and intellectual counselor for the Nazi regime, sought at one time to show a recasting of essentially theological themes into the great modern political and juridical ideas. To speculate from there, if one were to take a practical and concrete approach without considering the distinction between formal objects, it would be very easy to say that political realities are themselves of the divine and sacred order. This is the meaning that the German theorists contemporary to the "Sacrum Imperium" give to the term *politische Theologie*. They refer to the messianic and evangelical idea of the Kingdom of God, which they hope to find realized in time and history"]. See Jacques Maritain, *Humanisme intégral*, Œuvres complètes (Fribourg, Paris: Éditions Universitaires Fribourg, Éditions Saint-Paul, 1982—2007), vol. 6, 406–7.

6. The expression reappears in the current era in the German theology of the years 1960-1980, in particular that of Jean-Baptiste Metz and Jürgen Moltmann. For them, since they justifiably

Therefore, if we understand "political theology" to mean a theology concerned with the communal order, with the fact that people are called to live in human communities, we must recognize that political theology has been slow to emerge in the Tradition of the Church. Certainly, the communal nature of human life and the reality of human communities have not escaped the judicious attention of the Fathers of the Church, but it took centuries for the political order to be caught up in the light of Revelation. It is true that the foundations in the New Testament are scarce. The essential place is the word of Christ brought by Saint Matthew: "Render therefore to Caesar the things that are Caesar's; and to God, the things that are God's" (*Matthew* 22:21), to which we can add the words of Saint Paul when he invited prayers for political authorities. In fact, during the first millennium everything happens as though focused on the construction of a new body politic *sui generis*: the Church. Natural political communities are then only seen as the inevitable frame for this construction. It is evident in hindsight that primacy is given to Christian life in the heart of various political communities, and not to political thought in a Christian view.

Saint Augustine is very illuminating in this regard. He is undoubtedly the first to consider, in *City of God*, the meeting of a city of a divine nature—which one could view, in a simplified way, as the Church here on Earth—and Earthly cities. His treatise, and its title in particular, are, however, the source of a remarkable and long-lived misunderstanding: the idea that the *civitas terrena* which stands in opposition to the *civitas Dei* is not the political city, but the spiritual city through which man opposes the divine work. Of course, this is why he also calls it *the city of the Devil*. If we are not

---

affirm that evangelical principles cannot be satisfied with shaping an individual ethics or being limited to ecclesiastical communities, it must translate into political action. Various theologies of liberation fit into this perspective. In fact, this political theology searches to foreground a Christian praxis in the political life of cities. More precisely, it is not strictly speaking a political theology but seeks to be a Christian doctrine of political activity.

careful, we may take this to mean that many people spontaneously set up an opposition between the terrestrial city, understood as the political city, and the Church, understood as the city of God. This leads us into a dialectic of opposition which has nothing to do with Augustine's idea. For him, the fight between the two cities is spiritual, and that is what matters to him. This spiritual combat takes place within a political city, whatever its shape, but which is not defined in itself. Through a paradox which is undeniably underemphasized, Saint Augustine's *City of God* is characterized by the absence of political theology in the sense of theological thought about the political order. This absence is very significant, in a treatise which had the potential for such an approach. It demonstrates theological thinking which is not yet ready to deal with the political object, and perhaps, to some extent, because it does not have the tools to do so. Effectively, the philosophical instrument to think about the political city itself is lacking in Saint Augustine's work, and this only serves to highlight the contrast with the contribution of Saint Thomas Aquinas.

Before coming to the rise of political thought in the Middle Ages, with Thomas Aquinas, long centuries of Christianity pass where practical questions are dominant in the relationship between the Church and terrestrial cities. Here, we will take Christianity to mean a model of close cooperation between the powers, which depends on the argument that the civil authority, the prince, must cooperate in the construction of the Kingdom of God on Earth, which is in the care of the Pope. This context of Christianity, especially after the Gregorian reform in the twelfth century, encourages the establishment of a fairly common doctrine which was termed "political Augustinianism" by Mgr. Arquillière. It relies on the fact that divine law has often been imposed on, or taken the place of, the natural law which should govern the temporal order. Divine law, or something calling itself divine law, takes on such an authority by virtue of its origin that it is impossible to see how a human law could not yield to it. To speak of political Augustinianism is likely excessive, if we understand by this that the original source is the theology of Saint Augustine, but the term is justified if we consider certain Church practices as regards the temporal order. Beginning with Gregory VII, Popes were not content to excommunicate recalcitrant sovereigns, but rather aimed to depose them, which indicates a direct interference of ecclesiastical power in the temporal order. This all shows the absence of theological thought honoring the legitimacy of the temporal order, and only serves to highlight the contribution of Saint Thomas.

1. The Decisive Contribution of Thomas Aquinas

At a time when Christian human societies are in transformation, meaning the evolution of secular activities, and in a theological and spiritual context which has a tendency to subsume the natural order into the supernatural, Saint Thomas contributes, for the first time, political thought based on natural reason.[7] It is not an exaggeration to say that, in this domain as in others, Thomas shows an extraordinary trust in natural reason, because it comes from God, that it is, as contemporary language would have it, the honored image of himself that God placed in man.

This sudden explosion in political thought in the thirteenth century has a practical, almost material cause: the rediscovery of Aristotle's *Politics*, translated into Latin by Guillaume de Moerbeke, which quickly spread into sites of theological study across Latin Europe. Saint Thomas's assimilation of and adhesion to the main tenets of Aristotelian politics is clear throughout the composition of the second part of the *Summa Theologiae*, usually

---

7. I have discussed this point more in detail in: F. Daguet, *Du politique chez Thomas d'Aquin* (Paris: Vrin, 2017).

described as the section on morality. In Aristotelian politics, Saint Thomas has access to the philosophical instrument Augustine lacked, which allows him to think about the political order itself in the light of the Christian Revelation. In the view of the dominant thinking of his time, which bore the stamp of this "political Augustinianism" which I discussed above, the emergence of a moral and political thought based in nature, but open to the workings of grace, upends the way of thinking about the community order. It is the natural level which is the first consideration, all while honoring the perfection necessarily afforded by grace: *gratia non tollit sed perficit naturam.*

How then do we characterize Thomas Aquinas's approach to the theology of politics in a few words? We can identify two fundamental principles.

1) The political order is finalized by a moral good, itself controlled by the divine good.

Thomas shares Aristotle's firm ideas: communal life, understood on the natural level, is directed by a good of a moral nature which gives purpose to all city life, the life of all together and of each individually. Simply put, it is the search for happiness which drives the city; there is a political happiness, and it is even the result of singular happiness. Incidentally, this is why the political city is recognized to be, along with the family, a *natural* community, even the perfect natural community. That which Thomas calls, without defining it, the common good (*bonum commune*), which Aristotle simply called the good, without qualifying it, is for both men what we achieve in seeking to live, individually and together, a virtuous life. There are, of course, goods of the first order essential to communal life (peace, prosperity, wealth, culture): these allow us to *live*, according to Aristotle's terminology. Yet they are not sufficient to finalize the political order; they are themselves aimed at *living well*, that is, a life lived according to virtue and shared by the majority of the citizens. It is from this communal quest that friendship among citizens is born. There is therefore a happiness that comes from living together, and it is this which must be sought, constructed, and received all at once. It is important to note that this communal happiness is at once in the city and existing beyond it.

For Saint Thomas, as for Aristotle before him, the political order is therefore not a simple packaging of the private order dealt with by individual morality: it is rather the achievement of the whole moral structure. A very ancient tradition separated morality from politics, and often ignored the second. This is to deeply betray the ideas of the two great classic authors which I discuss: the study of individual morality is a prerequisite for studying the community order. Politics is the fulfilment of the practical order, of human activity, and not simply its inevitable packaging. One has only to carefully read the first book of the *Nicomachean Ethics* to grasp the ultimate nature of politics, which makes political science into an architectonic study par excellence, in the practical order.

Thomas Aquinas, far from relativizing such an idea, subscribed to it wholeheartedly: the political order is the final fulfilment of singular morality. Nevertheless, the Christian theologian adds an important aspect: this common good, this common happiness, which finalizes the city on the natural level, is not the ultimate good, which itself is given by the divine good, which is God himself—understood in an objective way—and the beatitude resulting from a vision of God—subjectively. The originality of Saint Thomas's thinking consists in his non-elimination of the temporal good, rather, by subsuming it into the supernatural good; he engages with the temporal good by placing it under the divine good. This is not a simple proposition made here, for theological charity, an expression of grace that effectively realizes here on Earth this raising up of the natural order. It does not disqualify it but rather corrects and elevates it from inside, as leavening does a dough. Thomas Aquinas reclaims space for political science, as we have noted, although he does it as a Christian theologian in such a way that nature cannot be considered without its connection to grace. It is the conjunction of these two which is at the heart of the divine and human work in the world, that is, the entire composition of the terrestrial city; this will not ever be more itself than when it opens itself up to the working of grace.

2) The Church and the city, on different levels, are empowered to cooperate.

Political Augustinianism stopped at the inclusion of the natural order within the supernatural one, and due both to this and a lack of conceptual means did not seek to consider the terrestrial city itself. Father Congar has showed how much the idea of *Ecclesia*, from the Gregorian reform onward, encompasses both the Church, as a hierarchically constituted society, and temporal sovereignties. Faced with this, as a theologian of Christianity, Thomas Aquinas uses Aristotelian instruments to produce a two-fold innovation. First, he thinks about the temporal city in and of itself, and secondly, he specifies more or less explicitly the relationship of the Church with it. He does not in any way place the Church and the terrestrial city on the same plane, but according to the conception taken up by the Vatican II, he sees the Church as a theological leavening agent within societies which are temporal by nature.

From this comes his idea of the relationship between the two powers, temporal and spiritual. Saint Thomas acknowledged the great autonomy of temporal power, as ecclesiastical authority does not intervene into the affairs of the city until it comes to the salvation of souls. In today's words, we would say that the Thomasian doctrine is a laic one which affirms the autonomy of temporal power in relation to the ecclesiastical sphere. It must be said that this free exercise of temporal power, on the basis of natural law, benefits from the support of grace, which perfects the natural order by correcting it where it may have gone wrong. I propose to present Thomas's approach by describing his doctrine as Chalcedonian, to describe the union, which prevails between the natural and super-natural orders without confusion or separation. For a theologian of Christianity, a pure separation of the two orders was unthinkable, and would be so up until the French Revolution which ended the era of political Christianity.

The theology of politics of Thomas Aquinas reminds us that the natural order, left to its own devices, cannot achieve the purpose for which it was made without divine help, and that it would not be able to fulfil the vocation of the human communities which live, ultimately, subject to a supernatural good that they cannot produce for themselves. However, there is a corresponding focus on the fact that communal life is first and foremost life in a political city, not the life of the Church. The latter is the interior leavening agent for the former. For the first time in Christianity, Thomas Aquinas's theology allows us to "think about politics" itself, in its connection with the theological order. The masterful treatise on the law, in *Summa Theologiae,* illustrates his idea of the whole, which makes space for nature, in its entirety—especially in his doctrine of nat-ural law—and for divine aid through divine law. We can see from this Thomas's reversal of Augustinian conceptions characterized by the primacy of the supernatural order, sometimes to the exclusion of all else.

2. The Posteriority of Thomasian Political Theology

It is difficult to appropriately judge the effect of the political writ-ings of Saint Thomas. The question is deserving of future study. On one hand, it is fairly clear that this incipient political theology is still an opinion, especially because, not being expressed in any larger work, it passes unnoticed by many. Augustinian ideas remain widespread during Thomas's time and after, encouraged by the practical affirmation of the papal prerogatives regarding temporal sovereigns. In terms of politics more than any other, historical reality is decisive and new ideas are slow to take shape. In the following centuries, Thomasian ideas are never formally taken up by the Church Magisterium which remains steadfastly distanced from political matters up until the collapse of Christianity beginning at the end of the eighteenth century.

On the other hand, despite all this, it seems today that Saint Thomas's work rekindled political science, strictly speaking, because it allows for consideration of the foundation of natural reason. The majority of the big driving questions of the following centuries, notably that of political systems, of the organization of the temporal city, and of the relationship between the temporal and ecclesiastic powers, have their source in the writings of Thomas Aquinas. We tend to say that modern political thought emerges, on the cusp of the 16th century, in reaction to the excesses of the ecclesiastical influence on the civil order. It is however fairer to say that these debates did not appear for the first time in the modern era. They were already present in the thirteenth century and Thomas Aquinas's works, by authorizing the idea of a profane political thought, contribute decisive elements to this turn in European thought.[8]

Within the Church, one can see the influence of Thomasian ideas in the questions debated in the sixteenth century during the controversy of the Reformation. It is quite clear, for example, in Robert Bellarmin's repeated presentation of his doctrine of the ecclesiastical authority's "indirect power" over the city. This is a balanced doctrine presented after the recurrent interference of the medieval era and during a time when the wars of religion were beginning to devastate Latin Europe. Of course, the real reach of this

---

8. See F. Daguet, "Thomas d'Aquin et la renaissance de la science politique au XIIIᵉ siècle," in *Le théologico-politique au Moyen-Age*, ed. D. Poirel (Paris: Vrin, 2020), 87-102.

spiritual power indirectly exercised *in temporalibus* is subject to multiple interpretations, but it is clear that the Jesuit doctor takes up Thomas's idea of it having no role except when the salvation of souls is immediately relevant. We can undoubtedly argue that the Thomasian conception of the relationship between the two cities progressively became, if not a dominant opinion, at least a common reference available to all.

In the same way and at the same time, it is clear that the development of the Salamancan school relies on the recognition of the legitimacy of the natural human and community order. Francisco de Vitoria contributed greatly to increased familiarity with the works of Thomas Aquinas, and from there the diffusion of his ideas across Europe, at a time when there was a huge expansion of human activity in economics, the new field of domestic and international law, as well as the juridical status of the person.

Certainly, it would be fair to speak of a general and diffuse fertility as regards the political theology of Thomas, rather than a formal and immediate posteriority. One could imagine that the collapse of the rule of Christianity in Europe from the end of the eighteenth century would definitively disqualify the ideas of Thomas of Aquinas, doctor of Christianity. Paradoxically, the reverse takes place. In effect, the French Revolution and its inauguration of the end of Christianity's rule crippled Catholic doctrine, both that of the pontifical Magisterium and that of theologians. Due to the continuing impoverishment of theology in the seventeenth and especially the eighteenth century, the Church discovered at the beginning of the nineteenth century that it had no useful conceptual instrument with which to think about the new situation. This situation is due to the fact that temporal societies then wished to be built on a profane foundation. The movement was long, but we can see that it reached its end at the end of the twentieth century. It is only with the papacy of Leo XIII that the Church took note of the now irreversible change and abandoned its desire to return to the *statu quo ante*. It then had to rethink the idea of political communities without postulating their immediate submission to the supernatural order. Thomas's theology was then rediscovered, a theology which gives ample space to the natural order, a useful instrument to deal with politics in the new context of contemporary liberal societies.

3. The Renewal of Political Theology in the Twentieth Century

Even if the pontifical Magisterium borrowed frequently from the Thomasian writings beginning with Leo XIII, they were still far from the elaboration of a complete political doctrine. Thomasian thought was only appealed to here and there: in reference to the freedom of choice of political systems, the basis of the legislative structure about natural law, the necessary opening of political orders to transcendence, etc. In truth, few authors sought to think about the new political order as a whole and in the light of Revelation.

One of the only examples is Jacques Maritain, supported by his friend the abbot Charles Journet. Taking note of the end of what he calls "sacral Christianity", Maritain looks to conceive of a political order in keeping with the Revelation which would also oppose the "political religions"—of the nationalist-socialist or Marxist-socialist type—as well as it did bourgeois liberalism. One of the bases of the Maritainian conception of politics is still the idea of the ontological subordination of the two cities, which his friend Journet shares, and which justifies for them the natural jurisdiction of the Church over the city. The idea of two analogical realizations of Christianity—one sacral and the other profane—is tempting and coherent. However, with hindsight, it seems that this conception of a non-sacral Christianity depends on the assumption of human

societies which remain Christian at their core, even if their institutions are not. This was still the case of the United States in the
middle of the last century, where Maritain lived at the time he was
thinking about the possibility of a new Christianity. It is difficult
to say that this is true for any place in the world today, and the
Maritainian political project, as tempting as it was, today appears
to us to be inoperative.

The Second Vatican Council is an essential milestone in
the Church's incorporation of political factors in its thinking.
Gaudium et Spes explicitly discusses the political community, and
asserts that "among those social ties which man needs for his development some, like the family and political community, relate
with greater immediacy to his innermost nature."[9] This echoes
the Thomasian doctrine of natural political communities, the family and the city. Despite introducing the topic, the Vatican II doesn't
offer a Catholic political doctrine taken in its entirety. However, it
does contribute several stones in the foundation for a future building. We can summarize the contribution of the Council by saying
that it places the foundation of a Catholic conception of laicity. The
term doesn't appear in the Council's text, but it would be expressly
stated by John Paul II and Joseph Ratzinger forty years later. This
idea rests on the following two principles:

1) In the wake of its recognition of the legitimate "autonomy
   of earthly affairs,"[10] *Gaudium et Spes*, which concerns the
   Church in the modern world, clearly states the principle of
   autonomy of the two spheres, the political and the religious:
   "The Church and the political community in their own
   fields are autonomous and independent from each other

9. Second Vatican Ecumenical Council, Pastoral Constitution on the Church in the Modern
World, *Gaudium Et Spes* (Vatican City, 7 December 1965), para. 25. Available online at: https://
www.vatican.va/archive/hist_councils/ii_vatican_council/documents/vat-ii_const_19651207_
gaudium-et-spes_en.html
10. Ibid., para. 36.

(*in proprio campo ab invicem sunt independentes et autono-mae*). Yet both, under different titles, are devoted to the personal and social vocation of the same men. The more that both foster sounder cooperation between themselves with due consideration for the circumstances of time and place, the more effective will their service be exercised for the good of all."[11] However, this recognition of the political order's autonomy does not stop the Church from passing judgement on the moral foundations upon which the political order is built: "It is only right, however, that at all times and in all places, the Church should have true freedom […] to pass moral judgment in those matters which regard public order when the fundamental rights of a person or the salvation of souls require it. In this, she should make use of all the means—but only those—which accord with the Gospel and which correspond to the general good according to the diversity of times and circumstances."[12]

2) In turn, *Dignitatis Humanae* discusses what the political community's stance towards the Church should be, in the eyes of the Catholics: the wish is for a guarantee of the right to religious freedom.

Thus on one hand, *Gaudium et Spes* recognizes the justified autonomy of the political order, without prejudice to the right to pass moral judgement on the *res publica*, and on the other, *Dignitatis Humanae* claims a guarantee of individual and group religious freedom from the political powers. On the part of the Church, there is an acknowledgement of an inability to directly understand temporal affairs; on the part of the State, a recognition of non-confessionality and an expectation of non-interference in spiritual matters and a guarantee of religious liberty. It is easy to see the far-reaching

11. Ibid., para. 76.
12. Ibid.

influence of Thomasian ideas. This reciprocal non-interference is indeed the expression of what current and legal language calls laicity. What the Council is advocating is thus a system of autonomy, or even separation, but not exclusively, since it calls for cooperation for the good of all. This can be seen as separation-distinction, which is not the same as separation-indifference or ignorance.

In this regard, the Second Vatican Council seems to be the one which takes into consideration the societal evolution of the past two centuries—in a word, the end of Christianity—and which seeks to present a fair ecclesiastical conception of the political community itself and of the relationship which the Church intends to have with it. Developed in practice, these are some essential elements for a theology of politics. However, many other elements, particularly as regards the basis of political communities are added during the papacies of John Paul II and Benedict XVI.

4. The Contribution of Saint John Paul II and Joseph Ratzinger - Benedict XVI

While taking part in the Church's integration of conciliar teaching, John Paul II and Joseph Ratzinger had to take into account a decisive political phenomenon: the general abandonment of Christian references in historically Christian liberal societies, and the explosion of moral references which the two Popes summarize in the expression "ethical relativism." Institutional questions are no longer the object of the Church's reflection, but also, and more radically, the ethical foundations of contemporary political societies. During the course of these two papacies, we can distinguish two large areas where theology was deepened in the political domain.

1) The return to the traditional doctrine
of natural law

The type of misunderstanding that this venerable doctrine, which owes a great deal to Saint Thomas, has been subjected to is well-known. This explains why it does not appear *expressis verbis* in the conciliar texts, even if its content is in fact present. During his political and moral Magisterium, John Paul II recenters it by making it one of the foundational aspects, not only of any singular moral edifice, but also of the laws of the city. The encyclical *Veritatis Splendor* (1993) reaffirms the necessity of a morality which unites liberty and truth as mediated by natural law. It refers explicitly to the "Thomist doctrine" revived by Leo XIII.[13] The repercussions in the political sphere are clear in his denunciation of "*the risk of an alliance between democracy and ethical relativism*, which would remove any sure moral reference point from political and social life, and on a deeper level make the acknowledgement of truth impossible."[14] At the same time, the *Catechism of the Catholic Church* (1992) shows the return to a doctrine well established in the Tradition, by avowing that natural law, in addition to providing "the solid foundation on which man can build the structure of moral rules to guide his choices. It also provides the indispensable moral foundation for building the human community. Finally, it provides the necessary basis for the civil law with which it is connected, whether by a reflection that draws conclusions from its principles, or by additions of a positive and juridical nature."[15] Here again we see the Thomasian affirmation according to which a positive law is not

---

13. John Paul II, *Veritatis Splendor* (Vatican City, 6 August 1993), para. 44. Available online at: http://www.vatican.va/content/john-paul-ii/en/encyclicals/documents/hf_jp-ii_enc_ 06081993_veritatis-splendor.html.

14. Ibid., para. 101.

15. *Catechism of the Catholic Church*, para. 1959. The full text of the *Catechism of the Catholic Church*, promulgated by John Paul II in 1992, is available online at: https://www.vatican.va/archive/ENG0015/_INDEX.HTM.

truly a law unless it is consistent with right reason and therefore the principles of natural law.[16]

Moreover, the *Catechism* again takes up the essential facts about the political order which follow both from Thomasian ideas and Tradition, on the basis of conciliar affirmations. People live in society by nature, primarily in families and the political community.[17] We see the ethical aim of communal life highlighted, through the notion of *common good* which owes so much to Saint Thomas.[18] Finally the necessary opening of the political order to spiritual realities is affirmed, along with the necessity of grace for a life in society which truly turns away from evil and violence.[19]

A *Note* from the 2002 Congregation for the Doctrine of the Faith, written by Joseph Ratzinger and approved publicly by John Paul II, is the result of these great principles for Catholic engagement in politics. Notably, it affirms that "for Catholic moral doctrine, the rightful autonomy of the political or civil sphere from that of religion and the Church—*but not from that of morality*—is a value that has been attained and is recognized by the Catholic Church, and represents a form of cultural heritage."[20] The *Note* carefully distinguishes the legitimate pluralism of options for governance and the illegitimate pluralism of moral conceptions of personhood: "Political freedom is not—and cannot be—based upon the relativistic idea that all conceptions of the human person's good have the same value and truth."[21] If we pay attention, the great principles of Saint Thomas's political theology have become those of the Church through the Magisterium of John Paul II and of Joseph Ratzinger.

16. Ibid., para. 1902.
17. Ibid., para. 1882.
18. Ibid., para. 1905-1912.
19. Ibid., para. 1886-1889.
20. See The Congregation for the Doctrine of the Faith, *Doctrinal Note: The Participation of Catholics in Political Life* (Vatican City, 21 November 2002), para. 6. Available online at: https://www.vatican.va/roman_curia/congregations/cfaith/documents/rc_con_cfaith_doc_20021124_politica_en.html. Here the English translation has been slightly revised.
21. Ibid., para. 3.

2) The call for a political order based on natural reason and open to the supernatural order

Joseph Ratzinger, having become Pope Benedict XVI, continues his reflection on the political order in his encyclicals, but also in his speeches given in the great liberal democracies (United States, Great Britain, and Germany). In an expansion of the conciliar teaching on the separation of the political and religious spheres, Benedict XVI justifies this separation by distinguishing the objects belonging to each. In *Deus Caritas Est,* he writes that it is for the State to establish and maintain a judicial order in the city, while the role of the Church is to live on charity. He does not hesitate in stating that: "Fundamental to Christianity is the distinction between what belongs to Caesar and what belongs to God (see *Matthew* 22:21), in other words, the distinction between Church and State, or, as the Second Vatican Council puts it, the autonomy of the temporal sphere."[22]

He goes on to wonder about the basis of the contemporary judicial order, that is the possibility of establishing a truly just political

22. Benedict XVI, *Deus Caritas Est* (Vatican City, 25 December 2005), para. 28. Available online at: http://www.vatican.va/content/benedict-xvi/en/encyclicals/documents/hf_ben-xvi_enc_20051225_deus-caritas-est.html. "In order to define more accurately the relationship between the necessary commitment to justice and the ministry of charity, two fundamental situations need to be considered: a) The just ordering of society and the State is a central responsibility of politics. As Augustine once said, a State which is not governed according to justice would be just a bunch of thieves: *'Remota itaque iustitia quid sunt regna nisi magna latrocinia?.'* Fundamental to Christianity is the distinction between what belongs to Caesar and what belongs to God (cf. *Matthew* 22:21), in other words, the distinction between Church and State, or, as the Second Vatican Council puts it, the autonomy of the temporal sphere. Justice is both the aim and the intrinsic criterion of all politics. Politics is more than a mere mechanism for defining the rules of public life: its origin and its goal are found in justice, which by its very nature has to do with ethics. [...] The Church cannot and must not take upon herself the political battle to bring about the most just society possible. She cannot and must not replace the State. Yet at the same time she cannot and must not remain on the sidelines in the fight for justice. She has to play her part through rational argument and she has to reawaken the spiritual energy without which justice, which always demands sacrifice, cannot prevail and prosper. A just society must be the achievement of politics, not of the Church. Yet the promotion of justice through efforts to bring about openness of mind and will to the demands of the common good is something which concerns the Church deeply."

order. At the Bundestag, in 2011, he shows the impasse faced by contemporary juridical positivism: "Where positivist reason dominates the field to the exclusion of all else—and that is broadly the case in our public mindset—then the classical sources of knowledge for ethics and law are excluded." At Westminster, in 2010, he had already spoken on this subject, showing the only possible solution, the recognition of natural law:

If the moral principles underpinning the democratic process are themselves determined by nothing more solid than social consensus, then the fragility of the process becomes all too evident—herein lies the real challenge for democracy. […] The central question at issue, then, is this: where is the ethical foundation for political choices to be found? The Catholic tradition maintains that the objective norms governing right action are accessible to reason, prescinding from the content of revelation.

In other words, he refers to the doctrine of civil law supported by principles of natural law, which Saint Thomas brilliantly developed.

Finally, as in 2002, Benedict XVI restates the necessary cooperation of the political and religious spheres. Indeed, no juridical order would be sufficient in and of itself. He calls for the necessity of transcendence through charity: "Love—*caritas*—will always prove necessary, even in the most just society. There is no ordering of the State so just that it can eliminate the need for a service of love."[23] His contemplation is far-reaching, suggesting that each of the spheres, one of reason and one of faith, contribute to the perfection of the other by purifying the corruptions which affect or threaten it.[24]

---

23. Ibid.

24. "It is a two-way process. Without the corrective supplied by religion, though, reason too can fall prey to distortions, as when it is manipulated by ideology, or applied in a partial way that fails to take full account of the dignity of the human person. Such misuse of reason, after all, was what gave rise to the slave trade in the first place and to many other social evils, not least the totalitarian ideologies of the twentieth century. This is why I would suggest that the world of reason and the world of faith—the world of secular rationality and the world of religious belief—need one another and should not be afraid to enter into a profound and ongoing dialogue, for the good of our civilization." Pope Benedict XVI's address to the Houses of Parliament in Westminster Hall on 17 September

Clearly, the united papacies of John Paul II and Benedict XVI show a unique elaboration of a Catholic political doctrine, conveying a true political theology. In hindsight, we see that it is a communal work, which addresses the demands facing the Church in the face of the evolution of the contemporary era. Remarkably, this political theology, based on conciliar statements, essentially fulfils this need and does not hesitate to draw from nor refer to Thomasian sources for its broad principles.

The assessment presented in the present contribution, while not immune the criticisms applied to any broad overview, suggests a few conclusions.

1) It must be recognized in no uncertain terms that the theological tradition of the Catholic Church has been lazy as relates to politics—and this is primarily due to the Thomist school. While the essential elements for the elaboration of a political theology were available in the writings of Thomas Aquinas, the Church preferred to depend on the pragmatism of a Christian system which thought itself immune to a radical challenge. At a time when modern thought, from the seventeenth century on, aims to emancipate its politics from the Christian order, theology is incapable of responding with a proposal which correctly understands the human community order. Things take a dramatic turn with the collapse of Christianity, as the Church shows itself incapable, not only of responding to events but even of understanding them: it does not have access to the keys of intelligibility which, paradoxically, its own tradition had provided. The extent of these consequences reveals itself over the course of the nineteenth and twentieth centuries. Indeed, theology

2010 is available online at: http://www.vatican.va/content/benedict-xvi/en/speeches/2010/september/documents/hf_ben-xvi_spe_20100917_societa-civile.html.

remains deaf to the transformational political processes of
the human world taking place in communal life, with a few
exceptions such as that of Jacques Maritain discussed above.
It is the pontifical leadership which, bit by bit, develops a
Christian response to the political challenges of the modern world. The Second Vatican Council is marked by this
weakness. If, on one hand, it places a few stones in the
foundation subsequently taken up by the Magisterium of the
Popes following Leo XIII, it gives only a general idea of the
political order.

2) In this context the work developed jointly by John Paul II
and Benedict XVI appears remarkable. It is the first sketch
of a true theology of politics, the work of two minds particularly aware of the *res publica*. However, this work remains
largely unknown for at least two reasons. On one hand, it
is dispersed in multiple texts, which means that the whole
is not visible to the eyes of the faithful. On the other hand,
it is an incomplete work, in the sense that it is constructed
through successive elements, not without a certain perfectly
legitimate pragmatism as regards political matters. It has not
been the object of a summary or of a major text such as an
encyclical, which appears to have damaged both its chances
of being generally known and its authority.

3) The two preceding considerations lead to a hope that theologians will—finally—take up this issue, shaking off the
lethargy that has affected them for the preceding centuries.
The stakes are no less important—at issue is the credibility
of a speech which the Church addresses to a world being constructed largely without it. At best, the neglect of
political matters limits Christian discourse to evangelical
pronouncements, which, while of course necessary, are
inadmissible to those without faith. It is sometimes limited

to simply providing a theological response to immediate political questions, as we see in the *Radical Orthodoxy* movement. This is, in fact, yielding to the temptation of a political Augustinianism, practical rather than conceptual, but as insufficient today as it was in the past to respond to contemporary political questions. It is past time to rediscover political Thomism.

FRANÇOIS DAGUET, O.P.—theologian, lecturer and award-winning author and researcher of ecclesiology and political doctrine of the Church. He received his doctorate in theology from the University of Fribourg and studied at the prestigious ENA in Paris. He is professor and dean of the Faculty of Theology at the Institut Catholique de Toulouse, where he also presided over the Institut Saint-Thomas d'Aquin. Author of the famous *Du politique chez Thomas d'Aquin* (2015), for which he received the Prix Biguet award.

CHANTAL DELSOL

THE END OF CHRISTENDOM

We have yet to fully realize the far-reaching transformation which our society is undergoing: the end of a sixteen-century old civilization. The death of Christendom is not, however, a sudden event. Apart from few exceptions, civilizations do not collapse unexpectedly: they break down and gradually fade away. During the last two centuries, Christendom has been forced to fight for its very existence—a moving and heroic agony indeed. Christian culture has put forth significant efforts to survive, having established a coherent world in all areas of life which is called "Christianity." Christianity has built a civilization that has existed according to distinct laws, principles and dogmas for sixteen centuries.

To some extent, the French revolution set itself to oppose Christianity; the latter has always been, perhaps sometimes mistakenly, considered as restrictive and antagonistic to modernity.[1] Historians have illustrated how the 1789 French revolution, which is the fourth of its kind in the West, was unique compared to earlier population revolts. In overthrowing the social order, like Archimedes balancing a lever in the right place, the Dutch, British, and American revolutions were able to rely on, and be supported

1. Here I use the term Christianity to refer to the Catholic and Orthodox traditions.

by, religion as a substantive base. Unlike these contexts where protestant reformation did not represent an obstacle to the development of new ideas, the French revolution did not have such a strong support to rely on, as in France the Catholic religion was opposing all of the principles, starting with freedom and equality, advocated during the time of the upheaval. Not only did the former three revolutions not conceive vengeful and delusive utopias, but they installed stable regimes where politics and religion could rely on bonds which tied them together. By contrast, the French Revolution resolved into acrimonious debates and constant conflicts between the Church and the State, with disastrous outcomes: entirely devoid of any religious values, the political sphere inevitably fell into dangerous extremes. The Church, reduced to a public enemy in revolt against the law and social customs, saw it pervasive force slowly withering away.

Christianity has been intricately intertwined with the history of Western society, and this is particularly true for Catholic Christianity, a religion which promotes a comprehensive view of society and challenges a culture of individualism. It is natural for Christianity to clash with modernity; having reached its apex, it has begun declining to finally disappear. Of course, several attempts have been made to adapt Christianity to the modern spirit; here I would like to recall, for instance, those pursued in the nineteenth century by Charles de Montalembert and the movement of liberal Christianity. Such adaptations, however, are unlikely to gain ground; any endeavor of this kind on the one hand involves accommodating but on the other hand scents betrayal. The essence of the Christian religion as an institution is such as makes it intrinsically and irremediably prone to oppose modernity, seen as a real threat to its bedrock principles: truth, hierarchy, authority and coercion. After the Second World War, the culture of late modernity has regarded the Church as an outdated, obsolete institution;

between the second half of the twentieth and the beginning of the twenty-first century, the gap separating the Christian and late modern worldview exacerbated. Liberalism and libertarianism are in exact opposition to ecclesial thinking. Today the overwhelming majority of the Christian clergy and believers are committed to modern principles of freedom of thought, conscience and religion—apart from some groups of people who, unlike those who openly disagree with its radical views, secretly value the so-called *Syllabus of Errors* but will not dare to defend publically this set of propositions, issued in 1864 by the Holy See under Pope Pius IX.

André Malraux, speaking in a kind of prophetic mode, said that the twenty-first century would be religious. Among Christians, we appreciate this observation, as it negotiates against time: "religion" can only imply "Christianity." Nevertheless, the spiritual scenario has not unfolded as expected: it is true that the twenty-first century is religious, but it is no longer Christian. The Western religious milieu has become richly plural and diverse. It is not peculiarly predictive to foretell that a century will be religious, for all centuries are. As long as humanity is imperfect and mortal (certainly until the end of time, despite post-humanist theories), it will always have a religious instinct and continue to create religious systems, wisdom and morals. Only the extremely scientific rationalization of the Enlightenment, detached from the real world, could support the naive view that religious beliefs will give way to atheism. Atheism represents a conscious act of vanity and egotism and is, at the end, unfeasible because as soon as Christianity falls, all other types of gods will replace it. No, the end of Christendom will not correspond to the emergence of an atheistic society, precisely because this latter does not exist. Societies are not constituted of a few intellectuals but of peoples who are at least agnostic if not believers, and whose common sense suggests that there is a mystery beyond life and the knowable. Habermas' pupil Hans Joas writes ironically:

"Perhaps a future without religion is conceivable, but is one without music and dance and theater, to mention other non rational forms of human communication?"[2]

Social and ethical values change and are reshaped throughout history, yet disenchantment does not coincide with atheism and all-powerful rationalism. Daily experience confirms that morality does not disappear with the fall of Christendom and, what is more, that morality pervades everything—but this is a different story. Neither civilization nor morality ends with Christendom: they reinvent themselves in a dynamic way and develop through other routes. We are not heading toward hell or going to suffer a total loss of what characterizes humanity; there is a paradigm shift happening before our eyes that, although it can be considered as radical and questionable, it nevertheless promotes some respectable principles. My teacher Julien Freund, troubled by the signs of late modernity of our decadent society, spoke of a New Age.[3] Here I also wish to use this expression: the new age will be the age of wisdom and paganism, inevitably rediscovered following the collapse of transcendence. I believe that we should understand the present age of transformation as a "revolution": the etymology of the word indicates a "revolving, turning back," and in the case here discussed is applicable to both the areas of morality and ontology. Since about the 1950s-60s, our Western society has undergone a complete inversion of the hierarchy of values and morals. It can be widely observed that, in respect to individual behavior and social norms, during the last decades what was considered as a bad thing has now become perfectly acceptable and, vice versa, a previously disliked behavior is now admired. There has been a dramatic shift in values. For previous generations, in the world of our fathers, colonization was a

2. H. Joas, *The Power of the Sacred: An Alternative to the Narrative of Disenchantment*, trans. A. Skinner (Oxford: Oxford University Press, 2021), 85.

3. J. Freund, *Le Nouvel Âge* (Paris: Marcel Rivière, 1970).

generous and admirable endeavor, torture and war were the last resort; today colonization, war and torture are diabolic acts to avoid by all means. Homosexuality was banned and despised, and today it is justified and acclaimed. Abortion, previously criminalized, is legitimized and advised. Pedophilia, always a prohibited contact but previously somewhat silently accepted to protect families and institutions, is now criminalized. Divorce, which was virtually almost impossible even to conceive, has become quick and easy to get. Suicide was illegal and despised (those who killed themselves were not offered a religious funeral), nowadays this type of death is considered to have some practical advantages, and in some countries the legal system helps citizens to accomplish it.

Morality refers to what societies sanction as right and acceptable. In a society, ethics, the system of moral principles and behavior, plays a major role in guiding and giving meaning to people's behavior. Moral principles tell us which acts are right and which are wrong; modes of conduct, acceptable or forbidden behavior, reflect the cultural sense of an era. Taboo and transgression must be understood from a socio-historical and socio-cultural perspective; they reflect long-held core ethical values. Radical changes in societal values have occurred within the lifetime of many of us; ethical behavior in general reflects what society values. As cultures evolve and societies develop, people change the way they think about life. Morality and moral sensibility are not rigid or monolithic; any signifying act reveals a conscious or unconscious belief. You may decide to try, sometimes unwisely, to stay with a difficult spouse instead of separating from them: it is because you value, perhaps unconsciously, a certain idea of loyalty to oneself, in other words of personal responsibility. When a woman decides not to terminate an unwelcome or unexpected pregnancy, it may be because she respects the embryo's dignity and individuality. Social and cultural norms are rules and expectations of behavior based on shared beliefs.

While often unspoken, norms offer social standards for appropriate and inappropriate conduct. Typically, our personal, and often unconscious, values dictate our actions. The norms that characterize our time, radically reversed according to adult generations, appear to be natural to the young people, who are increasingly influenced by the social environment and the media. It is true that coping with such dramatic changes is difficult for the elderly, but has it not always been an age-related characteristic to be nostalgic and feeling that anything in the past was better than the present days? The conditions of our post-modern society trouble some Christians, which explains the reason why people join the "Manif-pour-tous" and other pro-life associations.

It is about time for us to give a name to this inversion of values: I contend that this story brings to light the end of Christendom. I shall elaborate on this point by turning my attention to the origins of Christianity: Christianity itself was, in fact, established by a normative inversion, although in a different direction. The fourth century CE represented a break from the preceding paradigm, both in the philosophical and ethical sense. The Christian system of values was the opposite of that of the Romans': the former introduced a dualism between the temporal and the spiritual, humankind and God, whereas the ancient religious world was deeply unified. The Romans must have felt as if they were entering into a new intellectual and spiritual dimension, their familiar world being fully torn apart. Only within a few decades, a revolution of moral principles and norms took place: the old system of morality was being replaced; in the social context, there was an inversion of the system of values and principles of conduct. Everything was being reversed, as the second-century Christian theologian Tertullian wrote: "It is therefore against these things that our contest lies—against the institutions of our ancestors, against the authority of tradition, the laws of our governors, and the reasonings of the wise; against antiquity, custom, submission; against precedents, prodigies, miracles—all which things have had their part in consolidating that spurious system of your gods." Long before Christianity, the Romans were monogamous, but lawful divorce became more and more permissive over time to the extent that even women could ask for a quick and easy divorce. On the contrary, the Christian emperors penalized and finally forbade divorce. Abortion and infanticide had always been legitimate practices, except for Jews and Egyptians. The Greeks and Romans practiced them widely; for instance, unwanted baby girls were left to die and only the first-born female was to be kept and raised.

In the Roman patriarchal family law, according to the principle of *patria potestas* a women's fetus and child belonged to the father, who had full power over his children. The Jews and then the Christians rejected these practices.[4] Homosexuality, widely practiced and known in Athens as pederasty or pedophilia, was also perfectly acceptable among Romans. In a law of 390, Theodosius I declared that passive non-heterosexual male prostitutes should be burned alive. The new morality had started spreading from the center to the peripheries, being the countryside latter commonly behind—hence *paganus* ("peasant"), from which the word "pagan" derives. The term "pagan" was both convenient and inappropriate: it was created by the enemies. The dissemination of Christianity from the centers to the outskirts, and thus from places of sophisticated culture to villages, was accompanied by feelings of pride, as if the new was better. The "pagans" were considered as conservatives looking backward; Christians called themselves "modern"—notably, the term *modernus* appeared at that very time.[5] Paganism came to be

4. Philo of Alexandria explains that the foetus is "a living thing," in other words an innocent being: the act of killing a foetus is a murder. See Philo of Alexandria, *De Specialibus Legibus,* books 3-4, ed. and transl. A. Mosès (Paris: Le Cerf, 1970), 3:37-119.

5. See *Gelasius to Bishops Rufinus and Aprilis,* in *The Letters of Gelasius I (492-496), pastor and micro-manager of the Church of Rome,* transl. B. Neil and P. Allen (Turnhout: Brepols, 2014), letter 23, 195.

seen as superstitious and outdated.[6] The march of progress had started gaining ground: history is written by the winners, it is the winners' interpretation of facts that prevails.

The eighteenth century, a revolutionary period, represented what can be called the beginning of the end of Christendom: in the West, the decline and overthrow of the common civilization had just started. The whole process has lasted two centuries, and consisted of comings and goings and struggles between detractors and defenders. It looked like the siege of a town. One could tell the story of this succession of crashes; let us consider, for instance, the example of divorce in France. A law authorizing divorce was promulgated in 1792 during the Revolution; it was abolished in 1816 under the Restoration and reestablished in July 1884. On 2 April 1941, a law of the Vichy regime prohibited divorce. Finally, after the second world war divorce laws became more liberal. The fights against the principles of Christianity have suffered failures and setbacks. Christianity has defended itself and tried hard to keep the authority over legislative and moral power. Yet despite some episodic successes, for the last two centuries a rising wave of shifting social norms and cultural values have started sweeping away, never stopping, what were once key moral principles. The recent history of abortion laws elucidates well the turmoil which has accompanied a drastic change in moral attitudes and which has produced extreme reactions in both directions. When the law passed, some were crying out with joy and some with horror, and one could experience excess behavior everywhere. Emotional intensity is always present in crowd phenomena: women were marching by, screaming that their bodies belong to them, extremist groups were trying to block the operation of abortion clinics. The same can be said about the evolution of public opinion or protest against same-sex marriage, assisted reproduction or assisted suicide. Christians try to defend their traditional moral values relying

6. P. Veyne, *Quand notre monde est devenu chrétien (312–394)* (Paris: Albin Michel, 2007), 170.

on non-Christian arguments: they know too well that their dogma would not be heard at all. They strategically argue from the perspective of nature, natural law or related reasons which are not necessarily less important. In doing so, they even find sometimes unexpected allies, as when groups of psychoanalysts and psychiatrists with no religious beliefs join Christians in the defense of fatherhood. Yet with no practical meaningful results ever. Our society is not concerned with natural law: people widely believe that rules of right and wrong are created by society, and are not intrinsic to human nature. They also question the relationship between politics, power and traditional religion. Traditional morality is irreversibly declining. The crisis of traditional ethics is slow but persistent, radical and undeniable. Christian supporters struggle to construct compelling arguments and their style no longer appeals. Being aware of losing their case without obtaining the slightest concession, they find a certain justification in the application of the principle *ad majorem dei gloriam*. Countries that resist changes are singled out by others and treated as being backward looking, as if it were a matter of good taste, reasoning and intelligence to eradicate old values. Political movements that defend the old system of morality, although elected by many voters, have difficulty being represented by moderate candidates, and often end up only with extremist representatives, like Donald Trump. The fate of a movement condemned by history is to become increasingly extremist, its most reasonable supporters will inevitably walk out in protest over the radical views.

The normative inversion of the last two centuries is almost the exact opposite of what happened in the fourth century. Plutarch's cry "The great Pan is dead" might have anticipated the demise of paganism, or at least that is how Christians then interpreted it to their advantage. Pan, or Priapus, was the God of sex and violence. Today's society tells us the story of the return of the great Pan— the wheel has come full circle. In this paper, I have compared two dramatic normative inversions, which have taken place sixteen centuries apart and have moved in opposite directions, to emphasize that the current moral emancipation is pushed by a somewhat coherent social force. This emancipation is not sufficient to measure social progress, it does not necessarily champion an outward looking approach which will give us the gift of freedom; as highlighted above, in the fourth century the exact opposite movement took place, and it was as just as inevitable. In each era, "progress" consists in reconciling realities (laws, customs and moral principles) with widespread and sometimes unspoken beliefs, which are a driving force and evolve throughout history often silently. To put it differently, the global social situation is the result of a radical transformation of beliefs. A strong stream holding together collective shared values, the tenets which shape our society, flows before our eyes: why is such a stream invested with hopes for the future? Because people yearn to find meaning and achieve what has yet to come to fruition. In the fourth century, it was the Christians who invented the "modern," and pagans were on the defensive, opposite side of the social world. A normative inversion, especially of this magnitude, is intertwined with and rests on the basis of a philosophical inversion. This is quite natural: the system of morality is shaking because its foundations have been replaced. Each culture or civilization establishes, at some decisive moment in their history, a set of ontological choices which create and rule morals, laws and customs. For Christendom, this decisive moment was the time of the first ecumenical councils, which set out the first truths on which sixteen centuries of Christianity would survive: God, the person and the moral system.

There comes a day when trust in core principles breaks down. We are now living at a breaking point where ontological choices concerning the meaning and place of human beings, nature, and gods in the universe are overturned. If beliefs collapse, laws and morals will continue to have some power for some time without further justification and by the force of habit alone—this situation will not last too long, and they will eventually collapse being considered as illegitimate. Beliefs empower people; what we believe, we accept as our truth. Only beliefs can empower the set of original ontological choices. A first ontological reversal of a similar magnitude took place at the early stages of Judaism. Moses successfully, and to some extent fiercely, led the transition from polytheism to monotheism. Tacitus sums up this event as follows: "In order to secure the allegiance of his people in the future, Moses prescribed for them a novel religion quite different from those of the rest of mankind. Among the Jews all things are profane that we hold sacred; on the other hand they regard as permissible what seems to us immoral."[7] This story illustrates well the link between ontological inversion and normative, moral inversion. Historians of religions have differentiated between two types of religions: cosmotheist or polytheist religions, which are natural and obvious, and monotheist or "secondary religions," which are more complex constructions. The latter appeal to the concepts of revelation, faith, inner wisdom, and require to be constantly reaffirmed and nourished. By contrast, not only do polytheist religions arise spontaneously and proliferate without the need to be continually fed in order to survive, but also instantly reoccupy their social place as soon as it becomes available again. This is exactly what is happening today. Although Western society has been shaped by monotheism at all levels, cosmotheism has never fully disappeared from the scene. Several authors have been inspired by it to varying degrees: here it suffices to mention alchemy, the *cabbalah*, Spinoza, freemasonry, Lessing, German romanticism, Goethe, Freud, Nazism, the new age, and so forth. There is no doubt that cosmotheism neither disappears nor dies: it is asleep but always ready to rise and grow again as soon as the

---

7. Tacitus, *The Histories*, book 5: 4, trans. K. Wellesley (London: Penguin Classics, 2009), 252.

secondary religion shows signs of weakness. In his famous 1917 lecture, *Science as a Vocation*, Max Weber describes how monotheism has dethroned polytheism in the name of universal reason and how polytheism remains, lurking in the background, awaiting for revenge.

Christians have long believed that Christianity could only be replaced by atheism, nihilism or both; in other words, by negative forms that would bring darkness, which is a way of considering Christianity as irreplaceable. Péguy writes in *Dialogue of History and the Carnal Soul*: "There have been so many peoples and so many souls who have not been charmed or reached by Christianity; so many peoples and so many souls who have lived abandoned and who are not, who were not worse off, my friend; there, exactly there, there is, unfortunately, the secret, the hollow mystery."[8] Believing or making people believe that if Christianity collapses everything collapses with it is, in brief, talking nonsense. The Christian dominion has already been replaced by familiar and well-known primitive historical forms. While Christianity is collapsing, Stoic values, paganism and Asian-type spirituality are gaining ground. Nietzsche predicted this evolution when he wrote: "[...] a kind of European China, with a delicate Buddhist-Christian belief and, in the practical sphere, an Epicurean savoir."[9] At the start of the twenty-first century, the most established and most promising philosophical movement is a form of cosmotheism linked to environmental protection; one could also speak of pantheism or polytheism.[10] Most of our Western contemporaries no longer believe in a transcendent reality; the meaning of life must be found in this lifetime, and not

8. Translated in English from the original French; see C. Péguy, *Véronique. Dialogue de l'Histoire et de l'Âme Charnelle* (Paris: Gallimard, 1972), pléiade III, 70.

9. Translated from the French edition; see *Fragments Posthumes 1887-88*, trad. Jean Lacoste, Édition de Giorgio Colli et Mazzino Montinari (Paris: Gallimard, 1986), 86.

10. M. Tarrier gives an apology of pantheism and polytheism in *Les Orphelins de Gaïa* (Toulon: Presses Du Midi, 2012).

after or beyond it, where there is nothing. The sacred is already here: the sacred is experienced in nature and among us human beings. At the turn of the twentieth and twenty-first centuries, we look at and understand the world differently. Cosmotheism helps humankind to feel at home in the world, which represents the only existing reality and which contains both the sacred and the profane; from the monotheist perspective human beings are strangers in this immanent world and long for another, eternal and divine world. For the cosmotheist, this world is their home; for the monotheist, this world is only a temporary stay. The post-modern mind is tired of living in a temporary accommodation; it needs a proper independent home. The post-modern mind becomes cosmotheist again as it wishes to reintegrate and experience this world as a full citizen, and no longer as a sort of guest or "resident non-citizen," an expression denoting Christians as described by the anonymous author of the *Epistle to Diognetus*.[11]

The post-modern human being intends to overcome distinctions—their favorite adjective is "inclusive." Cosmotheism suits this mindset because it overthrows the old dualism characterizing Judeo-Christianity; it evades the contradictions between false and true, God and the world, faith and reason. Ecology today represents a religion and a belief, which does not mean that ecological problems should not be considered scientifically true, but rather that scientific data about climate and ecology produce irrational convictions, direction and certainty—in brief, religious beliefs, as these beliefs are endowed with all features of a proper religion. Today, ecology has become a liturgy: it is impossible not to speak about it

11. See the following passage in *Epistle to Diognetus*, transl. A. Roberts and J. Donaldson, in *Ante-Nicene Fathers*, vol. 1, chap. 5, ed. A. Roberts, J. Donaldson and A. Cleveland Coxe (Buffalo, NY: Christian Literature Publishing Co, 1885). "They dwell in their own countries, but simply as sojourners. As citizens, they share in all things with others, and yet endure all things as if foreigners. Every foreign land is to them as their native country, and every land of their birth as a land of strangers."

in any given occasion. It serves also as a catechism: it is taught to children since the kindergarten to help them to develop good habits of thinking and acting. It is also a consensual dogma: whoever asks questions showing doubts about environmental problems is considered as mad or judged negatively. Above all, and this is the clear feature of a strong belief rather than a rational science, a passion for the environment pushes us to accept what was challenged by individualism: personal responsibility, the legacy that we will leave to future generations and our duties towards the community. It is therefore in the name of this immanent and pagan religion that we are bringing together the basic dimensions of our human existence, which were previously cultivated by the system of Christian values.

The new ecological religion is a form of post-modern pantheism: nature becomes the object of a cult. Mother earth becomes a kind of pagan goddess, and not only among indigenous Bolivians but also among Europeans, to the extent that Pope Francis speaks today of "our mother earth," in a Christian sense of course, but using a language in tune with contemporary beliefs. Our human fellows are trying hard to protect nature overexploited by humankind, what is more is that they have also started, literally speaking, embracing trees. In the vast field opened up by the decline of Christianity, the set of new beliefs are still in the process of settling down. Disaffection with religious dogmas and truths, once presented as unquestionable, now gives rise to the triumph of morality: morality stands alone, independent. There is a kind of philanthropy unfolding before our eyes, the desire to promote the welfare of others and a love for humankind directly inherited from the teachings on love found in the Gospel, but without the same religious foundations. Late modernity gets back to the Gospel but deprives it of all transcendent aspects. For contemporary American political scientist Joseph Bottum, a deformed Protestant morality without transcendence dominates the moral sphere across the Atlantic. The number of Protestants have fallen from 50% to 4% in half a century; the deadly sins have become intolerance, power, militarism and oppression. In other words, a debased Gospel has generated the decolonial movement—and, one must add, after having generated the communist ideology. In pagan societies, religion and morality are separate: religion demands sacrifices and rituals, while the rulers impose the system of morality. This is exactly the formula we are about to experience again: our governing elite legislates and enforces morality. Our morality is post-evangelical and no longer based on religion; it is the same morality dominating the present media landscape, and which controls schools and families. When it needs some readjustments or redirection, it is for the governing elite to intervene. In this perspective, the European rulers represent the priestly tabernacle. In short, we are back to a situation of paganism: we have a state morality.

What will become of the Church without Christendom? In response to the current state of affairs, the Church as institution has shown several and diverging reactions. The most common, and especially among the clergy, are acceptance and surrender. The time is long past for the supporters of the *Syllabus of Errors*, although one still finds some traditional, and perhaps eccentric, sympathizers. Things go even further: not only has the Church, disarmed in every way, ceased to claim back the lost power but it also whispers a *mea culpa* for having abused it. Church leaders are now discreet apostles, nothing alike those proselytizers within the tradition we are used to. Conquest, no longer part of the agenda, has been replaced with humble testimony; evangelizers of the past are now often blamed for disseminating bad taste propaganda. Conquest is banned for both religion and states. Downgraded to the state of silent witnesses, Christians today are soldiers fighting a losing battle. Their social fights, especially those concerning principles and values, lead nowhere and have no chance of succeeding. I am not quite sure they got it right: Christians who fight and protest tirelessly against abortion or assisted reproduction laws should understand that they can win the battle only if they first initiate a spiritual revolution: convert people to Christianity, to the intrinsic dignity of each embryo, and only then you can try to abolish abortion. It does not work the other way around: imposing ritual confession on non-Catholics is extremist nonsense. Beliefs and the adherence to certain principles precede, in fact, acceptance of laws.

No longer planning to conquer the world, like the ancient Jews we will focus on living and surviving—and that will be enough. You can search everywhere but nowhere you will find somebody having a plan of conquest and, although this may be some hearts' secret, no one dares to share the dream. Many Christians are relieved to see the end of Christendom, and its hegemony and hypocrisy. We are all, Christians and not, the children of this era: we prefer gentleness to domination, imperfection to grandiosity. "When one cannot be a power, one can be an example," said Camus. Modernity, in fact, is probably both a rejection of Christian power (a challenge to societal laws) and a renewal and adaptation of Christian principles (especially social ones). In all its dimensions, modernity has developed against Christianity as a civilization rather than against Christianity itself. Modernity challenges the power of religion and not religion itself, as Tocqueville explains: "It was much less as a religious doctrine than as a political institution that Christianity had aroused furious hatreds."[12] In the end, it is pointless to press the question whether Christianity as a civilization was legitimate or not: today we are urged to think about how to approach the rest of this story.

We must, I believe, resist the temptation to transform Christian thought into ideology, creating a world which can be cut with a knife so to speak, and soon Manichean. New beliefs are taking shape, and tolerance is fading. A culture that feels threatened group

12. A. de Tocqueville *The Old Regime and the French Revolution,* trans. A. Goldhammer (Cambridge: Cambridge University Press, 2011), 16. First published 1856.

together its troops and country to prepare them for war. Yet some look with nostalgia at Christianity, wishing to preserve its last expression before the final disappearance: "Stop, oh Lord, the clock with which You measure our dissolution" (Lucian Blaga). For most of us, the past has become a foreign land and, I would add, an unwanted one. After the events, sometimes touching and sometimes deadly, of the last two centuries we have given it up. It is no longer Christendom leaving us: it is we who are leaving it. Why? Because we no longer choose (and accept) power, hegemony and coercion. In other words, are we not able to experience or identify Christianity with power and hegemony? Should mission necessarily be synonymous with conquest? One can think of Christianity by looking at the example offered by the monks of Tibhirine rather than the one presented by Sepulveda. It would be probably best if we were only silent witnesses, and ultimately secret agents of God, because despite the normative and philosophical inversion Christianity is still, in its way, the spirit of the place. Renouncing Christendom does not seem a painful sacrifice. The experience of our fathers provides us with a certainty: our aim should not be to produce societies where "the Gospel governs the States" but rather, as Saint-Exupéry puts it, to "walk gently towards the [ultimate] source."

CHANTAL DELSOL — born in Paris, France, in 1947. Philosopher, writer and professor of political philosophy. As a graduate of philosophy and art history at the University of Lyon, she received her PhD in philosophy at the Sorbonne under Julien Freund in 1982. In 1992 she became professor at the University of Marne-la-Vallée. Member of the French Academy. Winner of many awards, including the Academy of Ethical and Political Sciences Award (1993, 2002), Mousquetaire Award (1996), and the French Academy Award (2001). Her most recent book is titled *Fin de la Chrétienté, l'inversion normative et le nouvel âge* (2021).

RÉMI BRAGUE

THE PLACE AND RELEVANCE OF ART IN THE MODERN WORLD

1. A historical approach

We should begin by asking what we mean, exactly, when we speak of the "modern" world. There is a continuous flow of time and events as historians endeavor to reconstruct them. Where shall we draw the line? We commonly refer to the period after the Middle Ages as "modern." Moreover, we commonly distinguish between modern history and contemporary history.

Pinpointing the start of modern times after the Middle Ages is not easy, although it is supposed to begin with the Renaissance. But when did that begin? This depends on the country or city-state in question. The beginning of contemporary history is commonly accepted as the French Revolution and the upheavals that it brought about with the Napoleonic wars.

In Germany, things become even trickier, since Germans distinguish between *die Neuzeit*, which begins in the sixteenth century, and its subset, *die Moderne*, a common moniker for the arrival of new artistic practices, especially in Vienna or Munich, toward the end of the 19th century.

Be that as it may, modern times form a peak in the history of art. The arts flourished in every field and in every language. In literature, the novel appeared with Cervantes. Among the performing arts, theatre, both tragic and comic, which slumbered through the Middle Ages (except for the "mystery plays"), enjoyed a rebirth all over Christendom with artists such as Calderón, Shakespeare, and the French trio Corneille, Racine, and Molière. In music, polyphony appeared, along with new musical forms like the sonata, the cantata, and the symphony. Entirely new forms of art appeared, like opera, which blends theatre and music.

By and large, all the arts had Christian underpinnings. This burgeoning of the arts took place in Europe and therefore in a Christian context. This raises the issue of the relationship between art and Christianity. A historical approach is required, because Christianity is more a historical fact than a doctrine, given Jesus Christ's life, death on the cross, and resurrection. Furthermore, this fact is perhaps the only real event in history, the only thing that really "happened" and was not merely the kaleidoscopic reorganization of already existing elements of the world, the only fact that gave the lie to Schopenhauer's applying the motto *eadem sed aliter*[1] to history. Christian doctrine attempts to do justice to this fact and to translate it into an adequate conceptual vocabulary.

2. Before Christianity: Beauty without art

What was the state of art when Christianity became the leading factor in Western culture? Let us first consider the so-called pagan world. There is great evidence that in the pre-Christian world

1. A. Schopenhauer, *Die Welt als Wille und Vorstellung*, III, 38, in: *Werke*, ed. W. von Löhneysen (Darmstadt: Wissenschaftliche Buchgesellschaft, 1980), t. 2, 570.

decorative forms and art were present and commonly practiced across different societies. Ancient music was rarely noted on paper, and most ancient paintings were not preserved. But Greek architecture survived. So did Greek sculpture, mainly through Roman copies, barring some exceptions like the statues retrieved from the shipwrecked carriers that brought them from Greece to Italy. Greek and Latin literature produced masterpieces, some of which survived and remained models for later writers.

In our present-day common representation of the ancient world, especially the Greek one, this world was beautiful: not happening to be so, but essentially determined by beauty. The world was beautiful because it was good, and it was good because whatever exists, in so far as it exists, is good. This simple equation is to be found in each philosopher of the classical tradition, Platonic cum Aristotelian.[2] We identify the Greek world with a world of beauty because we see in it a world of art. For instance, in a late fragment, Hölderlin explains that the Greeks wanted to institute a reign of art, but failed to do so, so that what was supremely beautiful, Greece, disappeared:

Nemlich sie wollten stiften / *Ein Reich der Kunst*. Dabei ward aber / Das Vaterländische von ihnen / Versäumet und erbärmlich gieng / Das Griechenland, *das schönste*, zu Grunde.[3]

Nevertheless, a surprise awaits us that evidences a momentous shift in the understanding of art. We modern people speak of the "fine arts" in all European languages: *beaux arts, schöne Künste, belle arti, bellas artes*, изобразительное искусство, and of course *sztuki piękne*, demonstrating that art appeals immediately to the senses and that there is a strong perceived association between arts and beauty. For us, at least until a certain time that I will mention later, it was taken for granted that the goal of art should be the

2. See the texts quoted in my *Anchors in Heavens*, § 10.

3. F. Hölderlin, *Meinest Du es solle gehen...*, in: *Sämtliche Werke*, ed. F. Beissner (Stuttgart: Kohlhammer, 1951), t. 2, 228. My emphasis.

production of "things of beauty," to borrow John Keats' famous phrase, although the British romantic poet was referring to the sun, the moon, trees, and other natural phenomena and forms of life.[4] Yet beauty and art do not simply belong together as the goal and the means. They might even be in conflict. When Greek thinkers discussed the beautiful, which they often did, they seldom mentioned art as a means to create beauty.

In the *Phaedrus*, Plato saw beauty as being, among all the ideas, the most splendidly visible and worthy of being loved (εκφανεστατον και ερασμιωτατον); it sweeps us out of ourselves and brings us to another, higher dimension.[5] But Plato's opinion on art is anything but favorable. In his *Republic*, he hardly pampers poetry and painting. His Socrates expels poets from the ideal city he is sketching. He reduces poetry to a merely instrumental role and, if he supposed it could foster beauty, it would be the moral beauty of the virtuous warrior-citizen. As for painting, it is demoted to a mere way to ape things that are themselves images of true realities.[6]

Six centuries later, Plotinus, the father of what is known as Neoplatonism, wrote two treatises on beauty, I, 6 [1] and V, 8 [31]. A passage from the second treatise qualifies Plato's demotion of imitative arts by explaining that the sculptor does not copy visible reality, but rather the idea of it in his soul. Plotinus' idea of inner beauty and assumption that finding the way to true beauty requires first "an inner sight," already present in Cicero, and taken up by later authors, had a tremendous influence on Italian Renaissance artists and thinkers.[7]

The following passage is particularly revealing.

---

4. J. Keats, *Endymion* [1818], I.

5. Plato, *Phaedrus*, 250d8.

6. Plato, *Republic*, III & X.

7. Cicero, *Orator*, 2, 9; Plotinus, *Enneads*, V, 8 [31], 1, 34–40, ed. P. Henry & H.-R. Schwyzer (Paris: DDB, t. 2, 1959), 376; Macrobius, *Saturnalia*, V, 13, 23, ed. J. Willis (Leipzig: Teubner, 1963), 296; Proclus, *Commentary on the Timaeus*, II, ed. E. Diehl (Leipzig: Teubner, 1903), 265.

The soul must be trained, first of all to look at beautiful ways of life (επιτηδευματα); then at beautiful works (εργα), *not those which the arts produce* (ουχ οσα αι τεχναι εργαζονται), but the works of men who have a name for goodness.[8]

Plotinus is obviously alluding to the ladder of ascension that leads to the "beautiful" as it is presented in Plato's *Symposium*.[9] When he reaches a second rung, he is eager to remind the reader that the *ergon* he must contemplate is not the work produced by art. Later in the same treatise, Plotinus mentions sculpture, but only as a metaphor of the work we must do on ourselves to become adequate copies of the gods.

For Greek philosophers, if the beautiful was produced, this happened rather by action (*praxis*) than by production (*poiēsis*), if the distinction proposed by Aristotle can be applied in such a case. It could be argued that this view reflects the social conditions of the ancient Greek world, in which action—which by and large meant political action—was an activity of free citizens, while slaves performed the heavy physical work.

In any case, a moral meaning was associated with the "aesthetic" dimension, and even eclipsed it to the extent that *kalon* denoted "the noble" rather than "the beautiful." As a consequence, no full-fledged theory of the arts could possibly arise in this context. Several centuries later in Renaissance Italy, painters and sculptors had to salvage the dignity of their profession from the stain left on them by their alleged belonging to the "mechanical" or "servile" arts.[10]

In the Middle Ages, the "beautiful" is one of the transcendental properties of "being," at least if we are to trust Saint Bonaventure,

8. Plotinus, *Enneads*, I, 6 [1], 9, 3–5; tr. A. H. Armstrong (Cambridge, MA): Harvard University Press, 1966), 259.

9. Plato, *Symposium*, 210c (epithdeumata).

10. See, for instance, A. Blunt, *Artistic Theory in Italy 1450–1600* (Oxford: Clarendon Press, 1956), ch. 4.

who single-handedly added the beautiful to the classical list of four: being, one, true, and good.[11] For Aquinas, Bonaventure's contemporary, the beautiful is nothing more than a certain aspect of the good.[12] In brief, once again, the focus was not on art as such.

3. Ancient Israel

This "pagan" and medieval worldview was very much in keeping with the teachings of the Hebrew Bible, what we call the Old Testament. Mentioning it, let me remind you, is not a side issue to the task that was entrusted to me of speaking about Christianity. For Christianity has its roots firmly embedded in the experience the people of Israel had with God. Now, there are few references to art in the Old Testament. To be sure, the Torah mentions and praises the artists who crafted the special ceremonial vessels of the tabernacle. It even singles out two craftsmen whom the Bible calls by name, Bezaleel and Aholiab. It even says that they were "filled with the spirit of God, in wisdom, and in understanding, and in knowledge, and in all manner of workmanship" (*Exodus* 31:2–11, 35:1–2).

This passage is the first occurrence of the idea of inspiration given by some divine power and leading the recipient to artistic craftsmanship rather than to "prophecy." Interestingly, this biblical idea of divinely inspired art finds a parallel in the Greek idea of the divine inspiration, not of the prophet, but of the poet. Hesiod's narrative about the mission he claimed to have received from the Muses strikingly resembles the way the prophet Amos legitimized his own mission as assigned by the God of Israel. Both had to justify their activity as "amateurs" because they were not card-carrying members of an acknowledged professional guild of singers or prophets.[13]

11. See H. Pouillon, "La beauté, propriété transcendantale chez les Scolastiques (1220–1270)," in: *Archives d'Histoire Doctrinale et Littéraire du Moyen Age*, XV (1946), 263–329.
12. Aquinas, *Summa Theologica*, Ia, q. 5, a. 4, ad 1m. et al.
13. Hesiod, *Theogony*, 22–35 and *Amos* 6: 14–5.

Needless to say, this biblical passage, and the idea of "inspiration" in general, was heavily drawn upon by Christian artists who wanted to provide their trade with a theological foundation.

Nevertheless, the crucial utterance in the Hebrew Bible may be God's own satisfaction when constructing the world, according to the first narrative of creation in *Genesis*. On the end of each day, God looks at what He has just made and finds it "good" (טוב). On the sixth day, after the whole show has been completed, God adds that this is "very good" (טוב מאד) (*Genesis* 1:31).

It is interesting to observe that this judgement on the quality of the work completed refers precisely to a work (מלאכה) (*Genesis* 2:1–2, 3x), that is to say, something that has been wrought, brought into being, and not a fact that simply existed. I hesitated to use the word "quality," because the Hebrew adjective, for which I have kept the traditional rendering of "good," means "pleasant," "agreeable," and in many cases "beautiful". We can thus notice some closeness between the two ideas of "work" and "beauty."

In conclusion, in the ancient pre-Christian culture, the deep agreement on the fundamental goodness of whatever exists somehow places the Greek and Jewish worlds, "Athens" and "Jerusalem," side by side. This basic assumption was not challenged by the Christian revelation. Nevertheless, the Biblical tradition adds a rider: beauty can be fashioned not only by action but also by production.

4. The Christian revolution

There was great art in Christendom. This is a fact so obvious that nobody could possibly gainsay it. Yet a question should be asked: can we refer to this art as a Christian form of art? Was this a *Christian* art, properly speaking? To be sure, the bulk of the pictorial legacy of former generations is religious in nature, and specifically Christian. Scenes from the Old as well as New Testaments furnished a repertory of themes for classical painting and sculpture. But the same relationship between sacred scriptures and arts holds true for the Indian religions. Furthermore, classical China, Japan, South-East Asia, etc., produced masterpieces of art, but this art was certainly not Christian, and usually not even religious in nature.

The representative character of Christian painting mirrors the way in which God chose to address mankind, i.e., by taking a visible form. According to Paul, who incidentally never saw Jesus in the flesh, Christ is the one who makes visible the invisible Father, His image (εικων του θεου του αορατου) (*Colossians* 1:15) and, according to the anonymous author of the Epistle to the Hebrews, the effulgence (απαυγασμα) of God's glory (*Hebrews* 1:3). In the Fourth Gospel, Jesus said, "who saw me saw the Father" (*John* 14:9). The theologians who legitimized the use of icons drew heavily upon this argument.

Nevertheless, for Christianity, the "beautiful" is paradoxical in nature. It reaches its peak in Jesus' sacrifice on the Cross, hardly a beautiful spectacle. The crucified Christ suffered the punishment reserved for slaves, was whipped, ridiculed, and tortured. He was ugly, with not even a whiff of sublimity, and he was ridiculous, the summit of horror and scandal.

Furthermore, the model on which the narrative of the Passion was told, and perhaps even on which Jesus consciously molded himself, the Suffering Servant of the Deutero-Isaiah, is explicitly said to lack beauty and glamour (53:2) (לא תאר לו ולא הדר). The Septuagint rendered the second part of the same verse as "no beauty, that we should desire him" based on a reading (לא מראה), by the Greek concepts of ειδος and καλλος, which are heavily loaded terms for philosophers.

The German literary scholar Erich Auerbach (1892—1957), a Jew who taught comparative literature of the Romance languages at Yale, had a fascinating thesis on the origin of European literature.

He argued that literary realism, a tradition pervading the whole history of this literature, was not possible in ancient times. What he meant by "realism" is the sober description of the human condition and real world in all its dimensions. In the ancient world, a strict division of labor obtained. Two styles, two stylistic levels, divided the realm of narration. The stories of gods and heroes were told in the sublime style of epic and tragedy, whereas stories related to the lower class and the slaves were told in the vulgar style of comedy.

Christianity, specifically the central event narrated in the Gospels, pierced the border between the noble and the base. The Passion of Christ, a particularly base event, was related in a lofty, sublime style.

Doch nicht nur die Intensität des Persönlichen, sondern auch seine Mannigfaltigkeit und den Reichtum seiner Erscheinungswesen erschließt die Geschichte Christi, indem sie die Grenzen der antiken mimetischen Ästhetik überschreitet. Hier hat der Mensch keine irdische Würde mehr; es darf ihm alles geschehen, und die antikische Spaltung der Gattungen, die Scheidung zwischen dem erhabenen und dem niederen Stil existiert nicht mehr.[14]

Before Auerbach, another German, the philosopher and disciple of Hegel Karl Rosenkranz, published a work in 1853 whose paradoxical title adequately captured the author's intention: *Aesthetic of Ugliness*. In it, he wrote:

Mit der christlichen Religion aber als der, welche das Böse in seiner Wurzel erkennen und von Grund aus überwinden lehrt, ist das Häßliche nun vollends in die Welt der Kunst eingeführt.[15]

---

14. E. Auerbach, *Dante als Dichter der irdischen Welt* (Berlin: de Gruyter, 1929), 22. See also *Mimesis. Dargestellte Wirklichkeit in der abendländischen Literatur* (Bern: Francke, 1946), 43–52, 73–4.

15. K. Rosenkranz, *Ästhetik des Häßlichen* [1853] (Darmstadt: Wissenschaftliche Buchgesellschaft, 1983), 39.

5. Islam as counterproof

According to Islamic dogma, in principle, making images of any living being whatsoever is forbidden. This practice follows, to some extent, the prohibition in the Hebrew Bible, which forbade what it called "idolatry," the cult of images and consequently their production (Exod. 20, 4 and Deut. 4, 15–18). The Islamic objection to figurative representations is not explicitly mentioned in the Qur'an, but in some utterances ascribed to the Prophet Muhammad (see the corpus of *hadith,* reports about what Muhammad said and did).[16] The Islamic resistance to the representation of living beings stems from the prohibition of idolatry and from the belief that the creation of living forms is unique to God, which is why images and image makers have been controversial. The strongest statements on representational depiction were made in the *hadith*, where painters were challenged to "breathe life" into their creations and threatened with punishment on the Day of Judgment.

Islamic aniconism meant that, unlike in other parts of the world, no painting could develop, except the early Omeyyad period when the prohibition was not yet fully implemented or, more likely, when the *hadith* that forbade it had not yet been forged. On the other hand, miniature paintings became a significant genre that achieved exquisite refinement, mainly in Persia. But this consisted for the most part in illustrating literary narratives, such as Firdawsi's *Shah Nameh*. In compensation, Islam developed the art of calligraphy. To be precise, the art of beautiful writing had been known in China for centuries but used Chinese ideograms. Islamic calligraphy exploited the Arabic alphabet's inherent potential for writing as ornament.

Moreover, decoration with floral motives was quite common, as were geometric figures that didn't represent any definite object.

16. Hadith, for instance in *Sunan Ibn Majah*, XII, 5, no. 2151.

The philosopher Kant chose non-figurative art as the best example of what he called *pulchritudo vaga*, "free or floating beauty,"
in contradistinction to the *pulchritudo adhaerens* of figurative art.[17]
Interestingly, the typical form of Islamic art, whose name be-
trays its origin, the arabesque has become a favorite metaphor in
Christendom for the modern work of art that no longer must represent a concrete object. As for the word "arabesque," it may have been
first used as a book title by the painter Giovanni Paolo Lomazzo,
a so-called Mannerist, who penned a collection of pieces in the
Milanese vernacular and had it printed in 1589 under the title of
Rabisch.

In the first half of the nineteenth century, the word "arabesque"
became a favorite title in Romantic literature all over the Western
world, in Russia with Nikolaï Gogol (1835), and in the United
States with Edgar Allan Poe (1840). Similarly, this word was borrowed by classical musicians, again all over Europe, such as Robert
Schumann, Franz Liszt, and later Claude Debussy.

The theoretical use of the word had to await Friedrich Schlegel,
who wrote:

die Arabeske ist die älteste und ursprüngliche Form der menschlichen
Phantasie. [...] Ich halte die Arabeske für eine ganz bestimmte und wesen-
tliche Form oder Äußerungsart der Poesie.[18]

Both sentences are found in his *Dialogue on Poetry*, which to some
extent mirrors discussions held by male and female persons active in
intellectual walks of life: the philosopher Schelling, the theologian
Schleiermacher, the two Schlegel brothers. The first sentence is put
into the mouth of Ludoviko (most likely denoting Schelling) in a
"Speech on Mythology;" the second belongs to a "Speech on the
Novel" given by Antonio. (More on Schlegel below.) Two genera-

17. I. Kant, *Kritik der Urteilskraft*, §16.
18. F. Schlegel, Gespräch über die Poesie, in: *Schriften zur Literatur*, ed. W. Rasch (München:
dtv, 1972), 305 and 313.

tions later, Baudelaire, probably the most important and influential French poet of all time, followed suit, calling arabesque "the most spiritualist kind of drawing."[19]

6. Late modern times: art without beauty

Until the late modern period, beauty was assumed to be the supreme purpose of art and even synonymous with artistic excellence. With the early German Romanticism of the Jena period, what had been considered obvious for centuries, hence requiring no explicit mention, was challenged. A significant shift, and the reverse of what had happened earlier, took place in the understanding and evaluation of aesthetic values. The Greek philosophical inquiry into art and beauty, specifically Plato's approach, treated these two categories as independent, and spoke of beauty without associating it with art. Art, mostly denoting poetry, is closer to a greatest danger than any other phenomenon Plato mentioned, while beauty is closer to a greatest good. A new separation occurred, the same as in ancient thought, but in the opposite direction. Whereas Greek philosophy in the Platonic tradition had beauty without art, modernity has art without beauty.

Friedrich Schlegel took a momentous step at the end of the 18th century: he maintained that the proper object of art is no longer the "beautiful" but the "interesting."

Das Schöne ist […] nicht das Ideal der modernen Poesie und von dem Interessanten wesentlich verschieden.[20]

Here Schlegel was following Kant's proclamation of the autonomy of the "beautiful," the object of art no longer seen as a means:

19. See my *L'image vagabonde. Essai sur l'imaginaire baudelairien* (Chatou: La Transparence, 2008), 112–3. See also "Arabeske", in K. Barck, M. Fontius, W. Thierse (ed.), *Ästhetische Grundbegriffe. Studien zu einem historischen Wörterbuch* (Berlin: Akademie-Verlag, 1990), t. I, p. 272–86 [*non vidi*].

20. F. Schlegel, *Über das Studium der griechischen Poesie*, Vorrede [1797] in: *Schriften zur Literatur*, loc.cit., 89.

it pleases us as an end in itself, thus the aesthetic state is pleasure "without interest." The interesting can become the basic object of art precisely because Kant has freed the sentiment of the beautiful from its link with interest by defining it as "satisfaction without any interest" (*interesselose Wohlgefallen*).[21] He thereby made possible what I could call a "disinterested interest."

To be sure, what ignites our interest can be beautiful, but this is not a *conditio sine qua non*. The grotesque, the shocking, the monstrous, etc., can be as interesting as the beautiful, and perhaps even more so. Schlegel mentioned "the new, the piquant (*Pikant*), the striking (*Frappant*)."[22] The French poet Victor Hugo, in the preface to his verse play *Cromwell* (1827), explained this in a bombastic style, although he preferred to speak of the grotesque as the main aesthetic category he represented.[23]

What decides whether a production is a work of art is the reaction (not necessarily an active decision) of the viewer, reader, listener, etc. It is the impact on the audience, the audience's response that determines a work's aesthetic value. Art is yoked to subjectivity.

This leads to a bevy of consequences. First, the work produced must be able to arouse the subject's interest, thus being shocking in some way.

The artist's personality becomes more decisive than the works that he produces. The artist is swept into a whirlwind of concurring attempts to attract the subject's attention. This may be the case even when the "artist" must play the fool in order to be considered an artist, more precisely to lead the life of an artist. An artist without any work is no longer a contradiction. What really matters is that the would-be artist leads a bohemian lifestyle.

Beauty may even be banned from the realm of art and with it

21. I. Kant, *Kritik der Urteilskraft*, §2.
22. F. Schlegel, *Über das Studium…*, 100.
23. V. Hugo, Préface de *Cromwell* [1827], in V. Hugo, *Théâtre* (Paris: Hetzel, 1858).

what was commonly held, during the classical era, to be the highest example of beauty, i.e., the human body. Accordingly, whatever is human will be expelled, unless it is presented as a caricature, stylized, or even distorted. In an essay, originally published in 1925, the Spanish philosopher and essayist José Ortega y Gasset referred most literally to the absence of human forms in nonrepresentational art using the expression "the dehumanization of art."[24]

Beauty as such can be tolerated in so far as it enters the realm of technology. The name art takes when it accepts the yoke of technology is "design." A Frenchman who made his whole career in the United States, Raymond Loewy published in 1951 a book titled *Never Leave Well Enough Alone*. The French translation has, in my opinion, a more interesting title: *La laideur se vend mal* (Ugliness sells badly).

7. The end of art and Christianity

A first question to be asked is whether art still has a meaning in the modern period, regardless of the Christian, non-Christian, or post-Christian character of this period. A powerful voice answered in the negative. I mean the German philosopher Hegel with his famous thesis about the past character of art. Hegel reflected on art in a series of lecture-courses that he called Aesthetics. Notably, the term "aesthetics" derives directly from the Greek word for "sensory perception," αισθησις. But at the time its use in German was still recent; it was the German philosopher Baumgarten who coined the term "aesthetics" and established this discipline as a distinct field of philosophical inquiry denoting the general theory of sensory knowledge rather than a theory of art.[25] Hegel himself confessed that he would have preferred the word "callistic," meaning "theory

---

24. J. Ortega y Gasset, *La deshumanizacion del arte*, in: *Obras Completas* (Madrid: Revista de Occidente, 1950), t. 3, 353–86.

25. A. Baumgarten, *Meditationes philosophicae de nonnullis ad poema pertinentibus*, Halle, 1735.

of the beautiful." But his object was not the beautiful in the whole breadth of its manifestations, in nature for instance, but the beautiful in art.

Anyway, in the following passage, Hegel observed that, in its highest vocation and the highest form of consciousness of the truth, art is and remains for us a thing of the past:

Die Kunst ist nach der Seite ihrer höchsten Bestimmung für uns ein Vergangenes. Damit hat sie für uns auch die echte Wahrheit und Lebendigkeit verloren und ist mehr in unsere *Vorstellung* verlegt, als dass sie in der Wirklichkeit ihre frühere Notwendigkeit behauptete und ihren höheren Platz einnähme. Was durch Kunstwerke jetzt in uns erregt wird, ist ausser dem unmittelbaren Genuß zugleich unser Urteil [...].

Hegel clearly understood that this relative demotion of art's significance was the result of Christian faith:

Eine tiefere Fassung der Wahrheit, in welcher sie nicht mehr dem Sinnlichen so verwandt und freundlich ist, um von diesem Material in angemessener Weise aufgenommen und ausgedrückt werden zu können. Von solcher Art ist die christliche Auffassung der Wahrheit, und vor allem erscheint der Geist unserer heutigen Welt, oder näher unserer Religion und unserer Vernunftbildung, als über die Stufe hinaus, auf welcher die Kunst die höchste Weise ausmacht, sich des Absoluten bewußt zu sein.[26]

Art is not the highest way for modern man to enact truth. Martin Heidegger devoted a lengthy and deep article to the question of the work of art and its origin. The words "beauty" and "beautiful" are not in the center; what has this place is instead truth. In the version published in 1950, we must content ourselves with the short sentence, "*Schönheit ist eine Weise, wie Wahrheit west.*"[27] In the 1935 edition, those words are simply absent. But the focus is on art as "*ins-Werk-setzen der Wahrheit*," putting truth to work.

<hr>

26. G. W. F. Hegel, *Ästhetik*, ed. F. Bassenge (Frankfurt: Europäische Verlagsanstalt, 1955), t. 1, p. 22, then p. 21.

27. M. Heidegger, *Der Ursprung des Kunstwerks*, in: *Holzwege* (Frankfurt: Klostermann, 1950), 44; see also the Postface, 67–8.

Although the concept of truth may remain, to some extent, somewhat related to the concept of beauty, it has been separated from what is perceived as good: aesthetic values are independent of moral values; there is no moral dimension to art. A purposeless, aimless art becomes possible, the expression "art for art's sake" (*l'art pour l'art*) becomes possible. It illustrates that art is divorced from any utilitarian function, including moral and didactic functions. Art can't possibly be a window opening on transcendence. What is left receives the moniker of "culture."

In Thomas Mann's *Doktor Faustus*, a conversation takes place between the central character of the novel, the composer Adrian Leverkühn and … the Devil in person. The latter says of the separation between Kultur and Kultus, culture and cult:

Seit die Kultur vom Kultus abgefallen ist und aus sich selber einen gemacht hat, ist sie denn auch nicht anderes mehr als ein Abfall, und alle Welt ist ihrer nach bloßen fünfhundert Jahren so müd und satt, als wenn sie's, salva venia, mit eisernen Kochkesseln gefressen hätt […].[28]

8. Our present situation: art

We can hardly answer a question about art and the modern world without first defining "modernity" and examining how and the extent to which it affects our society and life. This is a tall order since the whirlwind of modernity draws all of human life into itself. I tried to do that elsewhere and need not repeat what was the topic of several books already.

In the present time, a time in which we can't help living, we must evaluate what in art is positive and negative for Christianity. On the one hand, art has lost its relationship to beauty for roughly two centuries. More generally, it has lost its possible relationship with the metaphysical dimension of reality. We saw that the fundamental object of artistic production was the interesting. Now, the

---

28. T. Mann, *Doktor Faustus*, XXV (Frankfurt: Fischer, 2003), 325.

interesting can't possibly be convertible with the other transcendental properties of being any longer. We can say that everything is one, true, good, etc. But we can scarcely say that anything whatsoever is interesting.

For we experience the opposite: the boring. And there are plenty of boring things. Rather, nothing is boring in itself, but we experience boredom, which is the flip side of our reducing the beautiful to subjectivity, to what we find interesting. The boring is the interesting that no longer arouses our interest, in the same way as the disgusting is what used to tickle our palate when we are no longer hungry.

At the beginning of the 19th century, more precisely between the Congress of Vienna and the revolutions of 1848, i.e., during the era of monarchic Restorations, the German *Vormärz*, for literary historians the Late Romantic period, we find all over Europe thinkers who gave the experience of boredom a literary or philosophical expression. Among writers and poets, let us mention Lord Byron on boredom, Alfred de Musset on *ennui*, Pushkin on *скука*, Leopardi on *noia*.[29] Among philosophers, Schopenhauer described human life as alternating between boredom (*Langeweile*) and pain; Kierkegaard meditated on *kedsomhed*.[30] This I can only mention *en passant*.

To stave off boredom, artists must change styles and subjects as quickly as possible, resulting in an unquenchable thirst for originality. The received definition of art was even enlarged to introduce into it practices that had, until then, hardly anything to do with art. The trouble is that, as Leopardi saw, the very variety in change produces boredom:

29. A. de Musset, *Confessions d'un enfant du siècle* (1836); A. Pushkin, *Evgeny Onegin* (1831); G. Leopardi, *Zibaldone*, passim.

30. A. Schopenhauer, *Die Welt als Wille und Vorstellung* (1818); S. Kierkegaard, *La Culture alternée*, in: *L'Alternative* [1843], French translation by P.-H. Tisseau and E.-M. Tisseau (Paris: L'Orante, 1970), t. 1, 267.

la continuità è così amica della noia che anche la continuità della stessa varietà annoia sommamente.[31]

I certainly can't demonstrate this by the methods of the history of ideas, yet it is my hunch that this overall experience of boredom is, a generation later, the consequence, the price to be paid, or perhaps the punishment for the reduction of the beautiful to the interesting in its various forms.

9. Our present situation: beauty

Beauty as such doesn't fare better in the other realm, i.e., in nature. The two uncrowned kings of late modernity, Arthur Schopenhauer and Charles Darwin, debunked natural beauty. Both contended, each in his own style, that beauty is in the service of reproduction and hence the will to live. This will does not consider the happiness of the individual, but its only aim is the survival of the species. This is Schopenhauer's thesis in his "metaphysics of sexual love." In his exposition of the theory of natural selection, Darwin maintained that, for instance, the bright colors of flowers are traps for insects that will be drawn to them, carry pollen from flower to flower, and ensure the reproduction of the species. Psychologists have shown through experimental research that we consider beautiful the faces of persons whose features suggest their ability to ensure the healthy reproduction of our genes or the protection of our offspring.[32]

Now, our current social and cultural context could be a chance for Christianity and thus may, if not foster, at least enable a renewal of Christian art. The temptation to idolize beauty has vanished. A sort of "religion of art" was dreamt of all over Europe in the late 19th century among some circles of refined aesthetes. Today, some people keep attributing to Dostoevsky the sentence "Beauty will

31. G. Leopardi, *Zibaldone*, 51, ed. L. Felici (Rome: Newton Compton, 2007), 35b.
32. Synthesis and critique in A. Nehamas, *Only a Promise of Happiness. The Place of Beauty in a World of Art* (Princeton & Oxford: Princeton University Press, 2007), 63–71.

save the world" (мир спасет красота). Those obscure words, which neither the author nor his character ever pronounce, are in fact ascribed to Prince Myshkin, the highly ambiguous central character of *The Idiot,* by the young nihilist Ippolít Teréntyev, who will end up committing suicide.[33] In any case, we should not take the Russian novelist for a prophet, let alone for a Church father, and handle this hackneyed quote with the utmost care.

These days, a religion of art is hardly thinkable. This doesn't mean that the temptation of idolatry has definitely been rebuffed. The famous sixteenth-century Protestant Reformer Jean Calvin put his finger on the sore point when he said that the human mind has always been a factory (*boutique*) of idols.[34] In fact, other idols have replaced what was once valued in art. And I'm afraid they may prove far more cruel and dangerous.

On the other hand, for Christians at least, art can develop itself as instrumental to revelation. Art must accept some humility, an ancillary function. This is exactly what it did during past centuries, by the way. There was no such thing as an "artist," a character invented in the Renaissance. There were craftsmen who did their job as well as possible and did not consider themselves entrusted with any sacred mission. They aimed to help the prayer of the faithful, which was the heart of the matter.

The leading metaphor could be an *objet d'art*, the monstrance. In this object, the rich splendor of the material and the delicacy of the ornaments wrought in valuable metal and precious stones don't have any other function than concentrating the onlooker's gaze on the small colorless host, thereby enabling Eucharistic contemplation.

---

33. F. Dostoevsky, *Идиот* [1868], III, v, in: *Complete Works in 15 volumes* (Leningrad: Nauka, 1989), t. 6, 382–3.

34. J. Calvin, *Institution de la religion chrétienne*, ed. F. Baumgartner (Genève: Beroud, 1888), vol. 1, ix, 8, 50a.

10. In conclusion: back to the problem
of the transcendental

In this essay, I mentioned the concept of the "transcendental" twice. First, I briefly recalled a classical doctrine: the medieval system of the main properties that run across the categories that divide Being. The "beautiful" was either one of the transcendental properties of "being," on the same footing as the other four, or a derived aspect of the "good" or the "true." I then observed that the "interesting," the central concept of modern aesthetics, doesn't belong among those transcendental properties. The trouble is that the older, more basic assumption, common to Greek and Biblical thought, on the fundamental goodness of being, is now facing a challenge. I have argued that renewing Christian art, retrieving both the sacred in art and art *tout court* would only be possible by rediscovering the transcendental aspect of art. Re-evaluating the "beautiful" and re-establishing the close relationship between beauty and art as conceived in the past would certainly be a fascinating and perhaps enjoyable task, yet not the best starting point. I contend that we should first reclaim the concepts of "true" and "good" as essential properties of "being."

My brief analysis has aimed to demonstrate that the problem of the relevance of art in Christianity today, if there is such a problem, is not to be solved at the level of art itself. No doubt art will continue to exist and, for better or worse, artists will continue to produce works of art. Would-be artists will certainly keep trying too hard to seduce the public and sell their works to the public, whatever they may be. Accomplished artists will continue to express their great abilities in their work and modestly ply their trade. But they will (whether or not they are realize it) need the support of the metaphysical dimension of art, which can be achieved by reasserting the transcendental characteristics of "being," "true," and "good." To accomplish this theoretical and practical task, we need philosophers and saints rather than artists. We have been blessed to witness these two categories combined in extraordinary ways in one person, Pope John Paul II. Therefore, I feel honored indeed to have had the opportunity to contribute to this volume, based on the JP2 Lectures held in Rome, and dedicated to his memory and work.

RÉMI BRAGUE—born in Paris, France, in 1947. Professor emeritus of philosophy at the Université Paris I Panthéon-Sorbonne and former Romano Guardini Chair of Philosophy at the Ludwig-Maximilians-Universität München. Renowned scholar of classical and medieval philosophy, culture, and philosophy of religion. In 2012 he received the Ratzinger Prize. His publications include: *Europe, la voie romaine* (1992); *La Sagesse du monde. Histoire de l'expérience humaine de l'univers* (1999); *La Loi de Dieu. Histoire philosophique d'une alliance* (2005); *Le Règne de l'homme: Genèse et échec du projet moderne* (2015).

RENATO CRISTIN

FORMAL EUROPE AND VITAL EUROPE: TRADITION AS GROUND OF IDENTITY

Many centuries ago and for a very long period, Europe was divided between an *actual or real Europe* and an *ideal Europe*: on the one hand, it was the Europe of empires, kingdoms, nations, principalities, and dynasties, in constant conflict with each other or at most in an "equilibrium" that was an ephemeral pause between wars; on the other hand, it was a united and peaceful Europe as conceived by seminal thinkers (including political exponents like Charlemagne) who looked beyond material contingencies and political needs, to reveal a potential, deeper sphere in which Europe essentially shows the spirit, the culture, in a word, the European soul. In this way the original foundation of Europe would come to light, the European spirit hidden by contingent interests but always alive and active.

In real Europe, this spirit was subordinated to national or personal needs, which placed it in a sort of oblivion. The Europe of reality—institutional and political—hid an impalpable Europe because it was spiritual, but concrete both because it represented a project, a vision in great style, and because it expressed a sense of tradition. It was not just a bizarre dream, but the vision of a possibility, which was opposed to reality but not totally opposed.

The expression *ideal Europe* does not indicate an imagined entity but rather a *potential* Europe, that is to say, a Europe that has not yet been realized but is possible. If, as Scholasticism taught, essence truly precedes the thing itself, then the possibility is, according to Heidegger, higher than actuality. The *ideal Europe* is therefore not unreal but potential, and a potential Europe would represent the higher degree of European being, the higher level of Europeanness. This ideal Europe was supported by a tension of the soul but it was not an abstraction, an imaginary place, a fiction of the mind. It was an aspiration founded on the peculiar concreteness of the spirit.

Among the multiple forms that have modeled this ideal or potential Europe, the religious tradition stands out for its intensity and pervasiveness, as it determined Europe before its political articulation and accompanied its social construction. This tradition, deeply intertwined with the political power of the various national states amd their dynasties, and despite the fact that religious wars were commonly waged in Europe, has at times exercised a unifying function and more frequently a function of defense not only of European identity in the abstract, but of Europe in its concrete territories, and on some occasions it has also exercised this function by opposing the fratricidal struggles that for centuries have divided the states and torn the continent apart.

An extraordinary example of this function dates back to 1683. On September 11 of that year, a decisive battle for the fate of Europe took place to defend Vienna as it was under siege from the Ottoman army. The Ottomans were defeated by a coalition led by the King of Poland Jan III Sobieski, set up at the behest of the Vatican, and animated by an Italian Capuchin friar, Marco of Aviano, who stirred up the enthusiasm of the Christian soldiers with his fiery preaching.

What happened on the Kahlenberg and on the plain around

Vienna that September 11 was not simply a war; it exemplifies a political and metaphysical event that enabled the power of the spirit to unite Europeans in fighting together against a lethal threat. It is not by chance that in 2003 Marco of Aviano was declared blessed by another great defender of the European spirit, Pope John Paul II, who, in doing so, clearly intended to reaffirm the power of faith and liberty and to corroborate the successful alliance between Poland and Christianity that saved Europe in 1683. It is therefore also in these underground intertwinings where the deep sense of European identity and tradition flows, which, beside the religious dimension, consists of a common ancient cultural heritage that is constantly renewed.

Today the conflict between a real Europe and an ideal Europe is different. While there have been a few intra-European armed conflicts in the last seventy years, such as those in the former Yugoslavia and the Balkans, or more recently on the border between Ukraine and Russia, they have been limited although painful. Other rifts, however, have emerged in the last century.

In the twentieth century, after the gigantic lacerations caused by the two world wars, yet another destructive result of a conflict between states that was also exacerbated by the toxic action of ideologies and savage nationalisms, and after the defeat of National Socialism, which posed a mortal danger to the European soul, Europe was divided into a free Europe and a totalitarian Europe, a division that forced more than one-third of Europeans into a sort of large Sovietic prison.

For almost fifty years after 1945, Europe was cut in two by the Iron Curtain, a hateful border splitting the European peoples who, despite their differences, particularisms, nationalisms, and even wars, for the most part wanted to live together freely and peacefully, an overwhelming majority of whom, both in the West and in the East, rejected the Communist ideology because they understood its dictatorial and criminal essence, because the East was unfortunately experiencing it.

The rift here showed a *normal Europe* (the western part, liberal-democratic) and *a dystopian Europe* (the eastern part, subdued by communist tyranny). In the first area, from the point of view of freedoms and respect for personal rights, people found a relative coincidence between their historical conscience and national political and administrative institutions; in the second, that is, in the part of the continent under the communist influence, the people were crushed, detached from their historical identity and traditions, primarily from the Jewish-Christian religious one.

During the Cold war, the "Church of silence" (an expression representing a paradox for the Christian and Jewish traditions, which teach that the truth will make humankind free) was a practice employed in Communist countries, whose leaders wanted to remove religion from the sphere of government and from the conscience of people. By eliminating the religious tradition, Marxist-Leninist ideology intended to disable the continuity of the European historical-cultural tradition, in favor of new values and a completely different world. Communist ideology also attempted to create a new type of man: the "homo sovieticus," who produced misery and destruction and caused the death of more than one hundred million people. This same type of man conceived the Gulag camps; they are, therefore, not different from the Nazis who conceived the concentration camp.

Even that division, a relatively short one from a macro-historical point of view, has been overcome with the decisive contribution of Pope John Paul II, who in my view can be seen as the Marco of Aviano of the twentieth century: the former saved Europe from Islamic invasion, the latter saved the continent from the communist plague. There are several obvious differences between these two figures, namely that every effort made by St. John Paul II marked a whole era at once, that the Communist armies were incomparably stronger than those like the army besieging Vienna in 1683, that John Paul II had powerful and loyal allies such as Ronald Reagan and Helmut Kohl, and above all that he was a great man of faith as well as a great theologian, philosopher, and political and moral personality who deeply shaped the last quarter of the twentieth century.

The reunification of the two halves of Europe—the most emotionally effective symbolic image is the demolition of the Berlin Wall and the consequent German reunification—was a milestone in the long itinerary of struggle against Communist totalitarianism and inaugurated a long process of intra-European reconciliation. From then on, it seemed that the dream of a united Europe could become a reality, the new European reality, one that could finally reconcile not only the division between the free Europe and the Europe that was a victim of communism, but also the gap between the real and ideal Europes. The pioneering work by Adenauer, Schuman, and De Gasperi, the pioneers of unification and major contributors to European unity, seemed likely to bear fruit: European integration of peoples and collaboration between nations.

Since a united Europe is a dream of more than a millennium, the need for integration is therefore not, in itself, a slogan of the bureaucracy or of the Europeanist ideology, but derives from an identity that precedes any ideology and which is irrepressible *despite* bureaucracy and ideology. Conceived in this way, integration would not be negative—quite the contrary, it would be a way of achieving an underlying identity and a purpose on the horizon.

Since 1990, there has been a great acceleration in the integration of European states, which has brought important achievements from an institutional perspective but which has, unfortunately, not involved the spiritual sphere except in an occasional, external, and extemporaneous form. These engineering results, although valuable in terms of organizational and operational levels, have not yet been able to connect with the tradition, spiritual dimension, and onto-logical ground of our civilization.

As a consequence, a new, third rift has appeared: the split be-tween what I call a *formal Europe*, the Europe of institutions, and a *vital Europe*, the Europe of life. This latter is not an imaginary Europe: it is much more real than Brussel's Europe. It is the Europe of real peoples, nations, their traditions and history. This gap sep-arates the political-bureaucratic class and the citizens, who, often unconsciously, are the real heirs of a long-standing European tradi-tion. Until this gap is bridged, it will continue to produce suffering and restlessness. European citizens long for a vital Europe and feel dissatisfied with the formal Europe and the current institutional situation. We can look at this pain or not, we can hear its lament or not, but the reality remains present, and it is incontrovertible: Europe is *tragic* today because it is traversed by pain and torn in its soul; and Europeans are, more or less consciously but mostly silent-ly, suffering from this laceration.

The current gap between European institutional actors and cit-izens is deepening and may never stop widening. Nations should care for their own citizens first. National governments should act as shock absorbers against tensions and protect Europeans despite all their cultural differences. Nations can protect their respective peoples and, consequently, the peoples of Europe in their plurality and their union. The dichotomy between a formal, legal, or institu-tional Europe and a vital Europe, which reflects the tradition and common history shared by its citizens, is dramatic and concerning.

Those centralistic and tendentially autocratic institutions, how-ever, wanted to weaken the nations, depriving them of many of their traditional prerogatives, attacking and delegitimizing the very idea of nations, so that nations can no longer fulfill their natural function, while the fracture between the Euroinstitutions and the people is increasing and may become irremediable. The portrait of the present time reveals to us a dichotomy between a formal, purely institutional Europe and a vital Europe that directly expresses the history and existence of its peoples.

And since peoples are made up of citizens, and since citizens today are people aware of their political rights, institutional Europe must initiate a great process of self-criticism and be in direct and close connection with citizens and their nations. Indeed, if action is not taken immediately and decisively, the fracture is destined to widen, causing further disorientation in Europeans, with two consequences, both catastrophic: on the one hand, the definitive entrenchment of institutional Europe in the bureaucratic and political ivory tower; on the other hand, the overreaction of the peoples who will reject Europe as a political entity and take refuge in nationalistic excesses.

And it is precisely to avoid these two outcomes that we must recover *a new European thought* that abandons the path of postmodern technocratic positivism. This way of thinking rejects the rhetoric of Europeanism with which the Eurobureaucracy tries to deceive the peoples, and also restoress the nations as individual homelands belonging to the greater *European homeland*, enhancing their spirits without falling into nationalism.

Only in this way can the sense of belonging to Europe be resurrected in the conscience of its citizens, and only in this way can the identity of Europe as a union of the identity of its peoples be preserved and strengthened. A united Europe is an ancient dream that must not, however, become a contemporary nightmare. It is a noble dream that must materialize in an equally noble reality, in order *to keep up with both tradition and the challenges of the current age.*

Today, after the integration process that led to the construction of the European Union (EU), the continent continues to be divided by a less visible but no less concrete gulf that *separates consciousness from function*: on the one hand, the consciousness of being European, and on the other hand the function of governing the Europeans. In the conscience of Europeans there is Europe, but not the administrative systems of the EU.

Let me explain: the institutional order of the EU is a necessary step toward better integration among Europeans, and is a useful tool for regulating important economic issues, but it is equally necessary and useful for Europeans to feel those institutions are their own, and for this purpose neither demagogy (empty Europeanist rhetoric) nor imposition (the maniacal regulatory network that catalogs and harnesses every aspect of its citizens' lives) is needed. What is needed instead is empathy and reflection, awareness of identity, and revitalization of tradition. Formal Europe is in fact distant from the sentiment of citizens because it is distant from their identity, which is not expressed by the European passport or by the right to vote in elections for the European Parliament, but is contained in the symbols and practices of tradition, in the sedimented consciousness that is culture, understood not as erudition but as existence and historical experience.

The EU has replaced *the sense* of being European with *the pragmatics* of administration, which has become the dominant form of institutional, social, and civil relations and even invades personal ones. Bureaucratization is the most evident reality of the European institutions, but it is also the negation of the European soul. Of course, the state administration also arose from this same soul structure, but the bureaucratic mentality is a deformation that spread with the twentieth century, with the affirmation of both totalitarianism (Communist and Nazi) and statism in liberal democracies as a pathological hypertrophy of management and control.

Today, bureaucratic European policies even try to invade the citizens' consciences, but the bureaucratization of consciences is an oxymoron and therefore an impossible undertaking. Conscience cannot be reduced to administrative management, so it will always remain a territory that is not completely conquerable. And so the fracture I am talking about is produced, and although they are not fully aware of it, Europeans feel this fracture painfully.

Formal Europe and vital Europe are two opposing entities: we could say that the first is factually the *legal representative* of our continent, of which it is the institutional and official face, but legal Europe is only the simulacrum of the vital, spiritual one, which contains and preserves the living tradition of the continent itself, and which is crushed or even disintegrated by legal Europe. And since tradition is not only a force behind it, which brings energy from the past to the present, it also enables the future, that is, a power that allows us to plan. To neutralize or paralyze it means limiting the potential of the future; it means asphyxiating the life project of the entire community of destiny that is Europe.

Europe, Romano Guardini said in 1946, will have to be Christian, or it will never exist again, because if it abandons its founding nucleus, "what still remains of it does not have much more to mean." Europe "is a living entelechy, an active spiritual figure," Guardini continues, and since its religious core is Christianity, without Christianity it will not exist or will become something else.[1] At the end of the eighteenth century, Novalis similarly linked the identities of Christianity and Europe. Now, in the wake of Pope John Paul II and the movement to mention European religious tradition in the Treaty for the European Constitution, I speak of *Jewish-Christian roots*, of the Judeo-Christian tradition. But the meaning of the discourse remains the same: detached from its cultural and religious tradition, an institutional structure withers, and can survive only as an inanimate form, as a pure technical construct.

---

1. Cf. R. Guardini, *Damit Europa werde. Wirklichkeit und Aufgabe eines zusammenwachsenden Kontinents* (Mainz: Matthias Grünewald, 2003).

This Treaty, signed in 2004, is an excellent example of the almost pathological dissociation between the two Europes. It was from the beginning an anomalous constitutional text; in fact, there was no concrete nation (and state) to which this Carta was to refer. It was not just a political deficiency, but also an institutional shortcoming, a separation between citizens and institutions, a failure to involve society in political decisions and, therefore, did not develop the essential prerequisite for the creation of a constitution: the popular will.

A constitution must in fact be rooted in the tradition of a people and in the history of a nation, because a constitution (as a *politeia* and as a fundamental charter) is an expression of the historical and ontological identity of a people, as in the first words of the Constitution of the United States of America, "We the People." But to clear the field of a possible misunderstanding, I specify that my theory (and therefore my use of the concept of people) has absolutely nothing to do with populism, which I consider a negative ideology, which flatters the people, deceives and uses it for purposes that are alien to their material historical and spiritual interests.

Therefore, if a constitution is drawn up starting from a break with the tradition of a people, as happened in the twentieth century with the constitutions of many countries after their fall into the Soviet sphere of influence, that constitution, even if legally sanctioned by a legislative body, will be illegitimate in terms of the spirit of the people, that is, in terms of history and national identity.

Ignoring or fighting this identity means doing violence to the history and sovereignty of a people. Sovereignty is a concept that can be defined according to perspectives and convenience, and therefore it is ambiguous, which risks leading to nationalism (such as the German idea of *Grossraum* for which the Nazis invaded half the continent) or, paradoxically, even in communism (in fact, think of the sovereign rhetoric with which communist ideology

has subjugated Cuba), If you combine it with the idea of a constitution, however, if you think of it in foundational terms of constitutional respect for the identity of a nation, without thereby losing
respect for the identity of the others, then *constitutional sovereignty*
becomes a good premise for developing a national identity in the
context of European integration.

What I call constitutional sovereignty differs from the "constitutional patriotism" theorized by Jürgen Habermas, which marginalizes the idea of a nation in favor of an idea of a superstructural
homeland: if, Habermas says, the conception of the people as a cultural identity (and, to some extent, an ethic identity) is pre-political,
it must be reshaped to more of an exclusively political and therefore
also multicultural vision of a homeland. What this and similar theories overlook is not only the concept of a people but also that of a
nation (and its sovereignty), which would be absorbed by a universalism that makes the concept of identity meaningless and formal-
izes the idea of a constitution. This is exactly what happened when
the anomalous majority formed of the European People's Party and
the European Socialist Party drafted the Treaty for the European
Constitution: the formalism of the rules crushed the vitality of the
people; *institutional supranationalism* seeks to cancel *national sovereignties*.

Much could be said to refute the validity of the supranational
approach the EU takes, but I choose to quote Pope John Paul II,
who in his 1980 speech to UNESCO passionately defended the
ideas of nation and sovereignty.

I am the son of a Nation which has lived the greatest experience of history,
which its neighbours have condemned to death several times, but which
has survived and remained itself. It has kept its identity, and it has kept, in
spite of partitions and foreign occupations, its national sovereignty, not by
relying on the resources of physical power, but solely *by relying on its culture*. This culture turned out in the circumstances to be more powerful than
all other forces. What I say here concerning the right of the Nation to the

foundation of its culture and its future is not, therefore, the echo of any 'nationalism,' but it is always a question of a stable element of human experience and of the *humanistic perspective of man's development*. There exists a fundamental sovereignty of society which is manifested in the culture of the Nation. It is a question of the sovereignty through which, at the same time, man is supremely sovereign. […] In the name of the primacy of the cultural realities of man, human communities, peoples and Nations, I say to you: with all the means at your disposal, watch over the fundamental sovereignty that every Nation possesses by virtue of its own culture. Cherish it like the apple of your eye for the future of the great human family. Protect it! Do not allow this fundamental sovereignty to become the prey of some political or economic interest. Do not allow it to become a victim of totalitarian and imperialistic systems or hegemonies, for which man counts only as an object of domination and not as the subject of his own human existence. For them, too, the Nation—their own Nation or others—counts only as an object of domination and a bait for various interests, and not as a subject: the subject of sovereignty coming from the true culture which belongs to it as its own.[2]

Here the great Polish Pope showed his commitment to the idea of national identity and sovereignty, exorting the world to protect and cherish the idea of a nation not merely as the sum of its heritage, but also as a homeland (Heimat, *patria*), nurturing a community that includes the values that make up the culture of a nation. Twenty years ago, John Paul II observed that European countries were in a "post-identity" phase. Today more than ever we should try to understand the far-reaching implications of the evolution of this post-identity process for Europe as a cultural and civic polity. For EU-level institutional actors, for Europe as a whole, *identity*, deprived of the ideological dangers of both cosmopolitism and nationalism, should be the most authentic value to implement, protect, and nourish. Identity reflects a collective awareness. It con-

---

2. John Paul II, *Address to UNESCO* (2 June 1980). English translation available online at: https://inters.org/John-Paul-II-UNESCO-Culture. Original French available at: http://www.vatican.va/content/john-paul-ii/fr/speeches/1980/june/documents/hf_jp-ii_spe_19800602_unesco.html.

nects heritage and memory and drives our actions, as it helps us to rediscover and tend our own roots. The EU needs to rediscover and value the concept of cultural identity, as its institutional structures are *hyper-bureaucratic* and *hypo-spiritual*.

Pope John Paul II was perfectly aware of this need. When he looked at Europe, he saw not only political and administrative structures, but overarching spiritual outlines, the features of the European soul, and therefore made an extraordinary effort (not crowned by immediate success but later proven prescient) to mention Jewish-Christian religious roots in the Constitutional Treaty, because he knew that without that explicit mention the European project would be doomed. He knew that any social construction intended for lasting results and general purposes must be founded on the cornerstones of its religious faith, if the latter is, as in the Jewish-Christian tradition, separated from the secular institutional body and respectful of its decisions. In fact, this approach, if applied with a religion like Islamism that absorbs the state into itself, produces fundamentalist effects that veer away from liberty.

Supporters of Europeanism seen as the bureaucratic centralism practiced by EU institutional actors promote the theory of post-identity, which I believe will destroy our various national identities. Post-identity will replace European traditional identity with human rights theories: the concrete traditional European identity will be progressively replaced by formal theories of human rights that have become politically correct dogmas. Here too, regarding the concept of a nation, the rift between the formal and the vital becomes clear: on one side is the EU with its formal supranational role, on the other side are the individual nations as vital cores.

Not only does the supranational defeat of national identities dismantle the idea of a nation, but it also damages Europe as a continent. It destroys each nation as well as the wider European sense of identity and conscience. It eradicates people's love for their native lands. Sovereignty is increasingly ceding ground to a supranational order, and there cannot become a love for the European homeland without the respect and love for each country that comprises the EU.

Pope Wojtyła was clear in defending the rights of nations. He never tired of reminding us that a nation is a natural community, because his ecumenical-evangelical anthropological vision does not disregard the human social structure, from the original foundation, inherent to humans, that is expressed in the minds of the nation as an institutional love for the homeland. He said that the cultural and historical identity of any society is preserved and nourished by all that is contained within this concept of "nationhood." As each nation creates a repository of culture, it enriches the treasure trove of national cultures we all enjoy. His emphasis on people and their real-life problems reveals the phenomenological character of his system of thought: Pope John Paul II used the framework of phenomenological thought (particularly as formulated by its founder, Edmund Husserl) aimed at the meaning and direct experience of life, in its immanence and transcendence.

In this context, the conflict between Europeanist and Euroskeptic arguments have intensified and spread. "More Europe" is the Europeanist slogan, meaning more concentration of power in the hands of the centralized political-bureaucratic structure; in contrast, Eurosceptics would like to see "less Europe," that is, less intervention by the centralized bureaucratic supranational structure. I add that "More Europe" should mean rebuilding a true European identity and decreasing the functional mechanism of the institutions: more thought and less positivism. Today, having yielded to the administrative-technocratic vision of centralistic institutions, culture has become an amusement park attraction, a tool for electoral advantages, while culture must instead be an aim in itself and not a means for other purposes; in any case, it is the soul that allows institutions to flourish. Every institution, even the coldest and most technical, can be virtuous if it respects this soul.

Relevant here is what Leibniz did in 1715 following the devastating War of the Spanish Succession between European powers. Instead of declaring war against the state, which would have violated federal clauses, Leibniz proposed establishing a European constitution. With a diplomatic and strategic vision, Leibniz chose efficiency and stability: a European central bank. He wanted a federal financial guarantee for any European central bank because certain nations could be powerful enough to disregard the European tribunal. For Leibniz, a financially backed agreement is an incentive to cooperate, while he recognized the political impossibility of establishing perpetual peace. Leibniz's vision for Europe forms a unity in virtue of the general societal goals it pursues and the intellectual ethics that govern it, an ethics of reciprocity and moderation. He saw the urgent need for stable peace in Europe, based on a less volatile foundation than the fragile treatises that were constantly violated, throwing the region off balance each time. Leibniz suggested a European deposit bank in order to establish a punitive mechanism:

[...] if two or three of the most powerful young monarchs grew tired of the prescribed laws and wanted to infringe them, what other way could this be prevented than by a war of doubtful success? This could be resolved by the General Council controlling the largest bank in Europe, in which all monarchs would have to deposit (proportionally) large sums of their money, which would remain there as safely as in their own coffers and even earn interest. Thus their capital would be productive and would serve as a kind of "bourgeois bond."[3]

Leibniz's proposal is revolutionary and worthy of a realistic politician who knows that control strategies must be implemented to prevent power from becoming despotic. Hence the need to restore dignity to faith and morals, and to create strong bonds such as

3. A. Robinet, *G.W. Leibniz. Le meilleur des mondes par la balance de l'Europe* (Paris: Presses Universitaires de France, 1994), 268.

economic ones, without, however, reducing the life of a group of peoples to a simple financial contract. In fact, the life of conscience, the life of the spirit, must rise above everything, as it is the only force that is never depleted and that, by virtue of the freedom that inspires it, is the source of every authentic human creation. This was the European Bank of Leibniz; this could be the European Central Bank today.

The current Europeanistic rhetoric proclaims: fewer nations, more Europe, compromising the only remaining possibility for the continuation of the EU, that is, the free will of the nations that *decide* to unite and act together. Probably, this anti-national obstinacy is not only motivated by intentions that are authoritarian design and, within the limits of bureaucracy, totalizing, but also by a bleak and embarrassing ignorance, a dramatic inability to understand the historical-conceptual. In fact, the Europeanistic ideology does not realize that in destroying the national spirit, it is also eliminating the only effective antidote to nationalism understood as national supremacism.

Despite the current scenario and the large crisis the EU is facing, I do not support the disintegration of the EU, which would indeed be perilous. Such a disintegration would leave a power vacuum that could easily be filled by brutal forces and driven by narrow-minded impulses, even external actors or Islamic integralism. A Balkan scenario is the most probable reality for a EU that has been dismantled without preparing a realistic, effective alternative.

Bureaucratization and centralization has produced a *Europe without identity*; Euroskepticism will only generate a sense of *identity without Europe* if not properly mediated. The first path should be fully rejected; the second must be reconsidered in view of broader aims, which should be *European* and not *Europeanist*. All supporters of a united Europe should start hearing the voices that the politically correct reject as sovereign, isolationist, and xenophobic, that is, the appeals of those who want to be European without becoming a puppet of the institutions, the peoples and nations who want Europe without losing themselves. This way, perhaps we could have a less abusive and more authentic Europe.

But precisely for this reason, authentic Europe cannot be understood, much less built, with the postmodernist and deconstructionist thought that, along with political correctness, forms the dominant paradigm in European questions. Everything in the EU procedures is postmodernized and postmodernizing, taking such an unconscious, internalized, and automatic form as to influence and determine every attitude, analysis, deliberation, and act. The EU is an agglomeration of twenty-seven nations that coexist within the institutional framework of a formally representative bureaucratic structure, but one that substantially lacks contact with citizens. In this space, an ideology has emerged that has erased the sense of nations and national identity. Identities are no longer valid, only procedures; there is no historical responsibility but only the contingent opportunities. This is precisely as deconstructionism wants: everything must be mixed up and confused, deprived of identity and emptied of meaning, to allow the new European sophistication to play its game undisturbed: this new class of administrators and bureaucrats constitutes, as Shmuel Trigano states, "the very example of the new post-modernist elite."[4] This is the ideological-political connection on which the European institution is based.

I therefore oppose a formal or official Europe in favor of a vital Europe, not in order to destroy the former, but to connect it with the latter and, even more, to bind them together in a historical-cultural pact that is incomparably more solid than any treaty and any constitutional charter. It is this renewed alliance between elites and peoples, between institutions and nations, that we need today.

---

4. Cf. S. Trigano, *La nouvelle idéologie dominante: le post-modernisme* (Paris: Hermann, 2012).

Instead, we mostly see empty rhetorical displays, as in the formula I mentioned earlier: more Europe. It is heard on every occasion, pronounced with the sacredness of a commandment or with the arrogance of a threat, depending on the circumstances. "More Europe" is the medicine for every ailment, the solution for every problem. Is unemployment increasing? More Europe will decrease it. Are people rejecting immigration? More Europe will make them accept it. Does bureaucratic centralism distance citizens from European institutions? More Europe will bring them closer. Does the pandemic hurt and kill people, damage and destroy the economy? More Europe will overcome the health emergency.

With this formula, ideological and instrumental goals are passed off as ideals of European civilization. This, however, risks destroying an intangible asset that was forged and rooted over centuries, one that may disappear due to a deadly mixture of political opportunism and spiritual sloppiness. The certainty of Europeans in their identity has disintegrated and the trust that they had in their *continental homeland*, despite all the conflicts, has been destroyed.

More Europe, then? If by Europe we mean the bureaucratic-technical structure, certainly not. But if by this abused yet noble word we mean the two-thousand-year history of the spirit that, while splitting into many peoples, forged the continent's general identity and the particular identities of its nations, then yes, we need it. Altered in character and transformed in meaning, this expression would affirm the opposite of what it now designates: that is, it would recover the identity value of Europe, of the historical and concrete existence of our peoples. Thus, with a completely different meaning, "more Europe" indicates an objective that all Europeans, as bearers of a national and continental identity, share: to reinvigorate original and forgotten sources, to regain the pride of our history, to reaffirm its values and recalibrate our practices to defend them. It does not mean the disintegration of the EU, but, on the contrary, its reconstitution on a nobler and more solid basis, its concrete *regeneration*.

I conclude by presenting two examples of empty formalism in the current era marked by the coronavirus epidemic: the first concerns the socio-economic sphere, the second, public health. Since coronavirus first emerged, the prolonged pandemic has spurred endless headlines about the virus: charlatans, deniers, and conspiracy theorists of every cultural orientation and every political color have been denouncing phantoms and hazily defined conspiracies as the basis of the epidemic caused by the Chinese virus. Ravings made possible by the neglecting authoritativeness (which is not mere authority) derived from a thesis, a theory, or a principle and spread by the capillarity of social media. We have witnessed a collective logorrhea, the result of ignorance and arrogance, that poisoned public opinion and polluted relations between individuals and social groups, producing a psychological destabilization and a political disorientation that will not be easy to remedy. In this situation, scientists too have increased the chaos by talking non-stop, often out of context and inconsistently.

On the other hand, this degradation of thought and language is accompanied by distortions and manipulations in economic and social theory. For instance, the World Economic Forum, headquartered in Switzerland but deeply linked to EU institutions, launched the so-called Great Reset, a technical initiative aiming to shape the global economy not according to peoples' real needs but molded on strong ideological tenets. I argue that the Great Reset combines and renews two nineteenth century left-wing ideologies, and influences ruthless financial practices responsible for this savage new era. These are not authentic capitalism but rather a degenerate form that creates a dangerous practical and theoretical hybrid. This scenario signals the return of the shadows of utopian socialism and the specter of Marxist communism adapted to the mental and operational schemes used by contemporary technocracy, the global players in the media and information technology, robotics, and artificial intelligence.

This global project supports and is a powerful ally of the formal Europe's goals and fights against the vital Europe: precisely like socialism/communism, it aims to defeat Western tradition and especially Western religion, reducing Christianity to a mere civic survival manual. Further, it aims to reduce the Church (both Catholic and Protestant) to an organization that simply provides social support. Judaism and Jews are tolerated only to avoid accusations of antisemitism, while they are attacked when Israel is criticized and boycotted, revealing that anti-Zionism is a form of anti-Semitism. This type of attack on Israel is symmetrically similar to those that various far-right and far-left conspiracy groups launch against the international Jewish world, believed to be heading a conspiracy, of which the Great Reset would also be part, to establish a new world order. To sum up, confusion, distortion, and conspiracy theories create chaos and are not worthy of any further attention here.

Along with this socialist/communist and anti-Judeo-Christian resurrection, the Great Reset initiated a technocratic farce managed by global elites. This scheme enforces political correctness and thus sympathizes with global left-wing stances. They bellow at us that only machines can save humanity and therefore we must rely completely on technology, or rather on technoscience, which will replace man not only in mechanical operations but also in more sophisticated ones, to the point of replacing thought and consciousness. It is just a short step from *post-modern to post-human*. This is the direction that global projects like this type pull us. They are the exact opposite of what Martin Heidegger thought (and which, fortunately, many still think) when, referring to the technique and its dangers, he said, "only a God can save us" ("nur noch ein Gott kann uns retten"). The second example of empty bureaucratic formalism

I would like to discuss is the EU's slow and disorderly response to the pandemic emergency. While the Great Reset features the dissolution of the Jewish-Christian religious tradition into a new *religion of technology*, the pandemic spotlights the bureaucratization that paralyzes public health responses, both institutional and individual. In fact, it should be noted how European institutions handled the health crisis caused by the pandemic. Without judging either the arguments for vaccination or those opposing them (with respect to both, I argue that it is fundamental to guarantee freedom of treatment and a free personal choice of accepting or rejecting treatments), I will simply note that the United States, Israel, and England, after deciding that in order to limit the number of victims as much as possible, to protect production systems and the economy in general, and not to provoke dangerous social entropy, mass vaccination was the most effective measure in the short term, they acted quickly and effectively, following the principles of freedom of initiative and without the brakes of bureaucracy, producing vaccines and quickly procuring the doses necessary to safeguard the population and to restart not only the economy but also a positive psycho-social dynamic.

The EU, on the other hand, has moved in ways typical of bureaucracy: slowly and awkwardly, issuing abstruse regulations and imposing abstract rules, prescriptions, and restrictions. My interpretation in this case is that technical formalism has replaced living tradition, because the European rulers have chosen, once again, the path of centralization, instead abandoning the traditional approach to social and managerial issues: subsidiarity in which an agency higher in the hierarchy replaces a lower-level one *only when* the latter is unable to perform its duties, and vice versa: lower- level agencies can legitimately operate and therefore operate freely in all areas and for all problems in their purview, including the decision-making freedom of the family as the original nucleus of communities and that of individuals as the original nucleus of conscience. The idea (and the consequent practice) of subsidiarity is perhaps the most significant sign of the fruitful union between conservatism and liberalism that has characterized, albeit sometimes in a subterranean and discontinuous way, the anti-totalitarian and anti-statist thought of twentieth-century Europe.

Subsidiarity has been the fundamental concept of the Church's social doctrine for more than a century, founded in 1891 by Pope Leo XIII's Encyclical *Rerum Novarum* and then fixed by Pope John Paul II's Encyclicals *Laborem Exercens* (1981) and *Centesimus Annus* (1991) II. It therefore represents one of the most influential expressions of the European tradition in the socio-economic field. And since subsidiarity arises from the idea of freedom, the EU should have simply, within the limits imposed by an exceptional situation such as the pandemic, allowed and practiced freedom, from the individual level to the highest social level. Instead, once again the bureaucracy, the administrative form of positivist thought, has destroyed tradition, deactivating the historical conscience and its living thought.

Almost a century ago, in 1930, José Ortega y Gasset warned that Europe is decaying because of the massification of consciousness, and this decay is linked to the progressive bureaucratization of life, and bureaucratization is the face of the statehood, of the state control of society. It is not the idea of the state and the virtuous state that I question, but the distorted notion of state produced by a statist ideology. This kind of state can become the worst enemy of society, communities, and peoples.

Starting as a means of achieving positive results for the development of society as a set of individuals, families, communities, professional associations, and interest groups, the state becomes an end in itself, and people become the means to ensure this end: the state no longer plays a service function for its citizens, but quite the contrary: the people are at the service of the state. Thus, when formal Europe, that is, the institutional structures of the EU, wanted to become a super-state, a mechanism was produced by which the citizens, peoples, and nations of Europe themselves are at the service of the European super-state, whose end is no longer a vital or ideal Europe as the only acceptable condition for European citizens, but is the state itself. Eventually, Europe becomes a means of strengthening this state, which is increasingly alien and distant from its citizens.

When the formal Europe, that is to say the EU's institutional structures, decided to become a super-state, it generated a mechanism whereby European citizens and nations become a means for the super-state to achieve its aims. The EU institutions are a powerful tool for furthering the power of this super-state. Only memory allows the roots to continue to be alive, because memory allows identity to be transmitted through generations. Since a dead root is a fossil, a mere archaeological find, the European identity must always be revitalized. And since it is plural and pluralistic in itself, we can speak of an *inter-identity of Europe*, an identity in which different forms of identification participate, all nevertheless bound by a common essence consisting of an original institution of meaning as the basis of all the cultural, religious, political, and juridical affinities between the European peoples. It is an original and metaphysical space from which all the structures of our civilization have arisen in an infinite series of branches.

But identity also involves transcendence, planning, and freedom. Here identity is combined with truth, with a self-awareness that derives from the search for truth, from a tension toward the other and toward the beyond, toward the limits of one's own being while giving us the criteria for our actions. Therefore, since vital Europe is the expression of the peoples of the continent, and since peoples can continue to live only if their national and continental tradition survives, Europe as such will only be able to live and progress if it again becomes an asset for its peoples, for its own community; if it is felt as a homeland, as a *European homeland* that continues to be founded on its nations, on its tradition, on its original values and on its authentic and founding principles, revitalizing them and thus regenerating itself. Otherwise, Europe will be only able to *continue to formalize itself* as an institutional bureaucratic entity, until it becomes a lifeless mummy, a mummy of itself or, at best, a museum of a perished tradition.

RENATO CRISTIN — Italian philosopher, professor of philosophical hermeneutics at the University of Trieste. From 2003 to 2006 Director of the Italian Culture Institute in Berlin; from 2007 to 2012 Scientific Director of the Fondazione Liberal in Rome. His research is focused on: phenomenology and hermeneutics, European culture, political philosophy, Western identity. Author of *Heidegger and Leibniz*, with foreword by H.-G. Gadamer (1998); *La rinascita dell'Europa. Husserl e il destino dell'Occidente* (2001); *Apologia dell'ego. Per una fenomenologia dell'identità* (2011); *I padroni del caos* (2018); *Quadrante Occidentale* (2022).

D A R I U S Z   G A W I N

THE PHENOMENON OF
"SOLIDARITY"

August '80, just like the whole "Solidarity" movement from the period between 1980 and 1981, escapes all clearcut interpretations.

This is because this historical phenomenon can be observed
both from the perspective of social movements, one can highlight
the worker and left-wing features of the movement, thus also its revolutionary character (back when it started Jadwiga Staniszkis talk-
ed about a "self-limiting revolution"), but one is also totally justified
in interpreting "Solidarity" in light of the spirit of the Polish tradition of insurrections.[1] I will propose one more possible perspective for interpretation: I propose looking at the August strikes in
the Gdańsk Shipyards through the lens of the republican tradition.
Thus, August will be analyzed through the eyes of one of the key
traditions of political philosophy—reaching all the way back to the
ancient tradition of reflecting upon politics.[2]

1. Cf. *Lekcja Sierpnia* [The Lesson of August], ed. D. Gawin (Warszawa: Wydawnictwo IFiS
PAN, 2002) and *"Solidarność" w imieniu narodu i obywateli* ["Solidarity" in the name of the nation
and citizens], ed. M. Latoszek (Kraków: Arcana, 2005); an interesting overview of Polish texts concerned with "Solidarity" is Andrzej Waśkiewicz's "Ku pokrzepieniu serc" [Toward the Raising up of
Hearts], in *Res Publica Nowa* no. 8, 2000.

2. Years ago, Paweł Śpiewak was the first to conduct this sort of interpretation in the text

This choice of a vantage point makes it into an interpretation that goes beyond the boundaries of sociological theory, or the typical historical narrative. Just as with any other interpretation, it is merely an attempt at getting at a phenomenon, which, because of its scale and historical meaning, exceeds all possible perspectives of interpretation.

At the same time, the phenomenon of August exceeds, as is the case with other theoretical perspectives, the hermeneutical possibilities contained within the republican tradition. To put it another way, the republican tradition does a great job as a tool for understanding certain especially important aspects of August, but at the same time, the events of the summer of 1980 expose the weaknesses and limitations of the republican tradition.

Even now the news from the coast hits us with an especially strong feeling of the gravity of the events, which are coupled with descriptions of the psycho-somatic sensations of the participants that are clear examples of limit situations. The strike is an existential border-experience for them. To illustrate these crucial facts let's use several quotes taken from the participants, "I was constantly moved. I cried throughout, but felt strange about it, so I turned away from people, covered myself up, hid myself from others, but I could not get a grip on myself." "I cried throughout the whole strike. Even now [in 1981] whenever I hear the word, 'strike,' tears well up in my eyes" "this was an incredible experience. Only once before, as a child during the Warsaw Uprising, did I experience anything like it. I remember how my mother was sewing armbands for the soldiers of the Uprising. It was also August, and also warm. They pulled down the fence between the yards, so there was a lot of space, and there young soldiers of the Uprising were walking around and singing: Poland has not yet perished. I remembered this experience and something similar happened right under this gate. It was an atmosphere of euphoria—of choking on freedom, one of our friends was literally in a state of shock. He had to return to Warsaw, because he was constantly throwing up."[3]

If we agree with Hannah Arendt—whose writings on the republican spirit will be the interpretive key for our explorations—that a remarkable feeling of "public happiness" is born when free citizens constitute political freedom and at the same time establish a political community, then we can recognize in what took place in the Gdańsk Shipyard the pathos which has accompanied the republican spirit from the dawn of Western civilization.[4] The spirit of civic action, the same spirit that once visited Athens, Rome, Philadelphia and Paris, demonstrated its power in Gdańsk in the summer of 1980. This really seems like a far-fetched perspective—someone could ask, what could the times of Pericles and the American Founding Fathers have to do with these shipyard masses dressed in gray work uniforms, their carts with accumulators, their halls that served to organize boring meetings, their factory fences and checkpoints? All these requisites appear to be in disharmony with the spirit that has encroached upon them. However, the power of politics encroaching upon the mundane reality of that time was capable of constituting the meaning of events totally irrespective of the context. This fact always seems to have the character of an epiphany. The power of politics sacralizes places that were totally submerged, without reserve, in the profane. Every scenery could serve as the backdrop for a historical drama whose theme is the struggle between freedom and tyranny.

---

3. These are fragments collected by reporters who participated in the strike, from: *Kto tu wpuścił dziennikarzy* [Who Let in the Reporters?], ed. M. Miller and J. Jankowska (Warszawa: Rosner i Wspólnicy, 2005), 69, 86, 245 ff.

4. This phrase was originally used by Hannah Arendt throughout the book *On Revolution*.

1. The Shipyard as *Polis*

Let us start with the shipyard—the setting of the drama of August '80. Classical politics was tightly bound to cities understood as the physical emanation of the political community. *Polis, civitas*—in these concepts the physical space gave way to the laws of symbolism. The Greek *polis* contains, in its Indo-european roots, a tie to fortifications, that is, a fenced-in place which can become a shelter during times of attack. Fortuitously, the Polish word for stronghold, "gród," in its archaic meaning, or at least in its archaizing translations, for example in translations of classical drama, is taken as an equivalent of *polis*, because it contains similar layers of meaning. Etymologically, it is directly connected to "grodzić," the establishing of boundaries or fences. At the same time the Polish word for city, "miasto," is the same as the Old-Slavonic for place. "Stronghold" and "city" point to the specific character of the physical emanation of politics, which appears where people want to be together, connected by a common political authority. The city-place, *polis*, should have clear boundaries, thereby tearing away the space of citizen's action from the homogeneous space of nature, in which nothing can be called acting in Arendt's sense, because everything is subject to the power of necessity flowing from biological processes. The sphere of biological compulsion extends outside the boundaries of the city—the vegetative kingdom of life, the eternal rhythm of circling time.

In August of 1980 the place-city, Gdańsk's *polis* was the shipyard. More live accounts, "you could breathe there just like in free independent Poland. I felt so well over there. It was a wonderfully organized city, our little headland;" "Strumff told me that there came to be a country within the country in the shipyard [...] one that governs by its own laws, it has its own intelligence services, its own minister of propaganda, its supplies people, its own security forces. Thus, it fulfills all the functions of a normal country [...]"[5] The fences of the shipyard were the physical barrier of the self-constituting political community. This was the wall of the *polis*. Spread out beyond it was the domain of necessity, the social controlled by the tyranny, that is, a totalitarian authority. To put it another way, one can say that beyond the wall of the shipyard there spread out an undifferentiated "society," controlled by the authorities, which reduced politics to a totalitarian managing of social processes.

This particular tension is born of the interaction of two spheres, on the one hand, that which is social, submerged in pre-political tyrannical state control and on the other, the sphere of free political community—the meeting of these two created the specific atmosphere at the gates of the shipyard. This is how the participants described the unique function of the shipyard's gates: "This passage to another world was simply miraculous, especially after the stifling atmosphere of Warsaw. All of a sudden I find myself in a place where everything seems obvious, everything is clear, peaceful." "We could feel that behind these gates a totally different world functioned, that totally different laws reigned there. This is indescribable. I just stood there and watched. I found myself on the border of a totally different world."[6]

In the gates, literally and symbolically, a primordial politics concentrated within the shipyard came in contact with the social, with the whole of social life that remained outside the ring of freedom created by the strikers. The unique atmosphere of the plaza in front of the gate, filled with thousands of people waiting for communiques, fliers, manifesting their support, and, above all, concentrating and gathering in that point, was documented in countless photos and many documentary films. The gate, covered with flowers,

5. *Kto tu wpuścił dziennikarzy*, op. cit., 240.
6. Ibid., p. 84, 86, 93, 98.

guarded by shipyard workers wearing white and red bands, decorated with flags and pictures of the Pope John Paul II, became one of the most important icons of August.

If the shipyard was a *polis*, then the equivalent of the Pnyx (the Athenian place where the *ecclesia*, the assembly of the people, held its councils) was the Shipyard's BHP Hall[7], where the national Strike committee held its councils. A reporter present at the shipyard recalls, "I had the impression that it was, well, I don't know, something like the conference hall of the United Nations."[8] This primordial form of politics had the power to morph places and events seemingly banal into a historical drama, and here it showed its power. Thanks to it, the BHP Hall in the Gdańsk Lenin Shipyard became a historical icon not only on a local scale, or on the scale of Polish history, but also in universal history. The history of freedom picks the scene where its drama is going to put on its show. In this perspective accidental places, seemingly unfit for the occasion, become necessary elements of the historical narrative. This is why the symbolic career of the BHP Hall is reminiscent of the tennis courts in Versailles—as distant from the pathos of grand history in 1789 as the Gdańsk Hall before 1980.

On the margins of the comparison of the shipyard to the *polis* one notices one more factor that strengthens the metaphor—the Greek *poleis* were far from the modern understanding of democracy, because they forced women, slaves and foreigners who were permanent residents, out of political life. The shipyard was specifically a place of work and the majority of its employees were men. Indeed, many women took part in the strikes, some of them played very important roles, like Anna Walentynowicz, Alina Pienkowska or Henryka Krzywonos, but the absolute majority of the strikers were men. Their families remained behind the lines separating what

---

7. BHP—Occupational Safety and Hygiene [trans.].
8. *Kto tu wpuścił dziennikarzy*, op. cit., 98.

is the political from the social, that is, the reality which remained outside the fences of the shipyard. Even here, in a surprising way, accidentally, August's reality intertwined with the classical tradition and the thought of Hannah Arendt. As one of the reporters recalled, describing the atmosphere by the gates:

On the one side were the husbands, on the other, the wives and children. The striking workers would come to the gates and greet their children, often they were little, in their strollers.[9]

2. "Solidarity," that is, the *Res Publica*

Into this place-city that was the shipyard, fenced off from the outside world by a wall, something poured in like a torrent, it engulfed people and took them much further than they could have imagined at the beginning of their united action. It was elemental, primordial politics, which transforms and changes people and reveals the proper meaning of events. This is how a participant of the strike in Gdynia recalled the strike's atmosphere:

A strange knot of unity tied the Polish nation together, we became closer, dearer, everyone respected their brothers more than they respected themselves [...] this was not an ordinary strike, this was an enormous school of educating noble human feeling from which we took away not only theory, but an enormous experience of the immense unity of the nation.[10]

The knot of unity was nothing other than the directly felt nature of that which is in common, or also, to use an idiom grounded in the Western tradition, the nature of "the thing in common," the republic. Our knee-jerk understanding of res publica causes us to see it as the concept which describes the form of a country. Here res means a thing, an institution. In its primordial sense res publica is not a thing, instead it is an event, thus it does not describe

9. Ibid., 86.

10. E. Bernatowicz, "Czarne chmury" [Black clouds], in *Sierpień '80 we wspomnieniach* [*Memories of August '80*], ed. M. Latoszek (Gdańsk: Wydawnictwo Morskie, 1991), 166.

something that exists beside citizens, instead it refers to relations that join citizens, thereby constituting the proper foundation for the state's institutions.

The pathos of the August strikes was the result of a leading affect which engulfed the people directly involved in fanning the flames of the common will and feelings. The community of will and affect allowed for the constitution of an event common to everyone, a res publica, that is, "Solidarity," because precisely this content is hidden in this remarkable word that was chosen as the official name for the movement born in the shipyard. The specificity of this name comes from the fact that it, and this is rare in modern politics, does not point to any political institution or ideology, but instead to a certain specific and universal human relation.

3. Equality and Solidarity, that is, *Homonoia*

Primordial political action, as its swift current poured into the *polis* of the shipyard workers, caused a rapid transformation of the drama's actors. Just the day before, submerged in the social (for the great majority the impulse that pushed them to join the strikes was material, the increase of prices by the communist authorities), but now, from day to day, they became citizens—free people who desired to constitute and regain their freedom at last. The rapidity of this change shocked observers. Many, up to this day, are inclined to instinctively explain the meaning of the August events by resorting to the category of "miracle." This is because a miracle is an act that just happens, seemingly out of nowhere, and is not the result of the past—it is something that cuts through time and makes possible the establishment of a new order.

Within these categories the proper meaning of the miracle which occurred in the shipyard was the sudden (yet peaceful) and unexpected birth of a political community of citizens. The crowd deprived of its own will, a population treated as an object of administrative procedures by thoroughly alienated rulers, changed itself into conscious and responsible citizens. The freedom that changed the anonymous crowd into citizens acts on two levels: it changed both individuals and the collectivity. In the first case, we are dealing with an ennobling of every individual, or rather, each person. On the other hand, in actualized socialism there was a dramatic divergence between the declared respect for the rights of the individual and reality, a reality over-saturated with contempt for anyone who found himself lower in the actual social hierarchy. Thus, the ethical postulate of guarding the dignity of the individual had deeply revolutionary political consequences. The power of this postulate was surprising and fascinating, because it ripped apart the cover of universally present lies and gave back social reality its proper proportions.

This precisely was the cause of the thing that made people cry and gave them lumps in their throats. Freedom is a miracle because with its mysterious force it changes the essence of a person right down to their core. This is such a substantial and rapid change that affect precedes reflection, feelings are faster than thoughts. When freedom is encrusted with institutions, laws, procedures, when it is hard to perceive it under the accumulations of politics understood as the craft of gaining power and ruling it becomes increasingly difficult to realize how special it actually is. In August freedom showed its power without any veils, in its whole, primordial, wondrous character.

The rapidity of that metamorphosis of individuals and the whole collective fascinated observers. In September of 1980, Ryszard Kapuścinski's report about the strike in Gdańsk appeared in the Warsaw-based "Kultura" weekly. Kapuściński was at the time one of the most renowned journalists in the world.

Its tone does not stray from the tone of other texts written by intellectuals from the capital reporting live about the strange strike-phenomenon, which they personally witnessed. What is most interesting about it is the direct way in which he grasped the ethical dimension of the workers' protests.

Kapuściński wrote that someone who:

> tries to reduce the movement from the coast to matters of pay and living [...] has not grasped anything. This is because the leading motive of these occurrences was the *dignity of man*, it was a striving to create new relations between people, in every place and in all ranks, there was the principle of mutual respect binding everyone without exception, a principle according to which one's subordinate was at the same time one's partner.[11]

Recognizing the dignity of every human person, recognizing their inborn right to be treated as a subject, not as an object, constituted the crucial condition this collectivity of individuals needed to raise itself up to a higher level—a collectivity composed of persons could no longer be just a crowd nor a mass of people. The collectivity had to transform itself into in a community of citizens. The ethical sense of August turned into its political sense—just as individuals were becoming persons, so also the crowd was becoming the People.

For this transformation to be complete another step was needed. A step that depended upon thinking through the logical consequences of the previously accepted conclusion about the inborn dignity of each and every human person. The conclusion had to be the presupposition that the collectivity of such individuals can be recognized as a valid subject of action only when it acknowledges the principle of equality as the main principle regulating their mutual relations. And again, just like with the surprise voiced at the unexpected eruption of general agreement to treat each other and everyone with respect, also the experience of the sudden, spontaneous community of equals caused wonder mixed with deep feeling. This mood resounds in the picture painted by the words of a reporter

---

11. Cited in: G. Pomian, *Polska "Solidarności"* [The Poland of "Solidarity"] (Paris: Instytut Literacki, 1982), 76.

written several months after his time in the Gdańsk Shipyard, "We sat on the ground, right by me there was some professor from the Fishing Institute. There were no barriers resulting from titles, positions, age, profession. Everyone was open." Someone else added, "It was a republic of equals. No rituals."[12]

The regained freedom brought out, from under the decks of social roles and social hierarchies, an inborn humanity. A female reporter who spent time in the shipyard recalls, "Faces were interesting […] I immediately realized that I couldn't tell the difference in professions from faces, and yet both workers, technicians, and engineers were there." This similarity was not the same thing as standardization—a loss of individual identity. On the contrary, resemblance in dignity allowed for a recapturing of authentic subjectivity. It seems that the classic conception of *homonoia*, that is resemblance, but also equality, is useful for understanding this aspect of the strike. The citizens of the political community, of the Aristotelian *koinonia politike*, as equals should at the same time resemble each other. This is due to the emphasis put on friendship between citizens by the Stagirite. That's because it fulfilled a unifying role, transforming a collectivity merely living together into a community ready to act as a political subject in solidarity.

This lead is quite interesting, because to a certain degree *homonoia* understood in this way overlaps considerably with solidarity understood as the tie of friendship. Friendship joining those resembling each other as the uniter of political community, or to put it otherwise, solidarity joining the free who recognize in themselves an inborn dignity, also expands and fills out the understanding of the shipyard as a *polis*. Plato and Aristotle underscored that a real

---

12. On the margins, with a certain bitterness, one can notice that from our current perspective years later this disappearance of all social barriers and hierarchies and all their attendant social rituals, it all seems all the more miraculous and extraordinary than it did then. Our democracy today offers us equality reduced to a narrow circle of formal procedures. We no longer have any chance to experience being in a universal community of equals.

polis as a political community is only possible in limited, small from our modern perspective, social frames. Several thousand citizens was the optimal number by their reckonings. The emphasis on this scale was the result of the conviction that a real community of citizens could only function where citizens know each other mutually and interact directly. Friends share the same interests, spend time together, and talk frequently. Since friendship is born of direct contact, thus, according to Aristotle, there arises the question about the possible number of friends:

Ten people would not make a city, and with a hundred thousand it is a city no longer.[13]

The reality of the August strike, in a curious fashion, can also be explained according to this aspect of classical political thought. The average place of work in the Polish People's Republic in its size was reminiscent of a Greek *polis*—at most it contained tens of thousands individuals. Therefore, one can say that the largest industrial behemoths of those times did not exceed the size of Athens from Socrates' and Plato's epoch. On this scale people could still know each other, and if they did not know each other directly, then they could recognize each other by sight, or could have heard about people with whom they did not run into during day to day situations. In such conditions it was easier to talk of friendship, or also, to use a more modern idiom, of trust and solidarity. The great "Solidarity," a union of tens of millions, which developed from the August strike reminds one of a large confederation, or as the Greeks put it, a *symmachia*, composed of thousands of city-states, of workplaces. This large union was composed of a thousand communities that each had its debates, its political conflicts, and its moments of political action. Precisely this circumstance was at the root of the unusual, even by modern standards, intensity of civic life which took place

13. Aristotle, *Nicomachean Ethics*, trans. H. Rackham (Cambridge, MA: Harvard University Press, 1934), 1170b.

within the union. In a normal parliamentary democracy conscious, intentional acting is needed to directly take part in political life— one has to sign up with a party, go to meetings, take part in discussions and pre-election meetings. To put it another way, one must find people and places that are "political." In the years 1980–1981 the vast majority of Poles participated in some workplace where they spent eight hours a day. Therefore, being political, as a way of collective acting and living, was really a universal and obvious dimension of their existence.

4. Language as the living element of Being Political

The element of the political is language, speech, democratic debate. To all the authors writing about August the talkativeness of those times stood out. The unbridled element of universal debate, of a general and uninterrupted talking, spilled out from the coast to the whole country. During countless meetings of work organizations of the union people could finally say what they thought and felt. The meaning of these monologues could not be reduced to its therapeutic function. Getting rid of anxieties or regaining psychological balance was not the thing at stake there. During them, opinions about public affairs hitherto hidden under the masks of the gossip, political joke, judgments made within the safety of one's own four walls, transformed themselves into public discourse. In the sphere of the political, speech stopped being mere blather, constantly buzzing, filling up everything, but unable to change anything.

Under the new conditions speech was becoming a tool of change, a weapon, even more, an inherently political form of acting. This helps us to understand why "Solidarity" sacrificed its efficiency on the altar of free speech. During the first convention of the union's delegates the super-democratic procedures allowed each delegate a chance to enter the discussion at any moment. Despite the fact that this usually resulted in a complete mess, this principle was carefully and seriously observed. Thanks to this "Solidarity's" republican democracy had a clearly substantial character. It treated procedures as a necessary evil.

5. The presence of religion

The republican tradition also allows for an interpretation of religion's presence during the August strikes. The unusual, mysterious character of the process of establishing the public sphere demanded a transcendent sanction. A reporter present in the shipyard said:

> How to understand this explosion, these explosions of religious feeling, this basically religious demonstration? All historical events demand a frame, ceremony. Right then the movement realized that its moral societal protest could not find any official form which was not compromised. The church proved to be the only institution that did not betray the interests of the nation. There was nothing to lean on and in the shipyard there was a great need for lasting things, a need for hope, and as we all know, God is imagined as the One who does not represent any group interests, because He is impartial. Masses had a significant meaning for the mood and for building up the dignity of people. People in the shipyard, irregardless of whether they were believers or not, found in them a kind of soundness which they wanted to serve.[14]

Thus, naturally, the boundaries surrounding this specific piece of physical space, which gained a totally new status thanks to civic action, had to be marked with religious symbols. On the fences of the shipyard, near national symbols, evoking political order, there spontaneously appeared crosses and pictures of the Pope John Paul II and of Our Lady of Częstochowa. What's interesting, this presence of religion was deprived of ideological variables. No one associated the crosses and pictures of the Pope with the stereotypical threat from the Catholic-nationalist rightwing. Just as the community had to first regain a primordial politics and an elementary public sphere, now the religiosity of its members first had to be rebuilt from a

---

14. *Kto tu wpuścił dziennikarzy*, op. cit., 156.

foundation of Christianity understood as the source of a sacred that sanctifies public space.

6. August and republican *Aporia*

August, as was underscored earlier in this paper, escapes all clearcut interpretations. Thus, the republican tradition cannot appear in a privileged position. Just like all the others, even though it is handy and useful when it comes to shedding light on significant aspects of those events, it is not capable of providing a hermeneutical key to all questions. With this the experience of August shows the limitations of the republican tradition. One of the crucial matters is the matter of violence.

For Arendt, in her reconstruction of the Greek model of political life, the exclusion of violence beyond the sphere of the political had substantial consequences. This thread returns throughout her work, but it plays an especially important role in *The Human Condition*. The point of departure of Arendt's reasoning is the way in which Aristotle bases politics upon the human ability to use language. Speaking gained a political character, because the Greeks identified speech with acting. If a political community's proper mode of existence is the gathering of citizens together, thereby constituting political space where the political appears, then speech is the living element of politics. Citizens appear in public space in order to make themselves present, to present their point of view and to let others judge them accordingly. Public speaking thus becomes the core of political acting through convincing others of your own point of view, or also, as the Greeks put it, through giving good council to the *polis*. The identification of political action with speaking is based upon the assumption that political virtue is the way of finding the proper arguments and words at the right time, thereby influencing the assembly. Physical power, violence or compulsion are mute, as Arendt puts it, "most political action, in so far as it remains outside the sphere of violence, is indeed transacted in words […] Only sheer violence is mute, and for this reason violence alone can never be great."[15] "To be political, to live in a *polis*, meant that everything was decided through words and persuasion and not through force and violence."[16] A leadership which cannot tolerate opposition, or does not allow discussion, which uses violence, always mute, is one that uses ways of governing that are characteristic of pre-political or extrapolitical forms of living together. Arendt contends that, on the one hand, the Greeks reserved this sort of conduct for family life, on the other, that it characterized tyranny, a political order based upon an unlimited power. The citizen of Athens, within the confines of his household, was a tyrant, he had unlimited power over the members of his family and slaves; his will was an order, and discussion with him was impossible. However, by crossing the threshold of his family home and by entering the *agora*, or any other place where people assembled, he stopped being a despot who reigns over a miniature monarchy and became a citizen, equal in his rights to others. He could no longer command, all that remained was the persuasion of equals.

The removal of coercion from the political sphere into the social sphere allowed Arendt to not only build a suggestive—the question remains how authentic—ideal model of the Greek city-state, but this also allowed her to criticize modernity, which according to her has confused these two spheres. By using society as the source of politics modernity made a mistake, because it let violence creep into politics.

However, there appears a very considerable difficulty: by construing her ideal model of a Greek *polis* she not only passes over in silence the true character of Greek politics during the classical period, which was full of violence, but she also passes over those

15. H. Arendt, *The Human Condition* (Chicago: The University of Chicago Press, 1958), 26.
16. Ibid.

elements of a Greek citizen's upbringing which were saturated by
the continuous presence of violence in Greek communities. We
should turn our attention to the references to violence in the models of a citizen's upbringing and civic virtues contained in the works
of Aristotle and Thucydides. This is especially significant, because
Arendt has her own specific way of choosing quotes from these
authors. Let's take, for example, the funerary speech of Pericles so
frequently cited by Arendt. Pericles says that before praising the
fallen he will first explain, "what the form of government under
which our greatness grew, what the national habits out of which
it sprang."[17] Pericles simply calls this political order democracy,
and marks out freedom as its leading principle. He suggestively describes the greatness and fame of Athens, which flow directly from
the spirit of its citizens. The glory of the country, above all, comes
from military victories. From Pericles' perspective the main advantage flowing from these victories is not prosperity, but glory itself:

> We have forced every sea and land to be the highway of our daring, and
> everywhere, whether for evil or for good, have left imperishable monuments
> behind us. Such is the Athens for which these men, in the assertion of their
> resolve not to lose her, nobly fought and died; and well may every one of
> their survivors be ready to suffer in her cause.[18]

Within all of this reasoning death has a key significance as a proof
of virtue—the one who does not fear to lay down his life for his native city does not only act on behalf of its material might, but also,
at the same time, is a witness of the power of its *polis*, of the power
of the ties binding the political community.

Thus, the virtue of courage does not have a purely military
character—it constitutes the highest realization of political virtue. Death on the field of glory in defense of a victorious father-

---

17. Thucydides, *The History of the Peloponnesian War*, trans. R. Crawley (New York: E.P. Dutton and Company, 1950), 123.
    18. Ibid., 126.

land constitutes the most perfect deed, the most perfect form of action for a citizen, and it deserves particular praise and memory. As Thucydides' Pericles says, the living should look upon the might of the country and fire themselves up with love for it, "and then when all her greatness shall break upon you, you must reflect that it was by courage, sense of duty, and a keen feeling of honour in action that men were enabled to win all this, and that no personal failure in an enterprise could make them consent to deprive their country of their valour, but they laid it at her feet as the most glorious contribution that they could offer."

Pericles concludes this part of his speech with the following words to the living, "These [heroes] take as your model, and judging happiness to be the fruit of freedom and freedom of valour, never decline the dangers of war."[19]

Pericles in his speech echoes Aristotle who placed death on the field of glory at the beginning of the catalog of virtues in the *Nicomachean Ethics*. Virtue of courage is related to danger, according to Aristotle, because the man who is valiant is the one who does not fear the greatest of all dangers. The deciding factor in the question about the essence of courage is the answer to the question about the things toward which man shows himself to be courageous:

What then are the fearful things in respect of which courage is displayed? I suppose those which are the greatest, since there is no one more brave in enduring danger than the courageous man. Now the most terrible thing of all is death.[20]

But not every type of death is intended here:

But even death, we should hold, does not in all circumstances give an opportunity for courage, for instance, we do not call a man courageous for facing death by drowning or disease. What form of death then is a test of

19. Ibid., 127–8.
20. Aristotle, *Nicomachean Ethics*, 1115a.

courage? Presumably that which is the noblest. Now the noblest form of
death is death in battle, for it is encountered in the midst of the greatest and
most noble of dangers.[21]

Arendt, in her convincing reconstruction of the nature of politics
and in her building up of a suggestive model of the ideal Greek
community passes over in silence the aims of these actions. Politics,
in the narrow meaning of the word presented by Arendt in her ideal
model, is concerned with the process of making decisions and desig-
nating the aims of common action. But one would be hard pressed
to find in Arendt's description what this whole process is concerned
with if not matters pertaining to maintaining and expanding the
might of the state (since this is obviously tied to violence). But when
one remembers the words of Pericles one cannot help but hold back
the impression that for real Greeks the establishment of ties and
new realities was inextricably connected with conquest and destruction, with the imposition of their will upon others. And not
even for material gains, but for glory, which confirmed their civic
excellence. The readiness to risk one's own life was the best proof
of having crossed the cramped confines of the biological nature of
man, which he shares with the animals. The most beautiful deed is
heroism in war, and the most beautiful form of "speech" is advising
the city in matters pertaining to war and peace.

If in the picture of the Greeks presented to us by Arendt we
notice considerable oversights, then there is a glaring contradiction
in her picture of the modern epoch and the place of violence in
modern politics. In her accounts of councils during the Bolshevik
revolution, or also councils during the Hungarian Uprising of 1956,
violence implicitly becomes a positive element.[22] Or to put it an-

21. Ibid.
22. The text itself is full of references to Marx and Engels, which brings up mixed feelings
today, as does *On Violence*, written under the influence of the counter-cultural student revolts of
the latter part of the 60's, where one can find, for example, the author's sympathy toward the Black
Panthers.

other way, it is hard to understand why criticism of the Jacobins and the negative appraisal of the violence used during the French revolution can go in hand in hand with a fascination with Russian workers' and military delegates councils. Arendt did not live to see 1980, but one cannot shake the impression that among all the 20th century political movements enlivened by civic cooperation, "Solidarity" was the closest to the ideal described in *The Human Condition*. This is because it was the only immense social movement totally devoid of violence. August, and later "Solidarity" between 1980 and 1981, was a political community whose main tool for achieving change was the element of speech, rather than physical force. And yet it seems to me that it is not possible to explain the republican political pathos which appeared in the Gdańsk Shipyard without acknowledging an element of violence.

The words of a reporter who was present in the shipyard are key to understanding this matter, "If one lives a bit with people who throw caution to the wind and are willing to risk their lives, then this has an effect." In an obvious sense violence was present in during August. It's true that violence was not directly present on the stage of the historical drama, yet, it was lodged within the reality of that time as a possibility.

Just the potential for violence, happily not actualized in August, decided upon the character of the pathos felt by the participants. It was also one of the sources of the extraordinary psychosomatic reactions described earlier in this lecture. The threat of intervention, internal and external, by the USSR, was both an obvious and deciding factor within the situation.

The nature of August's pathos seen in light of the republican tradition is based on the fact that a community of citizens, consciously and in solidarity, stood up against the threat of violence from a tyranny. This community itself did not resort to violence, but it did win a war of nerves; a war, because it consciously risked life. If

it was ready to risk its life in the defense of its freedom, then it fulfilled an elementary requirement of classical republicanism—it went
beyond the boundaries of its own biological necessity. By defeating
the tyranny it achieved the glory due to truly courageous people.

In 1972, in Toronto, during a seminar devoted to the thought
of Arendt, where the author of *The Human Condition* was present,
there came the question about where in the democratic and liberal world did she notice places where the spirit of ancient civic life
could come back to life. For the one asking the question it seemed
especially problematic, because the only thing "left to do for the
political man, is what the Greeks used to do, make war!". To this
Arendt replied that there are places where the spirit of civic debate
is still present:

Let's take, for example, urban public meetings. Let's say that building a
bridge is what's at stake. This can be decided from the top down, or through
public debate. If it just so happens that the building of a bridge is truly an
open matter, then it's better that it were decided upon by a discussion, rather than from the top down. I was once at such a meeting in New Hampshire
and was impressed by the reasonableness of those citizens.[23]

This whole example contains the core of the problem. Even though
local self-rule often remains—especially in countries where civic
culture is strong—a substantial element of civic activity, this form
of engagement is essentially different from the classical model of political community.

Civic life on this level, even though it is necessary and extremely useful, only with difficulty provides the stimuli necessary to feel
"public happiness" and also to feel the pathos which comes from
enacting freedom. It would be hard to imagine people who are constantly crying or throwing up at a vote for the county budget or
during a discussion about the renovation of a school.

---

23. Cf. "Seminarium w Toronto" [the Seminar in Toronto] in *Przegląd Polityczny* [the Political
review], no. 55/2002, 196 ff.

Local self-governance, free from pathos, directed at comfort and friendly cohabitation is always in danger of falling into the sphere of the social. This is not a catastrophe or an act of God, but a normal situation which is totally understandable in modern liberal-democratic societies. On the other hand, the appearance of the republican pathos requires a context, even just a potential, of violence, or at least a sharp existential conflict, which causes such situations to be treated by modern societies not as desirable, but rather as dangerous and threatening. The totality of social mobilization which appears during limit situations such as August '80 is hard to maintain for the long run.

Thus, the republican tradition is not so much a realistic project as it is a normative utopia, the measure for social and political reality, which serves as a tool to criticize them. Paraphrasing Arendt, who spoke of the "lost treasure" of this tradition, it is a treasure continually regained in history and also continually lost until its next lightning bolt, until the next historical revelation of primordially pure politics. It is true that each such bolt will fall back into the sphere of the social, but memory of the miracle of freedom and real community will constitute—for a time, for a generation, maybe for several generations—a continually present ideal that shows the measure of perfection possible for people. And one of such ideals— still present in our history—is the phenomenon of "Solidarity".

translated from Polish by Artur Rosman

DARIUSZ GAWIN—born in 1964. Associate professor at the Institute of Philosophy and Sociology, and director of the Department of Civil Society, both at the Polish Academy of Sciences. Deputy director of The Warsaw Rising Museum. His interests are political philosophy and the history of ideas. In 2006 he received the Andrzej Kijowski Award for the book *Polska, wieczny romans* [Poland, an eternal affair].

INDEX

A

Abraham 5, 59
Adenauer, Konrad Hermann Joseph 180
Aeneas 84
Aholiab 160
Alford, Helen, O.P. xiv
Amos 160
Anscombe, Elizabeth 25, 43
Archimedes 138
Arendt, Hannah 202, 203, 206, 214, 215,
    216, 218, 219, 220, 221
Aristotle 47, 87, 120, 121, 122, 159, 210,
    211, 214, 216, 217
Arquillière, Henri-Xavier 119
Auerbach, Erich 162, 163
Augustine, Saint 114, 118, 119, 120, 121
d'Aviano, Marco 177, 178, 179

B

Baudelaire, Charles 166
Baumann, Zygmunt 7
Baumgarten, Alexander Gottlieb 168
Bellarmin, Robert 125
Benedict XVI (Joseph Ratzinger) xiii,
    19, 79, 114, 115, 128, 130, 132, 133, 134,
    135, 136, 175
Bentham, Jeremy 91, 92
Bezaleel 160
Biggar, Nigel 53
Blaga, Lucian 154
Bogucka, Aleksandra xv

Bonaparte, Napoleon 89, 90
Bonaventure, Saint 159, 160
Bonino, Serge-Thomas, O.P. xiv
Bottum, Joseph 151
Brague, Rémi xiii, 83, 175
Broniewska, Marta xv
Byron, George Gordon 171

C

Calderón de la Barca, Pedro 156
Camus, Albert 153
Cavadini, John xiii, 114
de Chateaubriand, François-René 89
de Cervantes Saavedra, Miguel 156
Chesterton, Gilbert Keith 5
Chruścicka, Natalia xv
Cichocki, Marek Aleksander xiii, 94
Congar, Yves Marie-Joseph, O.P. 123
Comte, Auguste 92
Corneille, Pierre 156
Cristin, Renato xiii, 199
Croell, Benedict xiv
Crosthwaite, Alejandro, O.P. xiv
Cicero 2, 86, 87, 158
Czajkowska, Małgorzata xv

D

Daguet, François, O.P. xiii, 137
Darwin, Charles 172
Dawkins, Richard 10
Dąbrowska, Monika xv

Debussy, Claude 165
Delsol, Chantal xiii, 154
Demeter 82
Destivelle, Hyacinthe, O.P. xiv
Dionysius the Areopagite 72
Domarecka, Danuta xiv
Domarecki, Krzysztof xiv
Droste, Catherine Joseph, O.P. xiv
Dumouchel, Paul 56

E
Eagleton, Terry 65

F
Faust 170
Firdawsi, Abul-Qâsem 164
Finnis, John xiii, 50
Floridi, Luciano 14
Francis (Pope) 2, 9, 19, 108, 110, 151
Freud, Sigmund 57, 65, 148
Freund, Julien 141, 154
Fuchs, Josef 34

G
Galileo 15
de Gasperi, Alcide 180
Gawin, Dariusz xiii, 221
Girard, René 56, 57, 58, 60, 62, 65, 66, 70
von Goethe, Johann Wolfgang 148
Gogol, Nikolai 165
Görres, Joseph 90
Grabias, Karol xv
Gruszka, Jolanta xiv
Gruszka, Mirosław xiv
Gregory VII 120
Guardini, Romano 175, 184

H
Habermas, Jürgen 79, 140, 186
Hegel, Georg Wilhelm Friedrich 85, 90, 92, 163, 168, 169
Heidegger, Martin 169, 177, 195, 199

Heraclitus of Ephesus 5
Herbich, Tomasz xv
Hesiod 160
Hillesum, Etty 68, 70, 71
Himmelfarb, Gertrude 79
Hitchens, Christopher 10
Hobbes, Thomas 16
Holtz, Dominic, O.P. xiv
Hölderlin, Friedrich 157
Hugo, Victor 167

J
Janas, Piotr, O.P. xiv
John the Apostle, Saint 4, 6, 7, 60, 105, 106, 108, 162
John Paul II, Saint (Karol Wojtyła) xi, xii, xiii, xiv, 2, 4, 22, 23, 24, 25, 26, 27, 28, 29, 31, 32, 34, 35, 38, 39, 41, 42, 43, 46, 48, 74, 75, 76, 79, 86, 103, 105, 107, 112, 113, 114, 128, 130, 131, 132, 135, 136, 175, 178, 179, 180, 184, 186, 187, 188, 189, 197, 205, 213
John of Salisbury 86
Jesus Christ xii, 4, 6, 7, 35, 40, 60, 61, 67, 71, 72, 84, 97, 98, 99, 100, 102, 103, 104, 106, 107, 108, 111, 112, 113, 114, 118, 156, 162, 163,
Joas, Hans 140
Jobs, Steve 18
Journet, Charles 127
Justin Martyr, Saint 5, 113

K
Kadłubek, Wincenty 86
Kant, Immanuel 165, 166, 167
Charlemagne 176
Kapuściński, Ryszard 208, 209
Keats, John 158
Kierkegaard, Soren 88, 171
Kohl, Helmut 180
Krzywonos, Henryka 205

L
Leibniz, Gottfried Wilhelm 190, 191, 199
Leo XIII 126, 127, 131, 136, 197
Leopardi, Giacomo 171
Lessing, Gotthold Ephraim 148
Lewis, Clive Staples 67
Leverkühn, Adrian 170
Liszt, Franz 165
Loewy, Raymond 168
Lomazzo, Giovanni Paolo 165
Löwith, Karl 78

M
Madej-Wójcik, Monika xv
Muhammad 164
de Maistre, Joseph 89
Malraux, André 140
Mann, Thomas 170
Marczak, Mikołaj xv
Maritain, Jacques 127, 128, 136
Maurras, Charles 115
McGrath, Alister 67
McLuhan, Marshall 14, 15
Meier, John Paul 6
Merleau-Ponty, Maurice 62, 63
Milbank, John 53
Mill, John 92
de Moerbeke, Guillaume 120
Molière 156
de Montalembert, Charles 139
Morin, Edgar 17
Moses 21, 148
de Musset, Alfred 171

N
Newman, John Henry, Saint 67
Nietzsche, Friedrich 78, 92, 149
Nowak, Hanna xv

O
O'Connell, Timothy 34
Odifreddi, Piergiorgio 10

O'Donovan, Oliver 53
Onfray, Michel 10
Ortega y Gasset, José 168, 197

P
Paciorek, Joanna xiv
Palaver, Wolfgang 56
Paluch, Michał O.P. xiv
Paul, Saint xiii, 7, 20, 21, 37, 51, 52, 53, 71, 72, 118, 162
Paul VI 2
Péguy, Charles 149
Pericles 202, 216, 217, 218
Persephone 82
Peter, Saint 37
Peterson, Erik 115, 116
Piasecki, Wojciech xiv
Pienkowska, Alina 205
Pius IX 140
Pius XII 2
Plato 158, 159, 166, 210, 211
Plotinus 158, 159
Plutarch 146
Poe, Edgar Allan 165
Poniatowski, Stanisław August 79
Prensky, Marc 15
Pushkin, Aleksandr 171

R
Racine, Jean-Baptiste 156
Rajkowski, Mikołaj xv
Ravasi, Gianfranco xiii, 19
Reagan, Ronald 180
Renan, Ernest 92
Ricci, Matteo 5
Ricoeur, Paul 8
Rosenkranz, Karl 163
Rybka, Ryszard, O.P. xiv

S
de Saint- Exupéry, Antoine 154
Scheler, Max 23, 38,

von Schelling, Friedrich Wilhelm
   Joseph 165
Schembri, Justin, O.P. xiv
Schlegel, Friedrich 165, 166, 167
Schlegel, August Wilhelm 165
Schleiermacher, Friedrich 165
Schmitt, Carl 115, 116
Schopenhauer, Artur 156, 171, 172
Schuman, Robert 180
Schumann, Robert 165
Searle, John 13
Shakespeare, William 156
Skinner, Quentin 87
Sloterdijk, Peter 91
Sobieski, Jan III 177
Socrates 5, 158, 211
Spencer, Henry 92
Spinoza, Baruch 148
Staniszkis, Jadwiga 200
Stawicka, Izabela xv
Strachowski, Michał xv
Strauss, David 92
Strauss, Leo 78
Strumff, Tadeusz 203
Sullivan, Ezra, O.P. xiv

T
Tabaczek, Mariusz, O.P. xiv
Tacitus 148
Talarowski, Adam xv

Taylor, Charles 9
Teresa Benedicta of the Cross, Saint
   (Edith Stein) 63, 64, 65, 66, 68, 70
Tertullian 143
Thomas Aquinas, Saint xii, xiii, 20, 21,
   22, 35, 37, 38, 39, 41, 45, 46, 47, 50, 119,
   120, 121, 122, 123, 124, 125, 126, 127,
   131, 132, 134, 135, 160
de Tocqueville, Alexis 153,
Thucydides 216, 217
Trigano, Shmuel 192
Trump, Donald 146

V
de Vitoria, Francisco 126
Voegelin, Eric 78, 117

W
Walentynowicz, Anna 205
Weber, Max 149
White, Thomas Joseph, O.P. xiv
Williams, Rowan xiii, 73
Wittgenstein, Ludwig 62, 67
Wojciechowski, Krzysztof xv
Wolff, Larry 80

Z
Zdziebkowska, Dorota xiv
Zdziebkowski, Tomasz xiv